The F&RCC and Rock Climbing Guides
to the
English Lake District

The Fell and Rock Climbing Club, founded at Coniston in 1906, published its first rock climbing guide in 1922 and since that date has produced a continuous series of guides which are accepted as the definitive series on Lake District Rock Climbing.

The guides are written and published by a volunteer team of members who update the text and check new climbs, many of which have been, and continue to be pioneered by club members.

Enquiries regarding the F&RCC and its guide books should be addressed to the current Club Secretary or Guide Books Editor, whose addresses are available from the BMC.

Climbing Guides to the
English Lake District

Gable

by D. Kirby

Pillar

by J. Loxham

Illustrated by
A. Phizacklea

Edited by D. W. Armstrong

Published by the Fell and Rock Climbing Club
of the English Lake District

© ISBN 0 85028 033 8

Previous Editions

Pillar
1923	H.M. Kelly
1935	H.M. Kelly
1952	H.M. Kelly, W. Peascod
1968	A.G. Cram
1977	A.G. Cram

Gable
1925	H.S. Gross
1937	C.J. Astley Cooper
1948	C.J. Astley Cooper, W. Peascod, A.P. Rossiter
1969	P.L. Fearnehough
1977	P.L. Fearnehough

Present edition: Gable and Pillar 1991

British Library Cataloguing in Publication Data

Kirby, D.

Gable and Pillar. — (Climbing guides to the English Lake District)
I. Title II. Loxham, J. III. Armstrong, D. (David), 1953– III. Fell and Rock
Climbing Club of the English Lake District IV. Series
796.5223′0942784

ISBN 0-85028-033-8

Prepared for printing by Synergy, Royal Oak Barn, The Square, Cartmel, Cumbria,
LA11 6BQ.

Printed by Joseph Ward & Co. (Printers) Ltd., Wellington Road, Dewsbury, West
Yorkshire, WF13 1HR.

Distributed by Cordee, 3a De Montfort Street, Leicester, LE1 7HD.

CONTENTS

4 CONTENTS

PHOTOGRAPHS

INTRODUCTION

This is the final edition in the seventh series of Rock Climbing Guides in the process of publication by the Fell and Rock Climbing Club of the English Lake District. This series now comprise five volumes as follows;

1. Buttermere and Eastern Crags
2. Scafell, Dow and Eskdale
3. Langdale
4. Gable and Pillar
5. Borrowdale

It is now almost 14 years since the last comprehensive guides to the Gable and Pillar areas were published, then in separate volumes. A stop gap update was the production of the New West supplement in 1985, with new routes to both areas, a complete guide to Buckbarrow as well as stars, technical and 'E' grades for existing routes.

This long awaited guide combines and updates the crags of the past volumes and supplements into one edition, a task competently and enthusiastically undertaken by Dave Kirby who dealt with the Gable and Wasdale areas and Jim Loxham the Pillar and Ennerdale sections. (The crags of Eskdale, formerly part of the Gable guide are currently included in the Scafell, Dow and Eskdale guide.)

A wide variety of crags and routes are encompassed in this guide ranging from the smaller rarely frequented crags around Ennerdale, Mosedale and Wasdale; the sombre and neglected heights of Pillar; the magnificent routes of Gable Crag; the tremendous and powerful Tophet Wall climbs alongside the more friendly Napes and Kern Knotts classics. Last but not least the numerous small crags of Buckbarrow with their vast array of routes of all grades, all easily accessible on the sun-drenched southern slopes overlooking the south end of Wastwater. These provide an excellent poor weather alternative to the mountain crags around Wasdale such as Gable and Scafell.

Al Phizacklea's excellent maps and diagrams provide invaluable assistance for those seeking to locate the crags and routes and will be welcomed by all users for their clarity.

The Fell and Rock guidebook team must be thanked for their help together with all others who have assisted with the production of this guide.

D Armstrong, December 1990

General Notes

Adjectival Grades
These give the overall grade of the climb, taking into account such
factors as technical difficulty, rock quality and protection; and, of
course, they assume dry rock. The grades are:- Moderate, Difficult,
Very Difficult, Mild Severe, Severe, Hard Severe, Mild Very Severe,
Very Severe, Hard Very Severe, Extremely Severe. The standard
abbreviations are used for the grades in the text. The Extremely
Severe grade is divided into E1, E2, E3, E4, E5, E6, to date.
However, the system is open ended and E7 and above are available
for the future.

Technical Grades
Included for each pitch of 4a and above on all routes of Mild Very
Severe and harder (where known). This grade is an attempt to assess
the problems to be encountered on each pitch and once again is open
ended. The grades to date are:- 4a, 4b, 4c, 5a, 5b, 5c, 6a, 6b, 6c.

Aid
A few routes still require a limited use of artificial assistance and this
is indicated in the description where appropriate. Many aid reductions
have been made in recent years and routes are described in the most
free style in which they are known to have been climbed and are
graded accordingly.

Quality of Routes
A star system has been adopted to highlight routes of particular
quality, with three stars being used to indicate routes comparable with
the best in the country. The absence of stars does not mean that a
climb is poor, unless it is described as such. Black spots are attributed
to climbs of exceptionally poor quality.

Unrepeated Routes
Climbs which are not known to have been repeated, or verified by
the guide writer, are indicated with a dagger (†) and their descriptions
and gradings should be treated with caution.

Length of Climbs
The lengths of climbs and pitches are given in metres and this is
abbreviated to m in the text. Those who continue to think in feet will
unfortunately have to multiply the lengths given by $3^1/_4$.

Location of Crags
The location of each crag is indicated by its Ordnance Survey grid
reference. The aspect of the main faces have been included to aid the
choice of crags. The altitude given is based on the Ordnance Survey
datum, which gives mean sea level as zero. The terms 'true left' and
'true right' are used to describe the position of a crag in a valley or
ghyll relative to the direction of flow of the steam. The term 'left'
and 'right', unless other wise stated, mean as the climber faces his
climb.

New Routes

To aid future guide writers, please record descriptions of all new
routes in the New Routes Book in the Horse and Farrier Inn,
Threlkeld; Fishers or Needlesports in Keswick, or, Rock and Run in
Ambleside; the Log Book in the F&RCC huts, or send them to the
Guide Books Editor. Please include all relevant details in the usual
format. Information gleaned from magazines is not always sufficient
to identify routes.

Comments on any of the information contained in this guide, whether
thought to be inaccurate or misleading, would be welcomed for
correction of future volumes and should be sent to the Guide Books
Editor or noted in the above mentioned Routes Books.

Bolts

In the interests of care and concern for crags and the mountain
environment, and the belief that British climbing in general should
continue with the principle of leader-placed, removable protection, the
F&RCC are generally in accord with the guidelines on the use of
bolts for the protection of routes as set out by the BMC. It is agreed
that bolts are only acceptable on certain agreed quarried slate crags
and certain agreed limestone crags. This precludes the use of bolts
on any of the crags within this guide and we would ask that climbers
should adhere to this policy and refrain from the temptation to place
bolts.

Conservation

The crags of the Lake District are an important habitat for wild plants.
The lack of disturbance and the unique environment support the
growth of rare species. In addition, some crags have become regular
nesting sites for Peregrine Falcons.

To protect the natural environment, The Wildlife and Countryside Act
1981 makes it illegal to disturb nesting birds, such as peregrines, and

to uproot any plant without the owners permission. In designated 'Sites of Scientific Interest', which include a number of crags in the Lake District, any activity which damages vegetation or wildlife becomes an offense.

It is, therefore, important that climbers respect the natural environment and cause the minimum disturbance to crags to avoid future restrictions on access.

To avoid prosecution, climbers should avoid areas of crags where peregrines are known to be nesting and if, in ignorance, a peregrine is disturbed, they should retreat from that area.

On established routes, climbing can proceed without conflict if the plantlife is respected. Generally, gardening of new routes should be kept to a minimum and avoided altogether in Sites of Special Scientific Interest. Before developing new crags, or gardening routes, environmental considerations should be taken into account and the Nature Conservancy Council consulted on the importance of the vegetation in that location.

ACKNOWLEDGEMENTS

With the end in sight at long last I would like to take this opportunity to thank all those who have assisted me and without whose help this guide may never have reached completion.

This guide, which has been thoroughly revised and updated, was well founded on the excellent work of the previous guide writers to whom credit must be given; H S Cross, C J Astley Cooper, W Peascod, A P Rossiter and finally P L Fearnehough.

The F&RCC series of Recent Developments have proved to be most useful as has the New West supplement, compiled by W Young. This supplement created a breathing space prior to publication of the present guide and was a source of much valuable information.

I should like to thank Al Phizacklea for the fine new set of diagrams and perspective maps. These are once again of a very high standard and will help in providing easy identification of crags and access routes.

The production of any guide relies heavily on the good will and assistance of the writer's friends and fellow climbers for its success, the writer being simply the focal point, this edition is no exception. Their help with the climbing and checking of routes, the providing of descriptions, dates and grades plus their constructive, if sometimes sharp criticisms of the manuscripts have all helped to keep me on the straight and narrow. I would particularly like to thank the following for their involvement: Mike Lynch, Bob Wightman, Ian Turnbull, Bill Pattison, Bill Young, Jim Loxham, Colin Wornham, George Smith, Julian Carradice, Brian McKinley, Tony King, Steve Hubball, Steve Braily and members of the Ulverston Mountaineering Club,

A special thank you must go to Dave Miller who persuaded me that I needed the experience, Dave Armstrong for his excellent editing, encouragement and subtle pressures, Al Phizacklea for his infectious enthusiasm and patience when hauling me up many of the harder grades and to Andy Jones in getting me away from the Gable Area regularly thus preserving my sanity.

Finally, a special mention and thanks to my wife Penny for her support and total involvement in all aspects of this guide, the good and the bad. We can now climb elsewhere with a clear conscience.

Dave Kirby, January 1991.

I should have had more sense when accepting the invitation of the F&RCC Guidebook committee to attend a meeting to talk about the production of the new joint Gable and Pillar Guidebook.

A piece of cake, they said, living in the Valley with your local knowledge. After being overwhelmingly volunteered for the job, I accepted the task with grace.

So began the love-hate affair of guidebook production – I raise my hat to those who do it more than once.

What at first, I had been assured would be a straight forward job (There is no one as naive as the naive), turned out to be one of the most time consuming, frustrating, and also one of the most enjoyable experiences I have to date undertaken.

Pouring over old editions of the Pillar Guide it was a delight to find original descriptions as accurate then as now, or occasionally wildly inaccurate, like the three routes on Shamrock with the common top pitch, all three descriptions giving it different lengths.

In the revamping and union of Pillar and Gable into one Guidebook, some of the original charm has been regrettably lost, especially from some of the older route descriptions. The stringing together of short pitches into modern longer pitch lengths does not conjure up the same image in the mind of the earlier pioneers, clawing their way up the next ten feet (sorry 3 metres) of rock, but then that's progress.

This guidebook is of course based on earlier editions, especially the original editions by H M Kelly, and latterly with the more modern routes by A G Cram. A special note of thanks must go to that modern day 'Guru', Bill Young for his efforts past and present.

I am most grateful to Colin Greenhow and Sheila Maskrey for their combined efforts on the Bowness Knott and Anglers' Crag section of the guide. Also may I thank Colin Wornham and Dave Brown for their sufferance on the Pillar section. I must also thank Pete Botterill and Stuart Millar for their contributions.

Al Phizacklea is to be thanked for the excellent diagrams and also for recent contributions on the rock, especially on Haskett Buttress.

Checking routes for guidebook production can be a solitary experience, especially when undertaken on Pillar Rock.

Jim Loxham, December 1990.

HISTORICAL

Pillar

That Pillar Rock should have attracted mankind over one hundred years ago is not surprising in view of its situation and unique appearance – an isolated crag on the breast of a mountain flanking one of the most desolate dales in the Lake District. The very remoteness of its surroundings, as well as the apparent inaccessibility of its summit, doubtless fascinated as well as awed the shepherds and others whose work or inclination took them within its neighbourhood, and its solitariness naturally became a challenge. Farm fireside talk and inn gossip probably clothed it with a certain amount of romance, and early writers included it in their Guides as one of the notable features of the district. It also gained notoriety from Wordsworth, who indicated it, erroneously, as the scene of the fatal accident which inspired his poem, 'The Brothers,' published in 1800. So that, when the first ascent was actually achieved, it only increased the allurement of Pillar Stone, as the Rock was known in those days.

It is not very difficult to assign to this first ascent its due place in relation to our sport, for in it can be recognized the first seed of English rock-climbing. The climbing of rocks as an art in itself parted ways with mountaineering as then known, i.e., the attainment of a summit of a mountain by the least arduous route, for here was a definite attempt to get to a summit – not of a mountain – by way of difficult rocks.

John Atkinson, of Croftfoot, Ennerdale (variously described as cooper and shepherd), was the man who became associated with this landmark of British rock-climbing, and his feat was given due prominence in the two county newspapers of the day, the date of the ascent being given in both cases as July 9th, 1826. One of them stated that, "tho' the undertaking had been attempted by *thousands,* it was always relinquished as hopeless." Seemingly journalistic licence was known in those days. Still it is evident that the Pillar had a great reputation, and that many efforts had been made to reach its top.

Atkinson is believed to have used the way now known as The Old West, and it is understood that Messrs J Colebank, W Tyson, and J Braithwaite, all shepherds, followed his route the same year, though it is stated by a writer in the *West Cumberland Times,* of August 8th, 1891, that they reached the top by the East Side. There may be some ground for this statement, for shepherds must certainly have played the most prominent part in those early attempts. It seems very likely that they were on intimate terms with the crag, especially the east side of High Man, for the grassy ledges lying between the top of Walker's Gully and Low Man must have proved a great temptation to sheep straying from the fellside above, and consequently many of them would have to be rescued. Unfortunately, there is no record as to when the 'Old Wall' was built to prevent such straying; a knowledge of this might have thrown some light on the earliest ascents. Because of this early acquaintance with the east side, it has been hinted by R S T Chorley, in his historical investigations (*Fell and Rock Journal, 1926*), that even the first ascent may have been made from this and not from the west side.

For some unaccountable reason a period of twenty-two years elapsed before the next recorded ascent, when what might be described as the first tourist ascent, was made by Lieut Wilson (RN) He was followed by C A O Baumgartner, – Whitehead, and C W Hartley, all in 1850. These may not have been the only persons who had ascended Pillar by this time, as Mr Baumgartner says he found on the top "a bottle … containing a paper recording the names of preceding visitors," and it is to be regretted that he does not give their names.

The feat was now, by the frequency of its accomplishment, becoming less fearsome, and Mr George Seatree estimates that an approximate summary of ascents from 1826 to 1875 is as follows:-

1826 to 1850	6 ascents
1850 to 1866	22 ascents
1866 to 1873	31 ascents
1874	10 ascents
1875	50 ascents
Total	119 ascents

In spite of conflicting reports, it is traditionally held that the first few ascents were made by The Old West Route, with the possible exception of Baumgartner's, this, according to a letter of his, being by the east and north sides (which sounds rather like the Old Wall Route). Mr Whitehead also claims, according to Mr J W Robinson, to have done the Corner above the slab, i.e., the one into which the Pendlebury Traverse leads.

In the early sixties a little more certainty creeps in, and new courses were discovered. We learn from Mr Seatree's '*List of First Ascents*' that "the first known ascent of the east side" was made in 1861 by the Keeper of the Lighthouse, St Bees, and four friends. Messrs Conybeare, Butler and others also climbed the East Face, although there is some doubt whether they did the Notch on this occasion or went by 'Easy Way' variation. A still newer route was made in the early seventies by Gardiner and the Pendleburys, though one can only look upon this as substantial variation of the Slab and Notch Climb. An earlier guide stated that Messrs Barnes and Grave worked out the Old Wall Route in the early sixties. Further investigation proved this to be unlikely as, firstly, William Grave was only born in 1848, and, secondly, an extract from his diary (*Climbers' Club Journal*) gives his ascent with Matthew Barnes as being made on August 7th, 1870, 'by a slab on the east side.' Nevertheless, Seatree says, in the *Fell and Rock Journal* (vol. 2, p. 16), referring to 1866: "In that year also there occurred successful attacks on the 'Old Wall' and 'Great Chimney' route, now seldom climbed, by Messrs Matthew Barnes, A Barnes, W Grave, G Scoular, Hermann Woolly, R Whitwell, W G Holland, James Moore and Tom Leigh. The Rock now began to attract our womenfolk, and Miss A Barker had the honour of the first ascent for her sex in 1870. Miss Mary Westmorland accompanied her brothers (Thomas and Edward) up it in 1873 or 1874, and Mrs Ann Creer was the third in 1875. The latter year also saw the introduction to the Rock of that most interesting character, the Revd James Jackson, self and well styled the Patriarch of the Pillarites, a title which might now well be claimed by Mr Lawrence Pilkington, who as a boy of fourteen climbed the rock, with his elder brother, in 1869. It was also in 1875 that Mr Seatree himself became a devotee, and during the next ten years he guided many parties to the shrine on the summit. He claims to have made the first ascent of The Curtain (*F and R Journal*, vol. 2, pp. 15 and 17), with Stanley Martin, on September 14th, 1874, though it is hard to reconcile his description with the climb as we know it today. His devotion was wholehearted, and much of our knowledge of the early history of the Rock is due to the care with which he collected every scrap of information relating to his beloved crag."

An interesting point to note at this juncture is the fact, to which Mr Seatree called attention, that hitherto the climbing had been done ropeless, and this is probably the reason why there was not a great deal of variation in the quality of the routes taken in the first fifty years. One can, therefore, understand his surprise on seeing J W Robinson carry a rope when they first met in the eighties.

With the advent of that prince of pioneers, Mr W P Haskett-Smith, a change came over the scene, and, following the general new developments in rock-climbing, more difficult routes were worked out

(*Vide* List of First Ascents). Messrs J W Robinson (a name particularly associated with Pillar), W C Slingsby, and G Hastings, all assisted in the impetus which he gave to exploration. It was this decade which became memorable in the annals of climbing on Pillar Rock because of the long siege laid to the North Climb, for Haskett-Smith, along with his brother Edmund, reached the Stomach Traverse at least as early as 1884. Less than a year after the first ascent of the climb in 1891, G A Solly led a party up it, and proved that the descent into Savage Gully could be avoided by the Hand Traverse, a fact further emphasized by J Collier's successful attack on the Nose about twelve months later.

Exploration of the Rock kept pace with that on other crags in the Lake District, and 1899 and 1901 saw the fall of Walker's Gully and Savage Gully respectively, a fitting culmination to the gully epoch of the sport. The successful attack on the New West Climb by the brothers Abraham, in 1901, recalled the further possibilities of this almost forgotten face; but a more significant sign of the times (the development of modern rock-climbing) was the magnificent victory over the north-west angle of the Rock in 1906. It was ten years, however, before the west face was thought of again, when the South-West Climb paved the way in 1911 for the grand assault on it in 1919, with its afterthoughts in 1920 and 1923, though curiously enough the men who had shown the possibilities of this side in 1901 went to the north-east for their next conquest in 1912.

The High Man with its multiplicity of routes was becoming well-nigh exhausted, but Low Man had still secrets to reveal, and some homeric efforts at gardening on the West Wall of Walker's Gully, a labour which took the best part of two days, yielded in 1928 the magnificent Grooved Wall Climb. This was matched later by the two superlative routes on the north face, evolved in 1932 and 1933. These were, incidentally, the outcome of the Girdle Traverse, so ingeniously and fearlessly worked out a year earlier by its authors, a grand climax the girdling aspect of cragsmanship in the Lake District.

Before closing this brief history, the name of L J Oppenheimer should be mentioned. That Pillar Rock should have made an appeal to him was an inevitable reaction between such a striking natural object and a man of his artistic temperament. It was the lodestone of his wanderings in the Lake District, and though he did not achieve any of the glamour associated with being the leader of a first ascent, it was mainly due to his optimism that Savage Gully and the North-West Climb were done.

Finally one must recall the extraordinary demonstration of interest in Pillar Rock shown by both climbers and the general public on Easter Sunday, April 4th, 1926, a century after the first ascent. It is hardly an exaggeration to say that there were scores of climbers and non-climbers who reached its top by devious routes, whilst on the fellside ledges, above and on both sides of the Rock, were large numbers of lookers-on perched like so many sea-birds on their cliffs. The culminating moment of that day occurred, for me, as I reached the scree on the west side after descending the New West. It carried me back to days of veneration and awe, for before me stood a very elderly farmer and his wife gazing up at the great sweep of cliff before them. "Ay, it's a Grand Stone," he said simply. A sentiment, surely, that has echoed time and again in many a cragsman's heart.

H M Kelly, 1934

1934-1968

During the late thirties most of the exploration on Pillar Rock was done by parties led by A T Hargreaves and S H Cross, culminating in the ascent of Shamrock Tower. In this period A Birtwistle visited the Rock and climbed the difficult slabs on the left of the South-West Climb, naming the route South-West-by-West.

Then came an extraordinarily long period of inactivity on the Rock. For 18 years no new climbs were reported on Pillar although some routes were found on Black Crag and Haskett Buttress. The first route on Anglers' Crag was done in 1938 while the remainder were reported in the late fifties by climbers from West Cumberland. W Peascod led the most obvious routes on Bowness Knott in 1950 and the rest were discovered nearly 10 years later.

In the drought of 1959, G Oliver climbed the obvious line on the west face of High Man and named the route Vandal. This was, in fact, one grade harder than any previous climb on Pillar. On the same day M de St Jorre climbed Goth, the big corner on the west face of Low Man. Again came a period of inactivity until climbers who lived close at hand began taking an interest in the Rock. Beginning with Scylla, many of the most obvious lines on the north and west faces were climbed. The era of routes named from particle physics then began and a considerable number of climbs were found on Shamrock and the north face of Low Man, often only after extensive gardening. People were seen carrying ice-axes on hot summer days for this purpose. Some new ideas covered rock previously climbed, notably Bootstrap, and the final result has been a great deal of very pleasant climbing in superb and comparatively remote surroundings, always one of the unique values of climbing on Pillar Rock. Most of the best

lines appear to have been climbed but there is still a great deal of unclimbed rock in and around Ennerdale, although the prospective explorer may well require 'green fingers'.

A G Cram, 1968

1968-1976

The intensive development of the Rock reached a peak in 1968 with some ten major new routes being found. This development has continued with the discovery of a further nine routes, as usual mainly by local climbers. A notable addition is the Greater Traverse – a girdle of the main faces including Shamrock and totalling nearly 1,800 feet.

The dynamic Bill Lounds set a ferocious new standard with a free ascent of Black Widow, and also created the precedent of ten hard routes in one day! Other free ascents, including that of Scylla Direct by Jeff Lamb, have meant that the only aid on the Rock is now one sling on Gondor.

Two other less pleasant events should be reported. For some ten years it has been possible for the relatively small number of visiting rock climbers to drive up the Ennerdale Valley to a point below the Rock – particularly useful on a short visit. However, access is now banned (see approaches) beyond the car park at Bowness Knott. A second particularly sad event had been the annual destruction of Robinson's Cairn by mindless persons unknown.

On a more cheerful note, the 150th anniversary of the first ascent of the Rock was celebrated with great zest on the 9th – 10th July, 1976. Large numbers of people reached the summit, some by the original Old West Route and many by harder routes.

The recent changes have, of course, not affected the Rock at all. Pillar Rock is still a very pleasant and peaceful place to climb. Long may it remain so.

A G Cram, October 1976

1976-1990

Pillar Rock or 'The Rock' as it is affectionately known by local climbers has always been the 'Cinderella Crag' among the mountain crags of Lakeland. In the early days, its remoteness from centres of climbing popularity, bad communications and lack of transport held its development in check, and 'The Rock' has always lagged behind other mountain crags as standards have risen over the years. Even in 1990 it only boasts three routes harder than E2.

Development of the crag has been largely undertaken by locally based climbers and activity reached a peak in the 1960's when climbers could drive up the Ennerdale valley to below the crag. The loss of vehicular access spelled the death knell for 'The Rock' as ascents of new routes dwindled and, with the exception of the popular classics, the existing routes started to revert back to nature.

In H M Kelly's 1934 Historical Notes he makes reference to the Revd James Jackson, "self and well styled the Patriarch of the Pillarites." A century later that title may well go to Bill Young who has been actively involved in the development of the crag for some 20 years, being on the first ascents of Scylla in 1963 and Tapestry in 1982, with many in between.

The late 1970's saw the freeing of Gondor by the late Gordon Tinnings and until the exact line of his ascent became widely known, many epics ensued as climbers attempted to free climb the original way.

The 1980's opened with a quantum leap in difficulty. Tapestry, a bold E4 on the North Face of Low Man by local climbers Tony Stephenson and Chris Sice, re-kindled interest in new routes on Pillar and other routes soon followed. Cunning Stunts is notable and aptly named. This was followed in 1984 by The Straits of Messina (E4), the hardest route to date, climbed by Pete Whillance and Dave Armstrong.

Development then slackened somewhat, no doubt partly due to the wet summers in the second half of the decade. However, Jim Loxham was active during this period when weather permitted and notable additions were Over the Hill in 1987, a companion route to Soliton on the wall of Walker's Gully, climbed with Pete Botterill, and in 1988 Patriarch of the Pillarites with Stuart Miller. A notable event (for Pillar) in 1988 was the on sight lead of Pauli Exclusion Principle and The Terrorist, both E2 by Bob Wightman and Al Phizacklea, giving two new hard routes in one day.

There are still many new lines in the modern idiom (i.e. bold, short and hard) to be climbed on Pillar but until access improves, or climbers are prepared to make the long approach, new additions will continue at a trickle.

Two other crags worthy of mention are Black Crag in Wind Cap Cove and Haskett Buttress in Mirklin Cove. The former has seen attention from Jim Loxham and several worthwhile routes have been pioneered, making the crag well worth a visit. Haskett Buttress was visited by Al Phizacklea and Bob Wightman in 1988 and four new routes were climbed in one day, all named after the theme started by Don Greenop in the early 1970's. Thus, all the routes on this buttress have the initials DS, and rather peculiar names e.g , The Detrital Slide in 1969 and in 1988 The Dipso Somnambulist.

All the crags in the Pillar area are quiet and, unusual these days, one can often have them to oneself. It is expected that the new Guidebook will stimulate renewed interest in the area, I hope that it will still be possible to find peace and solitude on its crags.

Jim Loxham, December 1990

Gable

Seen from a distance, Great Gable has no great rock face to attract the eye, and it is therefore not surprising that some fifty years elapsed after the first ascents of Pillar Rock and Scafell Crag before the first climb on Gable was recorded. This was in 1884, when the Needle Ridge was climbed by W P Haskett-Smith.

It is true that in 1828 the Needle had been both observed and sketched by the father of J W Robinson, but no further attention seems to have been paid to this remarkable feature of the Napes Ridges until its first ascent by W P Haskett-Smith in 1886. This ascent, apart from it being a notable solo effort in itself, had a considerable influence on the future of British rock-climbing. It was the subject of an article in the *Pall Mall Gazette* in 1890, and there can be little doubt that its spectacular appearance in photographs drew wider attention to Cumbrian rocks as a climbing ground.

O G Jones, whose book did so much to stimulate British rock-climbing, was stirred to pay his first visit to the Lake District by the sight of a photograph of the Needle in a shop in the Strand.

The Needle soon commenced to be, as now, the most popular climb in the district, and the first ascent by a lady was made by Miss Koecher in 1890. During the next decade the pioneers completed the ascents of the main ridges; both the Arrowhead and the Eagle's Nest Ridges being climbed in 1892. G A Solly's lead of the Eagle's Nest Ridge Direct, on a cold April day, must rank as one of the outstanding feats of Lake District climbing history. In the same year Gable Crag attracted attention, the Oblique Chimney being climbed by Dr Collier. Tradition has it that the crag was used for business purposes by 'Moses,' the illicit whisky distiller, but no record remains of his routes. Other climbs on the crag soon followed the ascent of Oblique

Chimney, the fall of the Engineer's Chimney in 1899 marking the end of the first epoch.

Kern Knotts was the discovery of O G Jones, who ascended the Chimney in 1893 and the Crack in 1897 – having climbed the Crack on a rope the previous year. It may be of interest to record that in the early days a chockstone was lodged at the top of the niche, and was removed by S W Herford when found unsafe.

From 1900 to 1918, exploration on Great Gable remained almost at a standstill. A few new routes were made, but the only notable achievement was the conquest of the West Buttress of Kern Knotts in 1912, by Sansom and Herford; the climb being at that time the most difficult ascent in the district. 1919 was a notable year in climbing history, and Great Gable did not escape the wave of exploration which swept over Pillar and Scafell. Kern Knotts was converted into a boulder problem by H M Kelly, the possible moves being still further increased in more recent years. On the Napes, the energy of Fergus Graham, Frankland, Kelly, and others has left little for future explorers; although a few unconsidered trifles were picked up in 1934. Gable Crag remained in comparative obscurity, the last problem of interest, that of the Engineer's Slabs, not being solved until 1934.

Since the last guide was written two new climbing grounds have been developed.

Green Gable Crags were apparently visited as long ago as 1910 when Epsilon Chimney was discovered by a Fell and Rock Climbing Club party. No further interest seems to have been taken in the crags until the visit of Fergus Graham in 1925, but a fuller exploration was made by G G Macphee in 1927. There is little likelihood of these rocks providing any more new routes.

Boat Howe, on Kirk Fell, first attracted the attention of T Graham Brown in 1912, but it was not until 1925 that he, together with George Basterfield, actually visited the crags. In conclusion, it is not inappropriate to mention that the summit of Great Gable was chosen as the site of the Fell and Rock Climbing Club War Memorial, indicating as it does, the place which Great Gable holds in the history of British Climbing.

C J Astley Cooper, 1936

1948-1968

Ever since the sport of rock climbing began, Great Gable has been the practice ground of Lakeland cragsmen. The imposing nature of its walls and pinnacles attracted many of the early pioneers of the sport, and it is hardly surprising that most of the plums had been picked. Largely owing to the preparation of the new Guide, however, interest in the area was renewed and many more lines were discovered under the moss and heather. Kern Knotts, which had been dismissed as worked out years ago, yielded many variations on old routes plus an additional Very Severe, The Cenotaph; the direct finish to Sepulchre still remains an unsolved problem at the present time, however. Exploration on the Napes has been sparse, although the climbing of Crocodile Crack, Alligator Crawl, The Pod, and the Merry Monk, all in the Eagle's Nest area, have made that section of the crag a veritable maze of routes. The big overhanging crack of Tophet Wall still waits a first ascent, however. The often wet and forbidding Gable Crag has provided a variety of routes, including two new Extremes, The Tomb and The Slant, which must rank as hard as anything in the area. On Engineer's Slab, that magnificent wall of rock which was climbed well ahead of its time by Balcombe in 1934, two new Very Severes, The Troll and Interceptor, have filled in the gaps.

Boat Howe, Green Gable and Overbeck Crags seem to have survived the onslaught of new route finders, although some new lines have been climbed on Buckbarrow, the most notable being Witch, Harmony and The Mysteron. There is some confusion as to who did the first ascents, but the routes are very good, nevertheless. Across Wastwater, midway along the Screes, the hitherto unvisited Low Adam Crag has provided some routes for connoisseurs of steep, loose, lichenous rocks.

The popularity of Eskdale as a climbing ground is increasing enormously. This is largely due to the presence of crags offering easy access. Of these, the magnificently situated Heron Crag with its excellent routes has proved to be one of the greatest attractions of the district. The early pioneers on Heron ascended, in traditional fashion, the big breaks in the crag; Heron Corner, Babylon and Bellerophon were the result. Later, the ubiquitous Les Brown climbed Gormenghast, undoubtedly one of the great climbs of the district. Ascents of Hard Knott and Side Track on the left side of the crag virtually exhausted the supplies of clean rock, leaving the mossy right wall to the mercy of Allan Austin, who unearthed The Flanker and Spec Crack. A bold lead by Ian Singleton up the very imposing wall of the Central Pillar, Iago, and the Yellow Edge, led by Geoff Cram, seemed to leave very little rock still unclimbed. However, the judicious use of ice axes revealed Freak-Out and Kama Sutra, which were hiding beneath the foliage. The girdle was tidied up a little and the crag was virtually complete.

There are many more crags and outcrops in Eskdale, each with its own charm and atmosphere. As Eskdale gains in popularity as a climbing centre, we may yet see a guide to these.

P L Fearnehough, 1968

1968-1976

Since the last edition exploration has been rather sporadic, probably due to the scarcity of really good lines, However, some worthwhile routes have been found, particularly on Gable Crag. The mystery of the Unfinished Arête of Engineers Slabs has been solved; Paul Ross finished his Unfinished Arête way back in 1958. This is now incorporated into The Jabberwock. John Wilkinson, led by Rod Valentine and Dave Miller, found some more routes on Gable Crag, giving him a total of 9 routes on the crag, and Geoff Cram and Bill Young girdled the main buttress of Engineer's Slab.

Roper and Rogers found some good routes on Boat Howe and, although pitons were used for direct aid on the first ascent, Fangorn and Numenor are a couple of worthy additions.

A few more routes were done on some of the outlying crags, and another Hard Very Severe was forced between Spec Crack and Bellerophon on Heron Crag by T Martin. Colin Read put up Golden Eye to the left of Bellerophon.

Possibly the biggest breakthrough was The Viking on Tophet Wall, with an amazing free lead by Richard McHardy. I said in the last edition that this route was still waiting for an ascent and, sure enough, Richard rose to the bait, and across on Kern Knotts, Jeff Lamb knocked off the direct finish to Sepulchre. So maybe if I mention that the roof above Tophet Wall has up to now defeated would-be ascensionists, the new hard men may provide us with yet another plum.

P L Fearnehough, 1976

1977-1990

With the last recorded new route in the 1977 edition of this guide being in 1974 the Historical section of the present edition starts from that date. The Gable area was for many years, and still is, only to a much lesser degree, the habitat of the lower grade climber and mountaineer with its strong traditional links, restricted choice of routes and crags plus its remoteness from the 'scene' all contributing to suppressing its rate of development.

Prior to 1974 some interest had been rekindled as a result of guide book activities but the real wind of change started during that year when the local team, of Bill Pattison, Alan Dunn and Jim Bremner commenced serious excavation works in the Buckbarrow area. This was to become the main area of development over the next few years. Early exploration, which had its origins in 1973, unfortunately produced a crop of average quality routes, with the exception of Midsummer Madness (HVS) on Eastern Crags. It did, however, show that local alternatives to the often wet and cold higher crags did exist. Buckbarrow had been visited in 1962 by Pat Walsh and Mick Burke who climbed Witch (VS) but no one noticed or realized the potential.

During 1974 Kern Knotts was rudely, but only temporarily disturbed from its 12 years of hibernation by the addition of El Vino (E2) and The Kraken (E1) by Tony Stephenson and Stuart Miller, both in the same day. Gable Crag also receiving a rare new route during a visit by Pete Long and John Adams who climbed the very steep line of Vindolanda (E2) using a peg for aid.

1975/76 saw the continuing development of Buckbarrow by Phil Pattison and Alan Dunn, albeit at a much reduced rate plus the start of minor earthworks on Rough Crag by the same pair. It was late in 1976 that a raiding party from Carlisle gave a hint of renewed interest in the established crags of the area when Jeff Lamb and Steve Clegg added The Crysalid (E2) to Kern Knotts, a steep and fingery problem of excellent quality.

In most other guides the addition of only 3 new routes in any one year would be a non event, but in 1977 Pete Whillance and Dave Armstrong did exactly this and showed the real potential yet to be exploited on the traditional crags, that is if you had both the eye and the talent. Supernatural, which climbed a very steep and intricate line left of Tophet Wall, gave Gable its first E5. The bold Sarcophagus (E3) on Gable Crag and the Cayman (E2) on the Napes completed the trio. All these routes were of excellent quality. The locals who were shaken but not visibly stirred had no defence against such a talented and selective approach to poaching.

The Gable area came under scrutiny once again from Carlisle raiders during April and May 1978 when Jeff Lamb and Pete Botterill firstly added Triffid (E2) to Kern Knotts, then with the help of John Taylor, moved on to quickly and successfully take up the gauntlet thrown down by Pat Fearnehough in 1977 and climbed the very steep cracked headwall on Tophet Wall to give Sacrificial Crack (E4). Four days later Jeff Lamb and Pete Botterill returned to add another E4 to the left-hand end of Tophet Wall, Golden Calf.

The area was at long last slowly starting to take on a much needed character change with the addition of high quality routes in the extreme grades.

Any momentum gained over the previous few years quickly ebbed with 1979 and 1980 producing only four new routes, the best being The Angel of Mercy (E1) on Gable Crag by Jeff Lamb and Pete Botterill. The addition of Needle Front (E1) and Needless Eliminate (E1) on Buckbarrow failed to stimulate any further interest that year. Buckbarrow had to wait another year for its further development. Thus in 1981 Buckbarrow was re-discovered and the local teams became active; better late than never. Tony Stephenson and Jo Wilson started the ball rolling with Imagine (E1) giving good steep climbing up the obvious groove line then, supported by Bill Young and Chris Sice they went on to add a further five good routes. Not to be outdone, Dave Armstrong and Pete Whillance come in on the act and climbed two excellent, bold hard lines and left everyone with the problem of repeating Wild West Show (E5) and West Side Story (E4). During the same year kern Knotts finally and irretrievably had the cobwebs brushed away with the addition of five extremes, four in one day by a strong Carlisle team who also provided a solution to the problem created by the loss of Pitch 1 of Sepulchre in a rockfall. Kern Knotts had now become a balanced crag with climbing available at most grades.

The development of Buckbarrow continued through 1982 and 1983 by various local teams with their activities spreading on to the Pike Crag and Eastern Crag areas giving many short but good routes in the VS to E2 grades. A viable alternative to the often wet and cold higher crags was now a reality although the route information was very much a 'local affair'.

In May 1984 the pre-placed protection peg complete with long sling and pre-topproping techniques arrived on Buckbarrow, Tom Walkington and Barry Rogers had commenced on what was to be a short but fruitful period of exploration. In one season they added 15 new routes to Buckbarrow developing the Lakeland Pioneers area from scratch with the best being the Pinnacle Routes and Lakeland Pioneers (HVS). 1984 also showed another disturbing trend for the traditionalists, a hard new route on Yewbarrow. Ian Turnbull and Dougie Hall picked off Queen of Change (E3), an excellent route from a crag long associated with traditional dark chimneys and rounded polished holds. August of that year saw Pete Whillance and

Dave Armstrong in action again on Tophet Wall where they forced the superb line of Incantations, the first E6 for Gable. Many aspirant E6 mechanics have had the unusual opportunity, thanks to television, of rehearsing the route from the comfort of their armchairs, from where all things are possible. Don't be fooled it still requires talent and a lot of neck. At least we have all witnessed the fact that Dave Armstrong is not always cool and calm and does resort to the occasional expletive.

The next surge of activity was triggered off by the publication of the F&RCC New West Supplement in 1985, for climbers now had the route information which also showed up the gaps. In 1986 Long Crag was given a face lift by Dave Hinton, Joe Wilson, Alan Wilson and Pete Strong who added Just Good Friends (E2), Red Garden Massacre (E3) and The Movie (E2) all being deceptively steep.

Further routes appeared on the Eastern Crags, the best being Fall Out (E1) by Keith Phizacklea, Dave Greere and John Daly. But the prize of 1986 went to Colin Downer and Andy Hall who brought the Borrowdale scorched earth policy to Gable Crag and created Snicker Snack (E3), a superb classic crack climb left of Engineer's Slab. This beautifully cleaned strip of rock was to be a constant reminder to all of us of yet another lost opportunity.

1987 saw two new routes on Buckbarrow with the best looking to be Torch Song Trilogy (E5) by Martin Berzins and Chris Sowden, which up to date has not had a repeat ascent. With guide book checking, The Napes came under scrutiny and this, as always, results in a cluster of new routes with the best being The Tormentor (E4), a very committing slab climb, by Al Phizacklea and Tony Greenbank (yes, the original) and Amos Moses (E1) by Pete Long and Terry Parker.

Whilst attention was being focussed on The Napes, Colin Downie and Andy Hall came in on the blind side and scored two direct hits on Gable Crag with Dream Twister (E3) and Powder Finger (E3), once again producing routes of excellent quality and showing their ability to pick off the best lines and everyone else's inability to spot them before the event.

1988 saw a spread of activity throughout the area with parties touring the crags, mopping up and infilling during an excellent long Summer. Steve Hubball and Steve Brailey contributed eight new routes to Green Gable, the first new route activity for 55 years, at grades compatible with the existing, the best being Abacus (HVS).

Bill Pattison, who had been relatively quiet since the early days of Buckbarrow, teamed up with Pete Buckland to develop Great Knott,

Tapestry, Pillar Rock

a minor crag at the head of Overbeck. The crag offers 14 routes of widely ranging grades and quality the best being Mr. Softee (E2) and Wafer Thin (E2) both by Dave Kirby and Penny Melville. The good weather also brought Ron Kenyon to the valley where we at last sorted out the various options to Buttonhook Route on Kern Knotts by climbing Close to the Wind (E1).

Both Gable Crag and The Napes were to benefit from the good weather when Al Phizacklea, temporarily unemployed as a result if industrial action, added 6 routes to Gable Crag and one to The Napes as part of his 63 route bumper season in the Lakes. The Tombstone (E3) on Gable Crag was his best effort which filled in the gap between The Tomb and The Jabberwock.

Later that same year Yewbarrow was brought up to date by the addition of Femme Fatale (E3) that climbed the impressive overhanging prow left of Tim Benzedrino, and Catamite Corner (E2) by Al Phizacklea, Dave Kirby and Brian McKinley.

Ian Turnbull set the standard in 1989 when he and Jim Balmer climbed Final Curtain (E6) on Buckbarrow, a much fancied but frightening project up the centre of the detached pillar right of Wild West Show. The route has now had two ascents, both by Ian to confirm the grade. The rest of 1989 was to prove disappointing with very little activity, the only exception being that of Al Phizacklea, Dai Lampard and Bob Wightman who tiptoed across Tophet Wall on a very bold and sustained traverse line to create The Satanic Traverses (E5) (a very topical name at the time).

The general apathy of 1989 spilled over into 1990 when only Moggy Traveller (E4) and Fat Freddies Cat (E3) recorded during the summer months, both routes being variations on the left-hand end of Kern Knotts and climbed by Al Phizacklea, Andy Rowell and Dave Kells. A late development did occur during November when Don Greenop and party recorded 23 routes on Latterbarrow Crag, generally in the lower grades, their quality has yet to be confirmed. Personally 22 of the names are a complete mystery to me but I can at least identify with one of them.

In the 13 years since the last edition or more accurately the 16 years since the last recorded route in that edition development has been at best sporadic with one or two periods of more intense activity. The single largest addition to the guide has been that of Buckbarrow which now offers about 150 routes spread across the grades with an upper limit of E6 which should satisfy most. The quality of the routes is equally as diverse ranging from the hard, star quality, to the vegetated and loose variety. The easier and poorer quality products will no doubt dirt back into obscurity but at last they have been recorded. The same criticism cannot be levelled at development on the higher traditional crags where the new routes generally fit in well with their surroundings although this could be a function of the crag itself or the only available space left.

When looking through the first ascents list and route descriptions it soon becomes obvious that not all development is good or desirable development with the lines that are justifiably popular and here to stay having been carefully and selectively chosen for their quality and appeal, but not just to the first ascensionists. 1977 and 1981 were perfect examples of this selective approach when Pete Whillance and Dave Armstrong added routes to Gable Crag, The Napes and Buckbarrow which all carry star ratings and receive repeat ascents. This approach was by no means exclusive to them as born out by routes like:- Sacrificial Crack, Golden Calf, Snicker Snack, Dream Twister, Final Curtain, The Tormentor, Free Bird, Imagine, Fall Out and Lakeland Pioneers, all excellent routes that are guaranteed to get repeat ascents or at least attempts.

The other extreme to this will unfortunately always be found close at hand where many routes, although having been extensively gardened during their exploration, have still resulted in poor quality climbs with repeat ascent being rare. Nature has its own way of correcting this brief intrusion but over enthusiastic and often unnecessary gardening can and does create long term problems. The scars can take many years to heal and the critics are constantly in the wings waiting for the opportunity to prove their point.

The present edition, unlike its predecessors, now contains routes across all the grades giving a more balanced climbing picture but differs from many other guides in not being top heavy on both grade and quality. In spite of the modernisation process since the last edition the area retains its strong traditional links with many lower grade classic rock climbs on its mountain crags that can still provide superb days out in a relatively quiet mountain atmosphere. The difference now is in the choice of available crags and hopefully some of the increasing number of climbers will be tempted onto the alternative crags thereby reducing the pressure on The Napes and Tophet Wall.

Unlike the previous writer, I shall not be giving hints as to the remaining last great problems or 'plums', do it the hard way, go out and find them if they exist. Alternatively, try repeating any of the many fine recorded routes, the rewards for most would be much greater and the quality guaranteed. There can be few climbers around that have totally exhausted the available routes at their grade and below. Alternatively, work at it, and go up a grade.

It only now requires the armchair critics to adopt their usual and predictable positions when assessing the guides route descriptions, grades and star rating for the whole of the guide book production process to be completed.

Some things never change.

Dave Kirby, February 1991

ENNERDALE

Bowness Knott   (109 155)   Alt. 130 m   South West Facing

This is the collective name for a number of crags that lie on the south and south western slopes of Bowness Knott.

Above and right of the car park (109 154) are a number of outcrops including Oak Grove Crag, High Crag and Hollow Ghyll Crag. They have been well explored in the past, and are generally loose or vegetated and are not recommended; even the peregrines avoid them.

Left of the car park are Long Crag and Bowness Crag and comprise the main climbing area.

The crags face south and west across the lake and are easily reached via a gate opposite Bowness Cottage, 200 metres north of the car park. The climbing here is generally of poor quality, any good bits of rock or pitches, are far and away outnumbered by poor rock, heavily vegetated rock, or just the sheer poor quality of climbing. There are, however, one or two exceptions, i.e. Black Crack Route, and some of the harder shorter climbs on Long Crag. Green Gash and Labyrinth on Bowness Crag, are not without interest.

The crags do catch any sunshine going and have a pleasant, postcard outlook. Some holds need careful usage. Access is restricted during the peregrine's nesting season from mid-March to mid-July. Anglers' Crag is then the alternative. Swimming across the lake is forbidden.

Directly above the gate is Bowness Crag and the green wall of Labyrinth. Further into the quarry (left) a derelict stone-wall leads up to Green Gash. The track ends below a large, central scree slope which is unstable and best avoided, but it clearly defines the two crags. Long Crag is to its left and Bowness Crag to its right.

Descent Routes
The obvious gully just mentioned is **not safe** as a descent route, due to highly unstable material in the gully bed.

From the top of Long Crag, the descent is found to the left (facing in) by scrambling through the thick undergrowth of bilberry and bracken etc.

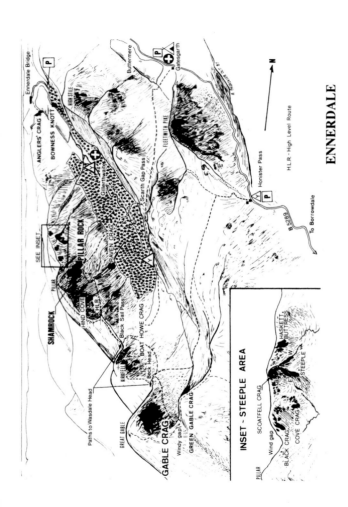

ENNERDALE

N

H.L.R - High Level Route

INSET - STEEPLE AREA

The descent route from Bowness Crag is either by abseil from a convenient tree about 3 metres back from the edge of Green Gash (double rope required), or, by scrambling up and slightly left to an old wall, and following this rightwards (facing in) until an arduous descent can be made down steep scree and so to the base of the crag (tedious).

Long Crag

Black Crack Route   80 m   HS   1950
Start at the base of Long Crag below a large tree.
1   20 m. Climb left of the tree and continue up the steep left edge to belay below the Black Crack.
2   15 m. A thin slab leads to the crack which has excellent holds. Belay on left.
3   20 m. Ascend the steep wall on the right to easy ground, then traverse right to a tree belay beneath Hyacinth Chimney.
4   25 m. Ascend the rib right of the chimney and continue up the fine crack, on hidden holds, to the top.

● **Snowstorm**   77 m   S   1957
Start as for Black Crack Route.
1   25 m. As for Black Crack Route to below the Black Crack. Then move right and up to belay on an oak tree in the corner.
2   16 m. Go up left, climb onto the Bos'n's Chair and up a steep slab to a belay in the Crow's Nest.
3   18 m. Climb the narrow groove, inclining to the right, which is awkward but has good holds to a block belay.
4   18 m. Easier slabs to the top.

Variation   Original Start
    The original start was 10 metres right and climbed the most appalling vegetated slabs to arrive at the same oak tree.

● **Tyrozet**   74 m   S   1968
A poor vegetated route which ricochets between Black Crack Route, Snowstorm and Hailstorm. Start 4 metres right of Black Crack Route.
1   30 m. Climb a short wall and vegetated rock to an oak tree. Continue up the broken crack to belay by a gnarled holly.
2   12 m. Descend left and make for a prominent block on Snowstorm. Climb over the block and go rightwards to Hyacinth Chimney on Black Crack Route.

3   12 m. Climb the wall immediately behind the tree and move right to belay above the chimney.
4   20 m. Step down to the left, then back right to a sloping ledge. Climb the overhanging wall and follow the slabs above to the top.

Hailstorm   78 m   HS   1950
Start 20 metres up to the right of Black Crack Route at a large block set against a short red wall.
1   20 m. Move upwards and left to a bracket, then climb direct to a ledge below a steep wall with a crack to its right.
2   20 m. Climb the fine wall left of the crack to the top of the pinnacle and continue to the foot of Hyacinth Chimney.
3   8 m. Climb the rib, right of the chimney, then move right to a stance below the final wall.
4   30 m. Cross the rough slabs to the right and up the corner crack, past a holly, to the top.

Wall Street   45 m   E1   1981
Start as for Hailstorm.
1   15 m (4b). Climb the short, red wall and continue to a terrace on the right below a black wall on The Marriage. Move 8 metres right to belay in a clump of trees.
2   15 m (5b). Climb the green wall by a ramp leading leftwards; when it ends follow a steep groove direct to a tree belay below a bulging wall.
3   15 m (5b). Climb up and right until it is possible to pull back left over a bulge and up a good jamming crack to the top.

Variation   15 m   1981
2a (5a). Start 10 metres right of the clump of trees. Climb the strenuous crack past a wedged block then leftwards to the tree belay.

The Marriage   48 m   HVS   1969
Start 4 metres up the scree from the Hailstorm block.
1   12 m (4a). Climb the impending groove which widens into a scoop. Move left and follow an indefinite rib to belay below the black wall.
2   12 m (5a). Climb the black wall strenuously to the obvious break. An easier scoop leads to the foot of Hyacinth Chimney.
3   24 m (4c). A fine pitch. The steep wall immediately behind the tree is climbed on small holds for 6 metres, then slightly right using a thin finger crack. Make an awkward step left round a rib to an attractive slab. Ascend diagonally left, then veer to the right

up a corner. Continue via a stepped nose on the right, a short wall and pleasant slabs to the top.

DON'T attempt the **Bowness Girdle** (100 m, S) until shovels become standard!

Bowness Crag

Scrambling by the old stone wall leads to the Green Gash, the obvious cleft tilted slightly right.

Skyhook   50 m   S   1964
Steep and interesting but spoiled by vegetation. Starts left of Green Gash at a large block below an overhang.
1   25 m. Climb onto the block, over the bulge and up a mossy slab to a ledge. Go up the short gangway on the left, then move back right across the slab above the overhang and up to a tree belay.
2   25 m. Climb straight up the slabs, keeping to the right edge overlooking Green Gash.

● **Left Wall**   40 m   E2
This hard and potentially dangerous route ascends a series of overhanging grooves on the wall between Skyhook and Green Gash at an overhanging corner.
   (5b). Climb the corner to an easier-angled section and gain the first of the grooves on the wall on the left. The overhanging grooves are ascended with increasing difficulty, and very strenuous moves have to be made on very suspect holds, until it is possible to pull out left near the top of Skyhook, and up to the tree belay at the top of Green Gash.

★ **Green Gash**   40 m   VS   1959
A rose amongst many thorns, this fine pitch cleaves Bowness Crag from top to bottom and although mossy, this does not detract from the pleasure of the route. Protection is good throughout. Start by scrambling to the foot of the obvious cleft tilted slightly to the right. The pitch can be split if necessary.
   (4c). Ascend the corner groove direct, moving left at the top and into the continuation of the corner. A bulge near the top of the climb proves awkward. Either, finish direct, or move right to the arête and finish up this to the obvious tree belay. An abseil down the route is recommended, double ropes required.

Labyrinth   55 m   MVS   1959

A meandering artificial climb, with some interesting bits, especially on the last pitch. Start about 300 metres right of Green Gash, behind a large block which is directly above the gate opposite the cottage.

1   25 m (4a). Follow a clean, pleasant gangway leftwards. Move out right at the top to a good ledge, climb directly up for a couple of metres to belay beside a mossy glacis.
2   15 m. Move up and right to climb a shallow slanting line with a detached block. After 10 metres, move horizontally right to jammed blocks, then down to oak tree belays.
3   15 m (4b). A good pitch. The overhanging crack behind the tree is climbed strenuously towards the top with some difficulty (large Friend, or awkward thread). Move left to finish on steep vegetation etc. The safest belays are to be found by scrambling up for about 15 metres to the next rock outcrop (tedious).

Grike   (081 148)   Alt. 200 m   North Facing

A collection of small buttresses in and above the forest planting are heavily vegetated, slow to dry, and although visited in the past, they are better left in the obscurity they deserve.

Crag Fell

The mountain falling into the south-west corner of Ennerdale Lake has four areas of cliff. The most obvious is the impressive ridge of pinnacles at half-height, well seen from Ennerdale Bridge. Unfortunately these can be ascended by easy scrambling and only offer short pitches.

The band of cliff below the summit ridge of the mountain and a similar band above the dam appear to offer nothing more than a few short vegetated pitches.

The spur of the fell protruding into the lake, however, has rock of a different calibre. This cliff, Anglers' Crag, which is often dry when Pillar Rock is wet, has many good short climbs, which are also some of the most low-lying in the valley. The rock is often lichenous and the climbs are shorter than the best routes on Bowness Knott. Anglers' Crag is, however, an excellent practice ground, especially for beginners, and for this reason many short routes will be described.

From Ennerdale Bridge take the first road to the Lake to a car park near the Pumphouse, (085 154). A track leads past the dam, round the south shore to the headland; approximately 1 km. There are some fine, little climbs with good rock and grand scenery, well worth a visit.

Crag Fell Pinnacles   (096 148)   Alt. 300 m   North Facing

The Pinnacles rise impressively at approximately half-height on the mountain and are best reached via the diagonal path to the top of Anglers' Crag, then by direct scrambling. The larger detached pinnacle at the east end is **Magog** (25m, MS, 1948) via the long arête. The isolated rock near the west end is **Robinson's Pinnacle**. Entertaining up its **Short Side** (16m, VD) and **Eastern Crack** (12m, MS, 1948). A fun place to boulder and practice leaping!

Anglers' Crag   (099 151)   Alt. 120 m   North Facing

Continuing along the lake shore path, Anglers' Crags two main buttresses are seen. The most westerly has a huge overhang which is turned by Hook, Line and Sinker and by Crystal Groove. Further left is an impressive, square tower with Angel's Step ascending its front. These climbs are more easily reached via a traverse in from the diagonal path over Anglers' Crag. The path continues under the lowest point of the crag to a wall approximately 40 metres high. The routes are described starting from the obvious chimney at the left (east) end of the wall – Dan's Mine and also with reference to Phantom Groove, an obvious V-groove in the centre of the wall.

Dan's Groove   18 m   D   1980
Start 5 metres left of Dan's Mine!
　　Move up left into a groove, then up this to the top.

● **Dan's Mine**   18 m   D   1958
　Well named.
　　Climb the obvious chimney to easy ground. A Severe finish can be made up the right wall.

Cow Pie   30 m   S   1980
　　Follow Dan's Mine to a grassy ledge, then transfer to the right wall. Climb up until a swing into a groove can be made and follow a crack in the groove to the top.

Desperate Dan 30 m VS   1980
A direct variation on Forgotten Wall, which is poorly protected, but nevertheless contains some good, clean climbing. Start immediately right of Dan's Mine on the arête.
   (4b). Climb the arête, to break through an overhang at 3 metres, climb the centre of the wall, crossing Forgotten Wall (runners), and then to the top.

Forgotten Wall 30 m HS   1958
Another pleasant climb, with adequate protection. Start 2 metres right of Dan's Mine, at a shallow crack.
   (4a). Follow the thin crack for 4 metres, and then move diagonally left up a shallow groove-line. Continue straight up. passing a huge detached block on the left, to an easy finish.

A few metres right of Dan's Mine, in the centre of the wall, is an obvious deep, 15 metre high V-groove, ending at the left side of a horizontal ledge. This is Phantom Groove.

A Face Remembered 35 m MVS   1985
A harder version of Shadow Wall and a more direct climb, with adequate protection. Start 5 metres left of Phantom Groove.
   (4a). Climb diagonally left up whitish rock to the edge of the face, and follow this directly, passing an in situ peg, to the top, finishing up the left arête.

Shadow Wall 35 m MS   1958
Good face climbing. Start 3 metres left of Phantom Groove. Protection is sparse.
   Climb the wall direct on good holds to an in situ peg at 15m, then steeply up, keeping just left of a shallow, vegetated depression.

Phantom Groove 38 m MS   1938
A pleasant, but not well-protected climb.
1   15m. Climb the groove to the ledge, then move right to obvious tree belays.
2   23 m. Move back left and climb the shallow continuation of the groove, then a wall, to the top.

Temptation 15 m S   1958
   Lies just right of Phantom Groove and is thin and tempting. Continue up Phantom Groove to the top or abseil off the tree.

A route has been climbed between Temptation and Phantom Groove – **Andrea's Revenge** (30m, HVS (5a), 1983). The main difficulty is the avoidance of the other two routes. It is possible to climb anywhere on the faces between Dan's Mine and Temptation, if you have the nerve (4c/5a).

A couple of metres right of Temptation is a dirty chimney/gully (M). Just right of this is a pleasant blocky ridge (just left of the lowest point of the buttress). **Like It or Lump It** (25 m, D) pleasantly follows the crest to the top.

Just right again, **Midge Arête** (25m, VD, 1982) climbs the obvious rightward slanting line up to the right of the obvious black overhang. The black overhang has been climbed and claimed on numerous occasions. The overhang is avoided by an awkward move right.

The rest of the lower crag offers many vegetated problems. The most worthwhile climb is up a shallow groove in a smooth face of rock at the extreme right end of the crag.

Shep 25 m VS   1959
A good pitch, with poor protection, above very steep grass and a very deep lake.
   (4c). Climb short overlapping slabs to a small overhang. Step right and up a wall to a ledge. Move right round a bulge, and climb a groove on good holds to a huge boulder belay. The huge boulder is a landmark and helps locate the route.

From Shep, scrambling up the fell rightwards brings into sight the largest and most impressive buttress (Angel's Step Buttress). This is best reached by taking the diagonal path which goes over the top of Anglers' Crag and traversing in (east). Hook, Line and Sinker Buttress is reached by descending a grassy gully (north) just before the top of the path.

★ **Angel's Step** 30 m VS   1961
An excellent and rather exposed climb on good rock, which starts at the foot of the buttress.
   (4c). Climb over bulging rock to a grass ledge. Continue up to the overhang, passing a peg runner. Move to the right and mantelshelf on to a small ledge (crux). Move up, then left to a grass ledge. Go straight up the wall above to the summit.

★ **Gog**   25 m   HVS   1959
Another good pitch. Start as for Angel's Step, but move right after 4 metres to climb a shallow groove with a crack.
    (5a). Climb the groove until it ends in a small overhang. On the left is the mantelshelf of Angel's Step. Move up delicately, then go to the right for 2 metres and climb the wall on small holds to the top.

Just right of Angel's Step Buttress is a short red buttress of rock. **Aneurysm** (10m, VS (4b),1982) ascends the middle of this buttress.

Between Angel's Step buttress and Hook, Line and Sinker buttress 100 metres across to the right, a number of very short problems on various bits of rock exist, most of which are not worth the effort.

Catalepsy Corner   40 m   HVS   1982
Start at the lowest point of the buttress left of Hook, Line and Sinker.
1   25 m (5a). Ascend the slab, trending right to greenery. Move left to below a reddish overhang. Traverse left under the overhang and up on undercuts to a tree.
2   15 m (4a). Climb the obvious V-groove to the top.

★ **Hook, Line and Sinker**   30 m   E1   1959
An interesting and rather exposed route, with a bold, unprotected start. Start 6 metres down from the large holly on the right side of the buttress, at a reddish break, which slants to the left.
    (5b). Climb the break to a grass ledge. Climb up the shallow groove above to a small stance. Step left and climb the groove to the overhang. Move out left underneath the overhang onto the wall.

★ **Crystal Groove**   30 m   HS   1959
An excellent little climb, which starts at the large holly on the right side of the buttress. Care is required with rope management, and the placing of protection, due to the awkward line of the climb.
    Climb out left along a sloping gangway until it peters out. Awkward belay possible. Gain the groove running up to the overhang; then traverse to the right, under the overhang, to the easy ridge leading to the summit.

Haskett Buttress and Steeple West Buttress

Haskett Buttress faces north-west and forms an impressive buttress among the crags at the head of Mirklin Cove. From some distance away the cirque of crags look quite impressive, but on closer acquaintance it is only Haskett Buttress along with Steeple Buttress to its left, that provides continuous rock for climbing. Haskett Buttress is recognized as being the central one of three buttresses at the head of the cove. On its immediate left is Haskett Gully and immediate right is Western Gully. The right wall of Haskett Gully is split by an impressive crack (the Dolorous Stroke), while the front of the Buttress holds two hanging corner grooves, and on the right-hand side at about one third height is a long horizontal overhang.

From Ennerdale the best approach is to cross the concrete ford on the River Liza before Gillerthwaite and take the path up onto Lingmell; follow this path eastwards to Low Beck and cross it to continue up onto the crest of the spur running north from Steeple. Either contour in from Long Crag, or more pleasantly, follow the main ridge over Steeple summit and descend to the col between Steeple and the Scoat Fell Ridge. Then descend the wide scree and rock gully (due west) and at the bottom of the gully turn right (north) for Steeple West Buttress, or left (south west) for Haskett Buttress.

From Bowness Knott car park, it's a 7 km walk with a 600 metre ascent to reach the crags in about 2-2½ hours (a cycle would reduce the time taken).

From Wasdale the crags can be reached in about 2 hours from Nether Beck Bridge. Follow Nether Beck for about 4 km and where Nether Beck veers north-east, continue north to the broad col between Haycock and Scoat Fell. From here follow the 700 metre contour across the Ennerdale side of the hill, first in a north-east direction, then easterly to the foot of the crags.

The routes are described from left to right starting with Haskett Buttress, followed by Steeple West Buttress which leads one back towards Haskett Gully.

The descent from Haskett Buttress is down the easy gully on the immediate right of the scrappy buttress to the right of Haskett Buttress (facing the crag).

Haskett Buttress   (155 114)   Alt. 750 m   North West Facing

★ **The Dolorous Stroke**   90 m   E1   1969
The right (westerly) wall of Haskett Gully is cut along its entire
length by a superb crack line. Except for the first pitch, it is a very
fine, if at present somewhat lichenous climb, and although it has a
serious feel about it, it is well protected by large friends. Well worth
the effort. Start immediately right of Haskett Gully at the lowest point
of the buttress.
1   30 m (4a). Climb an indefinite rib to ledges below a corner. Rock
    steps lead to a wall. Climb a vertical groove on the right, stepping
    right at the top to a bilberry terrace.
2   24 m (5b). The sharp rib on the left, overlooking the gully, has
    a slabby right face. Climb this to a niche below the crack proper.
    Surmount the first overhang (hard) and climb with difficulty to a
    poor resting place below the final bulge. Continue, still not easy,
    to a comfortable bilberry ledge.
3   18 m (4a). The continuation crack is followed more easily to
    another ledge.
4   18 m (4c). Traverse 3 metres left and gain a higher small grass
    ledge. The fine, open, and impending corner groove above
    provides a delicate and fitting finish to the climb.

The Devious Slash   75 m   VS   1969
The most obvious feature of Haskett Buttresses lowest band is a
vertical corner groove, situated in the centre. The climb starts some
9 metres below this, and about 20 metres up and right from the start
of The Dolorous Stroke.
1   24 m (4b). An indefinite rib and grass leads to a sloping terrace
    below the imposing vertical corner. Climb the corner groove; then
    scramble diagonally left for 6 metres to a terrace.
2   15 m (4b). Surmount two ledges to where the rock steepens. An
    awkward pull up to the left leads to steep slabs, which lead to a
    wall. Traverse 2 metres to the right to the corner crack and exit
    on the right; then move to the right, up slabs, to a grassy ledge
    with a large block.
3   36 m (4a). From the left end of the ledge, climb a steep wall to
    another ledge. An overhanging wall with good holds is followed
    by a pleasant ridge, which leads to the top.

The Detrital Slide   75 m   VS   1969
Start two paces right of The Devious Slash.
1   20 m (4a). Broken rocks lead to a sloping terrace. Ignore the
    corner-groove (pitch 1 of The Devious Slash) and climb straight
    up an enjoyable wall some 4 metres to the right to a ledge.
    Immediately above is a smooth-looking V-groove with an
    undercut start.
2   15 m (4c). A fine sustained pitch. The overhanging groove is
    awkward to enter and is climbed for 3 metres until a short,
    delicate traverse left leads to a smooth-walled sentry-box. Leave
    this via the rib on the left to reach a good runner. The steep slabs
    above lead to a grassy ledge at the top of pitch 2 of The Devious
    Slash.
3   40 m (4a). Climb the wall behind the block for 3 metres then
    traverse to the right, along a ledge for 6 metres to a clean, small
    buttress. Ascend this on fine rock; then continue easily, left of a
    chimney, to a short, delicate wall on the left. Scrambling leads to
    the top. (This pitch may be split).

The crag now swings right into a deep scree-filled cleft (Western
Gully), which has a left wall of immaculate clean rock, similar in
character to The Pinnacle on Scafell. At its lower edge is an obvious
roof above a great slab. The following route climbs above this.

★ **The Dexterous Shuffle**   65 m   E2   1988
A fine, intimidating route. Start by scrambling left from the foot of
the gully to belay below the left-hand end of the roof.
1   35 m (5c). Climb up the slab to a peg runner at the first belay
    on The Delectation Sinistrose, then up the bulging wall to another
    peg runner. Traverse right on undercuts, across the very lip of the
    roof to reach a good hold, and continue delicately rightwards to
    reach a vertical crack. Follow this to a ledge and block belay.
2   30 m. (4b). Pitch 2 of The Dipso Somnambulist.

★ **The Dipso Somnambulist**   63 m   E2   1988
A superb, steep climb on excellent rock. Start at the foot of the slab
below the right-hand end of the roof.
1   33 m (5b). Climb up to the roof, then swing right and follow the
    thin crack line direct to a ledge and block belay.
2   30 m (4b). Either climb the easy rocks behind to finish up the
    cleanest slab, or abseil from the block to the base of the crag.

★ The Deleterious Sting   60 m   E1   1988
Excellent wall climbing. Start just right of the previous route.
1   30 m (5b). A steep wall leads to the slab (crux), then move right
     across the wall and gain a good narrow ledge in its centre. Follow
     a thin crack to a bulge, then pull into a shallow scoop to a ledge.
     A crack leads to a ledge and block belay.
2   30 m (4b). Pitch 2 of The Dipso Somnambulist.

The Dactylic Springald   60 m   E1   1988
Although only a variation start to the previous route, it gives some
very good climbing. Start higher up the gully at a grassy patch below
an obvious clean groove.
1   30 m (5b). Climb out left to gain a small pinnacle on the steep
     wall. Step up to a crack, then traverse delicately left across the
     fine ramp to reach The Deleterious Sting at the scoop. Finish up
     this.
2   30 m (4b). Pitch 2 of The Dipso Somnambulist.

The Ductile Slant   50 m   MS   1969
Start 6 metres above the previous route, and some 6 metres below a
steep rib that divides the gully.
1   20 m. The left wall of the gully is climbed diagonally left,
     crossing the foot of a break in the wall, and continuing left to
     doubtful flakes and blocks. 3 metres after a small rock finger is
     passed, step right and ascend the blunt nose on good holds to a
     block belay on the ridge. The break crossed previously is now
     immediately on the right.
2   30 m. Step up and left on to a pedestal of rock; then swing onto
     the wall and gain the crest of the rib on the left. Climb this to a
     small ledge; then traverse left across a rib to a good ledge. Climb
     the wall behind the ledge; then follow the excellent and open slab
     on the right to the summit.

Almost opposite the start of The Dactylic Springald in Western Gully,
on the right or west wall, is a prominent crack line.

Steeple Crack   36 m   VS   1975
This short but interesting route climbs the prominent crack-line.
     (4c). Climb the wide crack past the initial steepening in the
     chimney. The crack and groove above are followed to the top.

The Delectation Sinistrose   103 m   VS   1970
A girdle traverse of Haskett Buttress giving sustained, delicate
climbing. Start as for The Dipso Somnambulist.

1   25 m (4a). Steep rock steps lead onto the slab proper. Climb
    directly up the right edge to the overhang, then, keeping as high
    as possible, traverse the entire length of the slab to a poor stance
    at its top left corner.

2   12 m (4b). Move across and down the small smooth slab on the
    left to moderate holds in the groove of pitch 2 The Detrital
    Slide. A short delicate traverse left then leads to a smooth
    walled sentry box; exit via the rib on the left. A block belay lies on the
    cramped overhung rock ledge above.

3   16 m (4b). An awkward movement is necessary before the ledge
    can be quitted on the left to an overhung groove; then step left
    again to the steep slabs of pitch 2 The Devious Slash. Ascend
    these for 2 metres then traverse 2 metres to the right into the
    corner crack, pull out of it and follow slabs up right to a grassy
    ledge with a large block.

4   26 m (4b). Traverse left along a diminishing ledge, and cross the
    top of a bottomless groove to the left edge of the buttress. Climb
    up over slabby rock to a rounded blistered nose, and ascend an
    exposed crack on its left side to a grassy bay containing a pile
    of large, rather doubtful blocks.

5   6 m (4a). Cross the blocks, swing left across the gully wall, and
    descend slightly to the rock crevasse below the last pitch of The
    Dolorous Stroke.

6   18 m (4c). Traverse 3 metres left and gain a higher small grass
    ledge; then climb the fine, open impending corner above. (Pitch
    6 of The Dolorous Stroke).

Steeple West Buttress   (156 117)   Alt. 700 m   West Facing

The easiest descent from Steeple West is down the obvious approach
gully.

Contravallation Ridge   70 m   MS   1969
The route takes a line of continuous rock running up the centre. A
pleasant climb on superb rock. Start 18 metres up and right from the
lowest point of the crag.

1   12 m. Climb the rough slabs. After 6 metres move to the right
    to an awkward scoop, with an exit on the left. Move left to a
    ledge with high belays.

2   18 m. Climb the slab line ahead to a grassy corner.

3   20 m. Follow the left side of the big nose ahead and traverse to
    the right to a perch on the ridge. The same point can be gained

via a gangway and groove on the right side of the nose. Slabs lead to a narrow ledge below a sharp, steep ridge.

4   20 m. The slabby rock just left of the crest is climbed on small holds to a grassy corner. A short wall is followed by scrambling to a block belay.

Moving Finger Grooves   65 m   VS   1969

This follows a discontinuous line of grooves and ribs up the right edge of the crag. Start some 12 metres up and right from Contravallation Ridge in a mossy bay below an unpleasant-looking, vertical, vegetated groove, which is usually wet.

1   25 m (4a). Avoid the wet groove by climbing vegetated, though more agreeable, rocks on the left to ledges with juniper. Traverse to the right past an inviting corner crack, and step delicately under overhanging rock to a poor landing in the groove on the edge of the crag, then up, steeply, to a ledge.

2   15 m (4a). Traverse left to gain the front of the exposed nose; then ascend directly to a wide ledge. Easy rocks and ledges are followed, bearing right, to the foot of a vertical rib on the right edge.

3   25 m (4b). Climb the awkward green scoop just left of the rib. Gain the crest; then climb up and right, over steep though easier ground, to a narrow ledge. Traverse to the right along this to twin V-grooves. Climb either groove to block belays.

Moving right (south) for about 200 metres brings one to the foot of the East Buttress. This broken crag has one route.

East Buttress   92 m   S   1942

The route starts at the base of the crag at the foot of a short rib. This route is not to be confused with Steeple East Buttress.

1   20 m. Climb the rib and step left at the top, then ascend an awkward corner on the right to a narrow ledge. From the left end of the ledge, work upwards to a block and continue straight up to a rib above and left to a ledge.

2   25 m. Easy climbing up rough rock to a sweep of slabs. Climb the slabs for a short distance, then make an awkward traverse right to climb a mixture of grass and rock to some blocks at the foot of a large steep wall.

3   22 m. Climb the wall above the blocks to a flake in the wall. Climb onto the tip of this and step right to a small ledge. Continue up the wall on good holds, and where the rock impends, work right and up a groove to a short wall (avoidable) which is climbed to blocks.

4   25 m. Scramble up the easy ridge to the top of the buttress.

Immediately right of East Buttress is **Haskett Gully** (1908) which is about 90 metres long and consists of appallingly steep vegetation, interspersed with bits of rock at a Severe standard.

Steeple East Buttress (157 117) Alt. 700 m East Facing

On approaching Black Crag in Windgap Cove from High Beck, the route is seen as the most obvious buttress rising direct from the right upper cove, Mirk Cove (158 115), to the summit of Steeple.

Steeple Buttress 154 m VD   1957

A long mountaineering route, very worthwhile in winter conditions. Scrambling over broken rocks leads to the foot of the buttress.

1 30 m. Climb easily up the first section of the ridge to a ledge at the foot of a steep wall.
2 15 m. Ascend the wall; then take a crack on the right and follow it to a recess.
3 25 m. Step left onto the ridge and climb it steeply to a grassy knoll.
4 30 m. Easy scrambling up the edge of the buttress. Move left to a belay.
5 24 m. Climb the stepped ridge to belay below the final impending rocks.
6 15 m. Move up into a groove; then take a steep crack on the left.
7 15 m. Easy scrambling to finish at the summit cairn.

Scoat Fell Crag (159 115) Alt. 750 m North Facing

The north-pointing spur of Steeple separates two hanging valleys: Mirklin Cove to the west, Windgap Cove to the east. Nestling in the westerly corner of Windgap Cove is a subsidiary hollow, Mirk Cove. Here, Scoat Fell Crag faces north just below the summit of Scoat Fell, and can be identified by an unpleasant gully, which splits the crag to form the tower-like east and west buttresses. Further right, the cliff develops ledge systems.

Travesty Cracks 57 m S   1971

Follows the prominent line of cracks to the left side of the east buttress. Start as for The Dream Merchants up the left of the twin chimneys.

1 14 m. Climb the chimney, past a capstone to steep grass. Pull to the right to a ledge on the rib, then climb a little slab on the right

to a large spike. Continue up the short, wide crack, moving left
to a ledge and little bollard belay.
2   23 m. Climb the layaway crack, immediately to the left of the
vertical crack on The Dream Merchants. Ledges are reached,
giving access to an obvious system of short, grassy grooves and
cracks trending left. Follow this line to a corner with a chock
belay.
3   20 m. The imposing chimney-crack ahead has an overhanging top.
Follow it past doubtful chockstones to a small ledge. Traverse left
for 2 metres to a rough, steepening slab. Climb this and veer left
up the final wall to the summit slabs.

The Dream Merchants   50 m   MVS   1971
A fine, open climb taking the prow of the east buttress. Start at the
left corner of the crag, where two short, though deep, chimneys are
divided by a vertical rib. Do not confuse with the gully's first pitch,
which lies further right.
1   25 m (4b). By using the left chimney for 3 metres attain a ledge
on the rib by stepping right. Climb the difficult shallow grooves,
then continue more easily up the ridge to a ledge, below a thin
steep crack which is awkward to approach and strenuous to quit.
Continue up the airy arête to a grassy ledge.
2   25 m (4a). A delightful pitch. Climb a short, thin, steep crack on
the ridge to small ledges, then bridge up the overhanging scoop
immediately above. Move slightly left onto a wall, which is
ascended direct to a gangway sloping right. Return to the arête
on the right, and climb past a huge block to the top of the crag.

The Faux Pas   58 m   VS   1971
A varied climb up the right side of the east buttress. Start just right
of The Dream Merchants' initial rib in a mossy chimney.
1   18 m. Climb the deeply-cut green chimney. A cave pitch followed
by 6 metres up steep grass leads to belays on the left wall at the
foot of a left-slanting fault line.
2   20 m (4b). The magnificent gnarled wall on the left is ascended
on small holds, first via the fault line for 4 metres, then straight
up using two thin and shallow cracks to a ledge. Climb the fine,
steep corner crack at the right end of the ledge. Grassy niche and
chock belay.
3   20 m (4a). Climb a rough slab on the left; at the top bear to the
right, up a groove, to a narrow, grassy ledge. Climb the exposed
wall, bearing slightly right, on good holds, to the top.

Two good climbs are to be found on the west buttress.

Twin Ribs Climb   84 m   HS   1945
The climb lies on the buttress to the right of the gully. Two prominent, steep, parallel ribs run up to a large overhang. Start 6 metres to the right of the foot of the ribs in a grassy corner.
1   20 m. Climb the wall for 3 metres, then traverse left to the edge of the right rib, which is followed for 6 metres. Cross the groove to the left rib and climb it to a small stance with a spike belay 3 metres higher.
2   27 m. Continue up the edge of the left rib for 4 metres, step right and follow a groove to a good ledge in the niche below the overhang. Swing out to the left under the overhang. Pull up on good holds, and climb a wall to a ledge.
3   12 m. Easier climbing up the broken edge of a rib leads to a large grassy ledge.
4   25 m. Rough scrambling leads to the top of the buttress.

Octopus   70 m   VS   1946
Start at the same place as Twin Ribs Climb.
1   23 m (4a). Climb the wall for about 3 metres and step to the right to the groove above. Climb the groove until it terminates at a small stance. Traverse left for 2 metres, then step up and back to the right to a small ledge.
2   10 m (4b). Swing out to the right, under the overhang, until a foothold is reached. Climb the vertical wall by means of a small crack until a short traverse left can be made to join Twin Ribs Climb.
3   37 m. As for Twin Ribs Climb, pitches 3 and 4.

Cove Crag   (162 118)   Alt. 660 m   North Facing

In the centre of Windgap Cove, 250 metres west and slightly lower than Black Crag, lies a low rocky spur which curves up to join the main Scoat Fell ridge (pleasant in winter conditions). The base of the spur terminates at a set of water-streaked slabs of immaculate rock. The routes are easily combined with a visit to Black Crag.

Prophylactics   45 m   VS   1988
This worthwhile route starts 15 metres left of the lowest point of the buttress at the left-hand of two converging ramps. Protection is sparse, but adequate.

1   25 m (4c). Follow the short ramp to the foot of a short vertical
     crack and scoop. Climb this with difficulty, then shallow ribs
     above lead to a large mossy ledge.
2   20 m (4b). From the left-hand side of the ledge, climb up to a
     slab and cross it leftwards until overlooking a black groove. The
     delicate rib above ends with a superb flake hold; finish at a higher
     ledge. Scrambling remains, or traverse left to descend.

No Ewe Turns   57 m   HS   †   1988
A climb with a dirty start which improves with height. Start right of
the previous route at the right-hand ramp.
1   15 m. Up the ramp to a ledge, follow the crack on the right of
     a smooth wall until it trends left, then climb straight up to a ledge.
2   20 m. Move up until 2 metres right of a detached block in a
     corner. Climb the slabby groove above to a diagonal crack, follow
     this left for a couple of metres, then continue up the wall above
     to a block belay.
3   14 m. Stand on the block, then climb the cleanest slabs above to
     belay beneath a cracked tower.
4   8 m. The left-hand crack provides a strenuous finish.

Black Crag   (165 117)   Alt. 650 m   North North West Facing

Black (or High) Crag is situated high up the north slope of Scoat
Fell, which goes down to Wind Gap. If approached from Ennerdale,
the most direct way is to ascend High Beck (a tributary of the Liza)
and in its upper part, the whole of which is marked on the Ordnance
Survey map as Windgap Cove, take the left fork of the stream
towards Wind Gap. The cliff lies a little to the right of this, and must
not be confused with the more broken up crags still further to the
right, or those encircling the combe (Mirk Cove) of the right fork of
the stream. From Wasdale the Wind Gap route to Pillar is followed,
and if a line is struck leftwards, at the same level as the Gap, across
the rather steep and rough fellside, the foot of the crag is reached in
less than 10 minutes from Wind Gap. The rock in the main is superb
and the routes vary in length from 30 to 60 metres. There are good
climbs at all but the hardest grades and the crag would well repay a
visit, especially in the afternoon and evening, with the sun upon it.

Black Crag conveniently splits into five separate climbing buttresses,
and the first marked feature encountered is a very wide stony gully,
which gives an easy descent from all the routes. The first buttress is
high on the left-hand side of the stony gully.

Evening Chimney   45 m   VD   1940
Start in the gully at the foot of a conspicuous chimney.
1   22 m. Climb the undercut chimney to grass ledges, and trend to
    the right over easy rocks to a grass corner.
2   23 m. Follow a broken slab to a corner with a block, climb the
    strenuous mossy corner on the left and continue up the V-chimney
    above.

The next route is immediately right of the wide stony gully

The Main Ridge Climb   96 m   D   1929
The route is artificial in that it is possible to turn difficulties on the
left and escape into the stony gully, but it does contain some
interesting climbing. Start at the foot of a short, steep buttress with
a huge block on top, and 4 metres left of a short chimney.
1   18 m. Climb the obvious line on the crest of the buttress on good
    holds, moving slightly right onto a grass ledge. Climb the short
    wall to emerge just to the left of a huge block.
2   15 m. Scramble right for 6 metres and cross the upper part of a
    wide chimney to another steep buttress. Move slightly down and
    right and traverse onto the ridge, then climb directly to the top
    of the buttress. The main difficulties end here.
3   30 m. Ridge scrambling followed by an awkward wall leads to a
    huge rock glacis (which descends into the stony gully).
4   18 m. Walk up the rock glacis to below a short crack.
5   15 m. A short crack, or rocks on the left, leads to a sloping rock
    ledge. This is followed by an angular corner and ends on another
    large rock glacis (which also descends into the stony gully).

20 metres right of The Main Ridge Climb is a superb face of rock
(Lower Slabs Buttress) about 35 metres high. It can be recognized
by a steep grassy recess on the right and some leftward trending
grassy grooves on the left.

Lower Slabs Ordinary Route   36 m   VD   1929
A good little route, which also gives an interesting variation start to
The Main Ridge Climb. Start 20 metres right of The Main Ridge
Climb and 4 metres left of the steep grassy recess.
1   12 m. Follow grassy rocks up left for 6 metres to an obvious foot
    ledge, which leads right to a low block belay.
2   10 m. From the left of the belay, climb a shallow groove with a
    crack to a rock ledge.
3   14 m. Move left onto the arête, and follow the crest pleasantly to
    the rock platform on The Main Ridge Climb.

★ **Lower Slabs Super Direct**   35 m   VS   1987
A fine direct line on excellent rock with a bold finish. Start at the
same place as Lower Slab Buttress Ordinary.
   (4c). Climb the wall direct via a small V-groove with an awkward
   move right to a grass ledge. Easier climbing straight ahead leads
   to a rock ledge. An upward traverse right is made to a hollow
   flake. From the top of the flake climb directly up the wall to the
   top.

Lower Slabs Climb Direct   38 m   MVS   1929
Another very pleasant climb which weaves its way up the face,
avoiding the main challenge but covering some interesting ground.
Start as for Lower Slabs Super Direct, 2 metres left of the large
grassy recess.
1   14 m. Climb a rightward trending dog-leg crack to reach twin
    quartz bands in a shallow corner, immediately above the top of
    the grassy recess. Follow these to a grass ledge on Lower Slabs
    Super Direct.
2   24 m (4b). Follow Lower Slabs Super Direct to the rock ledge
    and make an upward traverse right to the hollow flake. Continue
    the traverse until it is possible to move up and back left to finish
    in the same place as the Lower Slabs Super Direct.

Debutantes Slab   30 m   HS   1990
A good, but escapable slab climb, which is bold in the lower half
(no protection). Start right of Lower Slabs Direct above the grassy
recess at the right-hand side of the slabs, beneath a thin left-facing
corner. Or, use the start of Lower Slabs Climb Direct to reach the
same place.
   (4a). Climb the thin corner direct to easy ledges, continue up and
   slightly leftwards until it is possible to move back to the right
   along a short gangway to a blunt spike (first runner – protection
   is adequate from here). Ascend directly above the spike to finish
   just to the right of Lower Slabs Climb Direct.

The next climbs to the right are on the second terrace, about 30
metres higher, which can be reached via an opening a few metres
round from the large grass recess, or, from the top of the Lower Slab
Buttress by a short descent to the right. The cliff rises steeply to attain
its greatest height. On the left side, the crag is cut away in its upper
reaches by a large, leftward leaning, impending diedre or fault. Right
of this a small band of overhangs run horizontally across the crag to
peter out on the right side. Running down from the overhangs are a
series of ribs and corners.

Left Central Slab Climb   43 m   S   1929
An interesting and atmospheric, if somewhat mossy climb. Start at
the left-hand side of the face at a slabby wall, right of a fault running
up the left side of the crag, and in a grassy corner just right of a rib
with a small overhang at 5 metres.
1   15 m. Climb the slabby wall, right of the rib, to a grass ledge.
    Climb the narrow left-slanting slab above to a stance by perched
    blocks.
2   14 m. Move right, past the blocks, into a short corner, and trend
    left into a large recess under the impending head wall.
3   14 m. A good pitch. The leftward trending slabby corner is
    climbed to the top, ending on the rock glacis.

★ **Overhanging Central Slab Climb**   58 m   S   1929
A combination of two climbs to give the best route up the buttress
at this standard. The climbing is varied and gives a good if escapable
route to the top of the buttress. Start 5 metres right of Left Central
Slab Climb below two overlapping, leftward-slanting ribs.
1   12 m. Climb the first rib to a move right onto the second rib and
    follow it to a grassy stance.
2   15 m. Descend slightly and traverse out to the right over the arête
    onto a slab; the corner is climbed until it is possible to step out
    to the left edge. Climb the final bulge (a flake proving useful) to
    a ledge, and move right a couple of metres to a big grassy ledge.
3   22 m. Climb the wide slab with cracks in it (grassy gully to the
    right) to a rocky ledge. The slab narrows and finishes at the
    junction of the large rock glacis on the left (easy descent) and an
    easy grassy gully on the right (easy descent to Upper Slab
    Buttress).
4   19 m. A fine pitch. Follow a slab with a narrow crack to a large
    grassy corner on the right. A final slab and corner ends on the
    large rock glacis.

Variation   Central Slab Climb   27 m   S   1929
Not as good as the main route described but easier and more
escapable. Start 3 metres right of Poet Laureate, and 5 metres left of
a grassy rock rake, below a short shallow groove.
1a 12 m. Climb the groove for 4 metres to a slight overhang and
    traverse right along a narrow ledge to a grassy corner,
    immediately followed by another higher grassy corner.
2a 15 m. Climb a slabby corner by its left edge to a big grassy ledge.

Poet Laureate   46 m   E1   1987
A direct route up the highest section of Middle Slab Buttress. There
is a short, hard, bold section at the start of the second pitch, otherwise
the climbing is very straight-forward. Start 6 metres left of the toe
of the buttress at a clean arête, which bounds a right-facing corner,
and 2 metres right of Overhanging Central Slab Climb.
1   24 m (4b). Climb the arête direct (delicate at mid-height) to a
    block belay below a short V-corner/groove
2   22 m (5b). Make gymnastic moves off the block leftwards to the
    foot of the groove (small nut runner in the groove and in a small
    crack around the rib on the right). Climb the groove for a few
    moves before making difficult moves into a small crack in the rib
    on the right. Ascend the short, delicate slab above to easier
    ground. Follow the slabs pleasantly via a short left-facing corner.

Central Corner   24 m   HS   1987
The dirty corner is a fine line but unpleasantly vegetated and gives
a very direct start to Overhanging Central Slab Climb. Start
immediately right of Poet Laureate.
     Climb the corner direct with a move out right at the top to below
     pitch 3 of Overhanging Central Slab Climb.

● **Solo Slabs**   44 m   VD   1937
A very poor, escapable route that follows a parallel line to Central
Slab Climb. Start 5 metres up the grassy rock rake at a short corner.
1   24 m. Climb the corner to the top of the small buttress and move
    right to slabs, bounded on the right by a grassy gully.
2   20 m. Follow the slabs ahead keeping the grassy gully
    immediately on the right, to a junction with Overhanging Central
    Slab Climb.

From the right-hand end of the second terrace, a rock and grass rake
slants up rightwards to a third terrace, and a short upward scramble
leads to the foot of the impressive Upper Slab Buttress, which is
bounded on the right by West Gully. The buttress has a tower like
appearance with a hanging central corner and an overhang to its right.
On the left side of the crag lies a superb, hanging slabby corner and
left again an easy, leftward slanting, grassy gully which affords a
means of ascent or descent from the top of Middle Slab Buttress.

The routes are described from right to left from the foot of Tower
Buttress.

★ **Tower Buttress**   57 m   VD   1929
A fine climb on excellent rock and with pleasant situations. Start at
the lowest point of the buttress, which forms the left retaining wall
of the gully.
1   18 m. Pleasant slab scrambling to where the buttress rears up.
2   27 m. Climb the right edge of the buttress for 9 metres, then
    traverse left to the nose of The Tower, level with a rectangular
    overhang. Climb straight ahead to ledges below the final slabs.
3   12 m. Follow a slab to the left of the left-hand crack and a short
    delicate slab to finish.

Variation
3a Climb a crack (undercut at the base) right of the original finish
    and then a ridge to finish to the right of the original route.

★★ **Ode to Boby**   63 m   VS   1971
An excellent route which after an undistinguished first pitch provides
fine climbing and a challenging line. Start 7 metres left of Tower
Buttress at a stepped recess, which is in the middle of a small slabby
buttress leaning against the main crag.
1   15 m (4a). Easy rightward trending steps, to an awkward wall on
    the left, are followed by a rightwards leaning, corner gangway.
2   18 m (4c). A fine pitch. Make awkward moves onto the mossy
    gangway and follow it to the right-hand end of the prominent
    rectangular overhang (good thread). Traverse left under the
    overhang, step round the edge and continue a delicate traverse left
    to a triangular niche.
3   12 m (4b). Another good pitch. Climb the imposing corner above
    to a strenuous pull to the right to surmount its bulging top and
    reach a large grassy ledge.
4   18 m. (4c). Follow the grassy ledge left until it ends. Above is
    an obvious greenish, concave slab; climb the steep slab on small
    holds to a V-groove on the right, which is followed by easier rock
    to the top.

Variation   Direct Finish   15 m   VS   1987
4a (4c). Climb the rib to the left of a choked crack and follow it to
    the top of the crag.

★★ **Poetry in Motion**   57 m   HVS   1987
An excellent route with some atmosphere, which, except for the first
pitch (Ode to Boby), gives bold sustained climbing, with excellent
situations, up the hanging slab on the left side of the buttress. Start
as for Ode to Boby.

1   15 m (4a). Follow Ode to Boby to the grassy ledge below the
    corner gangway. Move left a couple of metres to belay under a
    large triangular block.
2   30 m (5a). Climb up past the large block and onto the left slanting
    corner slab. Climb the corner for a couple of metres (it is possible
    to climb the corner direct at a slightly harder standard). Traverse
    delicately left onto the edge of the slab and follow it to a move
    up to a small grass ledge to rejoin the corner. Continue to a small
    overhang (runners) and climb steeply but on good holds to the
    right, ending with an awkward pull out right to a grassy terrace.
3   18 m (4c). As for the last pitch of Ode to Boby.

Variation Finish   15 m   HVS   1988
3a (5b). Move left along a downward sloping ledge until beneath an
    obvious steep crack. Climb the crack with interest to the top.
    (This variation is incorporated into the following route)

★ **Limerick**   35 m   HVS   1988
Another good climb which follows an obvious stepped leftward
slanting corner on the extreme left side of Upper Slab Buttress. Start
about 30 metres up and left from Ode to Boby, near the top of a
grassy gully which separates Middle Slab Buttress from Upper Slab
Buttress. The route has excellent protection throughout.
    (5b). Follow the slabby corner to a small overhang. Step up and
right into another small corner, then climb this for a couple of
metres, until another overhang forces moves right into the final
corner. Climb this with pleasant layback moves to an obvious
grass terrace (possible belay). Immediately above is an
overhanging, slanting crack, which is both hard and strenuous.
Climb the crack direct, or the wall immediately to the left, with
long reaches required to overcome the difficult section of the
upper crack. The rest is followed more easily to the top.

West Gully (D, 1929) bounds Upper Slab Buttress on the right. It
offers about 40 metres of vegetated easy climbing. Right again is
Western Buttress, a very broken, easy angled area of rock. Crack
Chimney and Slab follows the left edge of the buttress and is
described, but two other routes, **Left-Hand Route** (D, 1929) and
Right-Hand Route (D, 1929) are so difficult to follow that they are
left to the exploratory skill of those who wish to climb them.

Crack, Chimney and Slab   35 m   VD   1929
This climb forms the right-hand ridge of the West Gully, and is a
traditional subterranean chimney climb. Start up and right from the
first chockstone in West Gully.

1   15 m. A narrow slab leads to the foot of a prominent black cleft.
2   20 m. The black cleft and through-route, which are often wet,
    leads to a continuation of the chimney, or a much more pleasant
    slab on the left.

West Cove   (172 125)   Alt. 750 m   North Facing

There is a fair amount of good climbing of an exploratory nature on
the crags at the head of the cove on the west side of Pillar Rock and
it may repay a visit in good winter conditions. The only route of any
worth is West Cove Eliminate.

Wide Gully (S, 1913) splits the crags from top to bottom, its start
being 90 metres from West Jordan Gully at a slightly higher level
than the foot of the latter. The way is obvious. **Branch Gully** is to
be found leading off right out of Wide Gully after about 10 metres.
It is easy scrambling.

Long Chimney (VD, 1908) starts 15 metres to the right of Wide
Gully. The chimney is followed, with some loose rock in its upper
part, to a ridge which leads past the top of Branch Gully. Straight
ahead is another chimney (VD), but an easier alternative chimney can
be found some distance to the right and round the corner.

West Cove Eliminate   55 m   HVS   1964
A technically interesting route, which follows the line of the
corner-groove rising from the junction of Wide and Branch Gullies
and is well seen from the West Face of the Rock.

1   25 m (5a). Climb a short groove and wall to a large grass ledge
    at the foot of the main groove. The groove is difficult to start.
    Climb over a small bulge to a larger one, surmount this, and move
    up to a good ledge.
2   30 m (4c). Move out to the right, up slabs, keeping near the right
    edge. Continue up easier slabs to the top.

Pillar Rock   (172 123)   Alt. 600m

North, South, East and West Facing

Pillar Rock is accessible from Ennerdale, Wasdale, Buttermere and Borrowdale. Any of the popular 1:50,000 or 1:25,000 maps will be found useful in this connection.

Approaches

Ennerdale – This is the traditional access route to the Rock for locally based climbers, and those having an extended stay in the area.

Vehicles are not normally allowed past the Forestry Commission Car Park at Bowness Knott. It is however possible to obtain a B.M.C. permit to drive as far as Gillerthwaite. To obtain a permit, contact the B.M.C. office in Manchester, Tel: 061 273 58351, who will give you the current name, address and telephone number of the permit distribution contacts in the area.

Another method, and one which is becoming extremely popular, is to cycle up the valley to the various walking points (take a good lock). Mountain bikes prove useful on this terrain.

At a point about 2½ km beyond Gillerthwaite (YHA) there is a fork in the road. The right fork leads directly to a concrete bridge across the River Liza. After crossing the bridge, turn left, and after 50 metres along the road a cairn marks the start of a good path which ascends diagonally through the forest, crossing the upper forest road, and continuing again diagonally before emerging, with fine views, at the base of the combe below the rock.

Wasdale – The traditional approach. From Wasdale Head take the path to Black Sail Pass. Head north-west past Looking Stead to pick up the well-marked track known as The High Level Route, which contours the northern slopes of Pillar Mountain.

Follow this route to Robinson's Cairn where the magnificent eastern profile of Pillar Rock can be seen. Continue the traverse to the base of the Rock (about 2 hrs).

Another more laborious route from Wasdale is to ascend Mosedale to Wind Gap, between Pillar and Scoatfell; then continue over the summit of Pillar and descend to the Rock.

Buttermere – From Gatesgarth Farm, follow the path to Scarth Gap. Do not descend to Black Sail YHA, but follow a path which starts a short distance down on the Ennerdale side and heads diagonally down in a westerly direction to reach the valley bottom opposite the memorial foot bridge. Cross the bridge and turn right (west) and after a few metres, go up a fire-break and ascend steeply to the combe beneath the Rock. (About 2 hrs).

Topography

Pillar Rock, as the name indicates, is a shapely crag, and is practically conical in appearance. Strictly speaking, there are two cones stuck together, one higher than the other, termed High Man and Low Man respectively. In plan it runs longitudinally north and south at right angles to Pillar Mountain, on the north slope of which it lies.

The south side is short and forms one side of Jordan Gap. This gap cuts Pillar off from Pisgah, which is part of the main mass. The north side is long and sloping, extending in an easy ridge from High Man to Low Man, thence dropping over the steep north cliff of the latter, and terminating in the Green Ledge, although traces of its massive form can be seen lower down the hillside in a plinth of lesser crags.

The east side is flanked by the Shamrock, which is in turn bounded by Pillar Cove, better known as Great Doup, and the deep cleft between the two is Walker's Gully.

On the west side, Low Man is cut off from the fellside by the waterfall, but the base of High Man is washed by the scree from an open gully which runs down from behind Pisgah. As the High Level Route will probably always be a popular line of approach, the routes to the various faces will be described from this direction.

From Robinson's Cairn, if the weather is clear, all the topography given will be seen, except that of the West Face, which, of course, is hidden from view. One of the first things to be noticed, apart from the towering mass of Pillar, is the Shamrock, which lies to the left and partly hides High Man. The notch on the left of High Man is Jordan Gap, whilst splitting the upper part of High Man itself is a cleft known as the Great Chimney, with a large sloping ledge on its right. The dividing line between High Man and Low Man is Savage Gully, with Walker's Gully running at an angle to it behind the Shamrock, but not visible from this point.

Coming back to the Shamrock, it will be noticed that this is split in two by a wide gully (Shamrock Gully). On the right is Shamrock Buttress, conspicuous with its diamond-shaped wall about half-way up. The Shamrock Traverse can be seen plainly running across a large sloping scree-strewn terrace on the top of the Shamrock. This is the easiest way, from the east to Jordan Gap and the short climbs on the East Face of High Man. To gain the Traverse, go along the path to the left, which makes towards the low but noticeable barrier of rock between the Cairn and Pillar. On reaching this still keep left and upward over the barrier into Great Doup, which is ascended until a short scree-shoot is seen on the right. The top of this is the start of the traverse. The track is followed, over the broad terrace mentioned previously, until it stops short at the top of an amphitheatre. This amphitheatre acts as a sort of funnel to the top of Walker's Gully and catches all the scree falling from the slopes of Pillar Mountain immediately above. A nearer view is now obtained of the east side of High Man, especially of the East Jordan Gully, which runs up into the gap, and of the prominent slab near its foot, which is the key to the easiest route to High Man. The descent into the amphitheatre from the traverse is somewhat awkward. The track continues across the amphitheatre into East Jordan Gully, a very easy climb with only one short pitch in it, and that of the chockstone variety. It should be remembered, too, that it is also possible to take an easy way over to the west side of the rock via this traverse; climb up a little out of the amphitheatre, about half-way across, whence the back of Pisgah is reached at the top of the open gully mentioned as running up from the west side.

It should also be noted that it is possible, by easy scrambling, to reach the top of Low Man from the Shamrock Traverse. The scree of the amphitheatre is descended on the left side (looking down) until the foot of the deep cleft (Great Chimney) is reached. A little ridge, which at one time had a wall on it, leading down to the top of Walker's Gully, is immediately in front; this is crossed, and easy ledges at the same level lead into Stoney Gully (upper part of Savage Gully), a scramble up which soon leads to Low Man. **The Old Wall Route** (1926), one of the earliest variations of the climbing on Pillar, goes by this way, except that shortly before reaching Stoney Gully a divergence is made to a wide square chimney, about 7 metres high, which is seen in a corner up on the left. This chimney is ascended, and from the top a junction is made with the ordinary ridge route from Low Man to High Man, which constitutes the finish of The Old West Route.

To reach the north and west sides of the rock from Robinson's Cairn, the best way, instead of making a bee-line to the Green Ledge, i.e., by descending the grass slope straight away, is to follow the same path as the one to the Shamrock Traverse, but before reaching the scree of the Great Doup take a turn toward the right over a grassy band on the rock barrier until the same scree-slope is reached lower down. A path descends across this, past the foot of the Shamrock, Walker's Gully, and other climbs hereabouts, and on to the Green Ledge. The latter runs right across the foot of the North Face, and a short descent at the end of it leads to the waterfall. It is possible to

MAP OF PILLAR ROCK

A High Man
B Low Man
C Pisgah
D Shamrock
E Jordan Gap
F Shamrock Gully (No descent)
G Walker's Gully (No descent)
H Savage Gully (No descent)
J Great Chimney (No descent)
K West Waterfall (No descent)
L Green Ledge
M The Waterfall Crossing
N Shamrock Traverse
O The Old West Route
P Old Wall Route
Q Path to Robinson's Cairn
R Path to Scarth Gap and Buttermere
S Path to Gillerthwaite
T Traverse to Wind Gap
U Path to Pillar summit
V The Low Path (Avoiding the waterfall)
W West Jordan Gully (No descent)

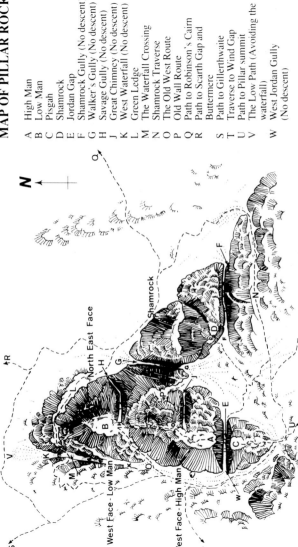

avoid crossing this by climbing up the rocks which bound it on the left side; these rocks are Difficult in standard. At first appearances the way across the waterfall looks the harder of the two, but it is a simple matter to reach the bed of the stream, and though the short climb out on the opposite side demands care, it is soon accomplished; after which easy ground is ascended until a more commanding view of the west can be obtained. To reach the West Faces from the combe below the Rock, when approaching from Ennerdale it is best to scramble up the fellside just on the right of the waterfall.

Unlike the east side, whose innumerable ledges and terraces catch the light from above and cast many shadows, the West Face, as a picture, is flat and stark, and assumes a sterner aspect, though the profile has a certain amount of grace. For, while the angle of Low Man is akin to that of the view from the east, the outline changes into a beautiful parabolic curve from its summit to that of High Man. Jordan Gap, too, is more impressive, whilst Pisgah itself has a toothed aspect like that of some snarling beast.

Despite the general flat appearance of this face, it will be noticed that where the right wing of Low Man rests against High Man, the rock becomes more broken up, forming an easy rake, known as The Old West Route. To those who wish to reach High Man by this route, there should be no great difficulty in locating it and following its course as far as Low Man. From there the way goes up the main ridge on the right by a series of ledges, corners, and short chimneys of moderate quality. The climb is well scratched throughout. It has a variation from Low Man, and Slingsby's Crack may be used instead. This crack, which is only short and of Moderate difficulty, starts a few metres to the right of the ordinary route and somewhat enhances the merit of the climb.

A most striking feature of this side is the cleft (West Jordan Gully) separating the main rock from the Pisgah West Ridge. It will be noticed, too, that high up on the right of Pisgah is a little gully. This provides an easy way to the east side. A mighty rock fall took place here in the summer of 1920. Thousands of tons of rock fell and scoured the west scree to such an extent as to lay bare a tiny feeder of the waterfall, which must have been buried under much debris. Owing to the flatness, already referred to, the characteristics of the climbing on the West Face are different from those on the others. Whereas in the main there are gullies and chimneys on the latter, here the climbs are chiefly composed of slabs and walls, and in consequence they are cleaner, if more exposed.

High Man

Jordan Gap

This is the South Face of High Man.

Far West Jordan Climb   24 m   VD   1909
Start at the same point as West Jordan Crack.
> Climb as for West Jordan Crack to the grassy corner. A short
> slab on the left leads to a small pinnacle. Above this a narrow
> crack is climbed, and the route finishes as for West Jordan Crack.

West Jordan Crack   24 m   VD   1909
Start from a poised block just to the left of West Jordan Climb.
> A delicate move to the left across bulging rock leads to a grassy
> corner. Climb a short slab to a steep crack; up this, then easy
> scrambling to the top of High Man.

West Jordan Climb   15 m   D   1882
Start from the highest point of the gap immediately to the left of
Jordan Bastion.
> A wall with an awkward start leads to a ledge 3 metres up. A
> shallow scoop is succeeded by a difficult crack on the right, which
> ends at the top of the flake; the Central Jordan Climb is joined
> here.

Jordan Bastion   15 m   HS   1919
The route climbs the obvious, steep crack between Central and West
Jordan Climbs. Short but sustained and strenuous.
> From the middle of the gap, move up right and approach the crack
> from the left. Climb the crack, on good holds, to a step out left;
> either climb the continuation crack to the top, or move right along
> a sloping gangway to finish in the same place.

Central Jordan Climb   15 m   D   1882
Start immediately to the right of the highest part of the Gap. The
descent furnishes a quick route off the Rock.
> A corner with a crack in it leads to a big sloping ledge. Another
> crack is followed, which starts from the left-hand corner of the
> ledge. From the top of the crack a low wall leads to High Man.

East Jordan Climb   30 m   MVS   1884
Start from the top of two jammed blocks, directly in line with a
right-angled corner, which marks the line of the climb.

(4a). From the blocks, climb direct to the foot of the corner. Make awkward moves to get established in the corner and climb it to a move left onto a ledge. Make another awkward move up and right onto the wall, and then climb direct to the top.

East Jordan Wall   25 m   HS   1919

Starts at the point where Shamrock Traverse meets East Jordan Gully, below a short corner. The upper section contains some suspect rock, but this does not spoil the route.

Climb the corner and then an open groove, leading to a niche 10 metres up. Trend up and right out of the niche, and then climb directly up the wall to the top.

★ Slab and Notch Climb   50 m   M   1863

One of the easiest routes of ascent and descent on the Rock; it is described in both directions. Numerous belay possibilities exist en route. Start at the foot of East Jordan Gully.

Walk 5 metres to the right to an easy step up and move right onto the Slab. Follow the base of the Slab horizontally right to a step. (The Notch is directly before you.) Climb the step to a short corner at the foot of the Notch. Up the corner, steeply, on good holds to the Notch (20 metres). Move horizontally right for 4 metres and climb the arête direct for 5 metres to another near horizontal ledge. Move right to a stepped slab overlooking a grassy gully (Upper part of Great Chimney). Climb the slab for 4 metres and then move right into the upper part of Great Chimney, to finish at a deep notch. Scramble left to the top of High Man (10 metres).

★ Slab and Notch in descent   50 m   1863

From the Summit of High Man move north for 10 metres to an obvious notch and chimney (Great Chimney) splitting the East side of High Man. Descend the chimney, easily, for a few metres, move right (facing out) onto a stepped slab, and descend this to a good ledge which leads left, to a short, steep arête. Descend the arête for 5 metres to another ledge. From the ledge move left to the Notch and descend the corner beyond, then down a short step and onto the slab. Traverse the slab left to a crack on the edge and descend left onto a good ledge, which leads to the foot of East Jordan Gully. Or, from the crack on the edge of the slab, climb the easy-angled slab for 3 metres and descend to the foot of East Jordan Gully.

There are variations possible both in ascent and in descent, but the route described gives the easiest way up to and down from the summit of High Man.

Pendlebury Traverse   20 m   M   1872
Start at the Notch on Slab and Notch Climb .
> Follow a grass ledge on the left to a short chimney. Climb over or round a block at the top of the chimney onto a moderate upward traverse, then follow a chimney in the corner.

Two easy routes, **The Curtain** and **The Arête** are best taken in combination, and give a pleasant alternative to Slab and Notch.

The Curtain and Arête   50 m   D   1887
The climb runs up the left side of Great Chimney, starting by a wall on a broad grassy ledge.
1   18 m. The wall with good holds (some loose) is followed to a crack which starts from a poised block on the right.
2   15 m. Follow a staircase, which is succeeded by an easy arête, which finishes on the ledge below The Notch.
3   17 m. Climb round to the left and up to The Notch. Just beyond The Notch, follow a slightly overhanging corner on good holds. An easy rock ridge is followed by a sharp arête with a level top, which leads to High Man.

The Great Chimney   25 m   D   1887
Much better as a reference point than a climb, this prominent cleft which splits the East Face, runs down from High Man to near the top of Walker's Gully.

North East Side of High Man

This face can be traversed at a higher level than the Old Wall Route. Well up the recess leading to the foot of The Great Chimney, an easy crack will be seen on the right. This leads to a broad ledge which has some large blocks resting on it. Just beyond this is the foot of **North-East Chimney** (16 m, D) whilst about 15 metres further on the Square Chimney on the Old Wall Route is reached. **North-East Arête** (16 m, D, 1909) climbs the slanting crack right of pitch 1 of North-East Chimney.

Pisgah

The next routes are on the south side of Jordan Gap.

Pisgah from Jordan Gap 6 m S   1898
Start from the top of a big block, just opposite the Central Jordan
Climb.
   By the aid of a small foot hold a long stride is made to a thin
   crack on the right. A groove is entered with a distinct lack of
   holds; a good one, however, is found for the finish. Hard when
   wet.

There are two chimneys on the east side of Pisgah, **East Pisgah
Chimneys** (1892), neither of which is of much interest, the climbing
being short and of poor quality.

Shamrock

This crag is very large, up to 180 metres high, with several long and
interesting routes, in the main on excellent rock. There is,
unfortunately, an excess of grassy ledges, and dry conditions are
therefore desirable before the routes are attempted. The Shamrock is
split by the Great Heather Shelf, which is reached from near
Harlequin Chimneys by easy scrambling.

Some routes such as Photon, Eros, and Thanatos do dry quickly
however, as this section of the crag catches the morning sun.

The easier climbs are not as good as climbs of comparable grade on
the North and West Faces of the Rock. The easiest descent is by the
Shamrock Traverse (see introduction).

The climbs are described from left to right.

East Side of the Shamrock

● **Sirloin Climb** 120 m S   1939
A poor route, which follows a fairly prominent series of ribs
bounding the left edge of the sweep of slabs, which form the left
wall of Shamrock Gully. If you must, it starts at the exact corner of
the Gully, which is also the lowest point of the Rock.

● **Shamrock Gully** 160 m S   1890
This gully, although of considerable length, offers very little real
climbing, the greater portion of it being composed of grass, loose

earth, and shifting scree. A very poor route of little merit – climb it at your peril!

★ Kipper's Chimney   30 m   HS   1967
The climb takes the obvious square-cut chimney on the left wall of Shamrock Gully and starts about 30 metres down from the top of the gully, just above the first steep step. Classic, steep, hard, on good holds, and a little worrying; worth the effort.

Climb the groove to the foot of the chimney proper. The square-cut chimney above is climbed using parallel cracks, and anything else which makes upward progress possible. Exit left near the top, or with more difficulty on the right.

Shamrock Buttress   148 m   VD   1909
The climb improves with altitude but is never very good. Start immediately to the right of Shamrock Gully.
1   75 m. Easy scrambling (with belays at will) leads to a large bilberry-covered platform.
2   25 m. From the ledge, climb the small buttress straight ahead and traverse into the gully (the diamond shaped wall is on the right). Climb a mossy wall on small holds to regain the ridge.
3   20 m. Follow the ridge to a grassy walk into the gully, to arrive opposite Kipper's Chimney.
4   18 m. An entertaining pitch. Enter a small niche which is left awkwardly to the right; a steep wall is then climbed with the aid of a crack, to a small cave just below the ridge. Exit right to gain the ridge.
5   10 m. Follow the ridge to the 'Tea Table' block.

● Variations. Route 1   1902
It is possible to climb the whole route at moderate standard by avoiding all the reasonable rock – not recommended unless botany is your bent.

4a   A few metres further up the gully, a narrow chimney is seen 4 metres up on the right wall. This is entered with some difficulty and followed to a ledge, about level with the cave on the original pitch. Climb straight up to another ledge on the left, passing a large detached block to finish on the ridge near the top of the climb.

North Side of the Shamrock

Harlequin Chimneys   150 m   D   1928
Starts right of a huge overhang, a prominent feature at the foot of
the Shamrock. The chimneys form a continuous fault from the foot
of the crag to the Shamrock Terrace.

Route finding is obvious with belays en route. In the middle it is
possible to climb the imposing rib on the right (Severe) which
entails a run out of 30 metres.

★ **Photon**   137 m   MVS   1967
A long and varied climb of a mountaineering character, which is the
forte of Pillar, and the Shamrock in particular. The stances are large
and the protection good. Start 6 metres to the left of the foot of The
Shamrock Chimneys at the foot of a cleaned groove. This is reached
by scrambling for 60 metres up the Great Heather Shelf.
1   25 m (4b). Climb the steepening groove.
2   30 m (4c). Move right, and go up a slabby corner to the foot of
    the groove. Ascend the steep corner to a bulge, climb this
    (lay-back proving useful) using the steep crack on the right.
    Continue up the crack to reach a good ledge on the left.
3   12 m. Climb the corner above and continue up to a good ledge
    and spike belay.
4   25 m (4a). Climb straight up the pleasant slab on the left to finish
    on a ledge overlooking Shamrock Gully.
5   25 m (4b). Climb up a couple of metres to the left of the steep
    wall of the final tower, then traverse 3 metres left into a broken
    groove, which is followed to the crest of the ridge. Alternatively,
    gain the groove direct by climbing the steep wall on good holds.
6   30 m. Easier climbing along the ridge to the 'Tea Table' block.

★★ **Eros**   90 m   E2   1968
An extremely good climb, taking the bold ribs right of Photon. It just
warrants its grade due to the sustained nature of the climbing and the
relatively poor protection on the second pitch. Start up the rib on the
immediate right of the first groove of Photon.
1   25 m (5a). Climb the rib direct to a mossy slab, which leads to
    a good ledge.
2   30 m (5b). Traverse left to gain a steep rib which is climbed on
    its right side for 18 metres. Continue up the slab above to a ledge,
    then traverse left to a grassy corner – a fine pitch.
3   15 m (5b). Climb the corner-groove above (the right edge of the
    diamond-shaped wall) with difficulty, using the rib on the right
    as necessary. Continue to a ledge on the right.

4   20 m. Step left across the groove and climb the left edge of a
     slab to a ridge, which leads to beneath the final tower. Pitches 5
     and 6 of Photon may be followed to the top.

● **The Shamrock Chimneys**   150 m   VD   1894
It's routes like this that give climbing on Pillar Rock a bad name!
    To the right of Harlequin Chimneys, beyond the mass of
overhanging rock, a grassy bay will be noticed. After scrambling
60 metres up steep grass, two chimneys, some distance apart, are
seen, the more conspicuous being the one on the right. The start,
however, is up that on the left.

Positron   124 m   MVS   1967
Takes the buttress between Shamrock Chimneys and Electron in its
lower half, and a rib and crack line in its upper half to reach the
ridge between Shamrock Gully and Shamrock Chimneys. This rather
contrived route starts as for Electron.
1   24 m (4a). Gain the upper grass ledge and, from its left end, climb
     diagonally left to gain a grassy crack. Climb this for a short
     distance and step left to a grass ledge. Ascend diagonally left to
     a good crack, which is climbed to a ledge and flake belays.
2   20 m (4b). Ascend the steep parallel cracks behind the belay. Near
     the top, step left to a ridge on the edge of Shamrock Chimneys.
     Climb this to a grassy bay.
3   20 m. Traverse left into a slabby scoop and ascend this directly.
     Near the top, move left to a small grass ledge and swing round
     to the left to gain an easy crack, which is followed to a grass
     ledge.
4   20 m. Climb a rib, keeping to its crest. Until a grass ledge is
     reached.
5   20 m (4a). Climb the corner for a couple of metres; then step on
     to the right edge and climb this to a ledge. Take the crack line
     behind the belay, which widens into a corner at half-height. This
     leads to the ridge between Shamrock Gully and Shamrock
     Chimneys.
6   20 m. Easy scrambling along the ridge leads to the 'Tea Table'
     block.

★★★ **Electron**   100 m   HVS   1966
In its own right, but especially if combined with Thanatos, one of
the best and longest routes on the Shamrock. The layback crack,
although not technically difficult, is bold and intimidating and the first
pitch is hard, especially if wet. The route starts 15 metres right of
The Shamrock Chimneys at the foot of a vertical right-angled corner,

which is reached by the inevitable scrambling up The Great Heather Shelf or, much better, by climbing Thanatos.

1   25 m (5a). Climb the right-angled corner to a chockstone at 6 metres. Continue over an awkward bulge, up the corner, with another awkward move higher up. Belay on a large grass ledge.

2   25 m (4b). Continue up the groove for 12 metres, then cross the small grass ledge, and ascend the wall at the back to belay on a large block just below and to the left of a prominent crack.

3   20 m (4c). The imposing crack, with resting places and protection en route.

4   30 m (4b). Move right and go up the grey arête to a cairn. Move 6 metres right and ascend a second arête on good holds to the 'Tea Table' block.

● **Tower Postern**   85 m   HS   1941
A poor route, grassy and vegetated. Starts on the Great Heather Shelf, 15 metres to the right of The Shamrock Chimneys, at a grassy groove just right of Electron.

1   25 m. Easy scrambling up the grass corner, then climb the corner crack ahead, which leads to a grassy stance below an apparently impossible finish. By a long and awkward step round the arête on the left, the upper section of a steep corner (Electron) is reached which leads to easy ground. By walking to the right an excellent thread belay is reached below a vertical crack.

2   8 m. Climb the crack, which is hard, strenuous and exposed, but on good holds, to an excellent stance.

3   25 m. Ascend a steep, turfy corner. Continue up the steepening corner; the difficulty increases but, after an awkward movement, the final section of the crack is more easily climbed.

4   15 m. Climb some ribs on the right to the foot of a tower.

5   12 m. The Tower. This is climbed to the main Shamrock ridge which is followed more easily to the top.

Lepton   100 m   HVS   1968
Ascends the buttress to the right of Tower Postern. A contrived climb which nevertheless contains some interesting climbing. Start just right of Tower Postern, below a short, square-cut groove.

1   23 m (4c). Climb the square-cut groove for 10 metres. Traverse diagonally left to the edge of the buttress and climb straight up to belay on the edge of the buttress below a prominent groove.

2   20 m (5a). Mantelshelf into the groove above and turn the overhang on the left; a long reach gives access to a sloping grass ledge. Scramble up to the left and belay below a large corner.

3 27 m (4c). Climb the slab on its left side to a short crack; climb this, then traverse right to below an obvious crack, which splits the left wall of the groove. Climb the crack to a slab.

4 30 m (4c). Traverse left into The Shamrock Chimneys, which is crossed above the chockstone. Climb diagonally left, up the left wall, to a crack, which is followed to the summit ridge.

Bosun 92 m HVS   1968
A poor, unbalanced climb, whose justification lies in pitch 3. The rest of the climb is a vegetated Hard Severe. The route follows the obvious corner to the right of Tower Postern, and starts to the left of the line of the corner at a square-cut groove.

1 12 m (4a). Climb the square-cut groove and move right to belay at the foot of the corner.

2 20 m (4a). The corner above is climbed direct, moving out left to a rib near the top. Then climb the wide crack on the left, to belay just to the left of a steep rib.

3 30 m (5b). Climb the steep rib near the right edge to a thin crack, which is followed to a recess below an undercut groove; fingery and strenuous. Attain the groove above, with interest, (not obvious) and climb it to a ledge. Climb another groove just left of the arête to belay by a dubious spike.

4 30 m. Climb the rib on the left to the top.

★ **Pauli Exclusion Principle** 75 m E2 †   1988
A fine, bold climb. Start just right of Bosun.

1 25 m (5c). Climb the arête, on its right-hand side, to a good hold at 10 metres. Step right to a small spike runner and move up the thin crack for 2 metres, then traverse back left to the arête and follow it to a grass ledge.

2 20 m (4b). Climb the large flake crack above, until easier ground leads to a belay in a diagonal chimney at the top of pitch 2 of Vishnu.

3 25 m (5a). Pull out right, onto the slabby base of the buttress. Move up left to almost reach a grassy gully above the chimney, then pull back right, and climb the arête on the left-hand side of the buttress directly on superb holds.

4 15 m. Climb the slab and corner to the top of The Shamrock.

Vishnu 90 m E2   1968
A serious climb, which is reflected in the overall grade, the main pitch being bold and not well protected. Start 6 metres to the right of Bosun, beneath a 6 metre high, right-angled corner.

1   25 m (5a). Climb the corner and continue up the crack above until it steepens, then make an awkward move left to a mantelshelf. There is a ledge a little higher and, 4 metres above this, another ledge is reached with a belay below a steep crack.

2   18 m. Climb the crack, avoiding a poised block on the right. 10 metres of easier climbing leads to a belay in a diagonal chimney, which bounds the left edge of a large prominent buttress.

3   30 m (5b). Pull out right on to the slabby base of the buttress. Move up to the left for a couple of metres, then traverse back to the right to the foot of a blank groove. Climb the rib on the right to a mantelshelf. Make an awkward move back left, across the top of the groove to gain a small ledge in the centre of the buttress. Climb the final wall, trending slightly to the right, on good but widely-spaced holds, to a large ledge.

4   17 m. Climb the wall behind the belay on the left, then continue up a pleasant slab, which forms the left wall of the corner above, to the top of the crag.

The next routes of any merit start at the lowest part of The Shamrock in the vicinity of where the rescue box 'used to be'. The best reference point is the large left-facing corner with the left-facing double overhangs at the top (Thanatos).

★ **Thanatos** 58 m HVS   1968
A good pitch, which when combined with Electron provides one of the best outings at its grade on the crag. Start just right of the lowest part of the crag, beneath the large corner.

1   18 m (4b). Climb a slab and vegetation to a corner. Go up this for a couple of metres, then move left onto the steep slab, which leads to a bilberry ledge. Continue to the base of the corner to belay.

2   30 m (5a). An excellent, well protected pitch. Climb the corner to some jammed blocks below the first overhang. Traverse left onto a rib, and enter a groove below the second overhang. Make difficult moves on the left to reach a good ledge.

3   10 m. An easy groove leads to the Heather Shelf just right of the big corner of Electron.

Shamrock Tower 168 m MVS   1940
A nomadic route, which provides enjoyable climbing in dry conditions. The lower half is improved by a direct variation on pitches 2 and 3. In common with all the routes starting on the lower tier of the Shamrock, it is split at mid-height by the Great Heather Shelf.

1   20 m. As for pitch 1 of Thanatos to the bilberry ledge and belay
    in a small corner on the edge of the arête.
2   18 m (4a). From the belay, step round the arête on the right, then
    climb up and rightwards for 6 metres to a traverse right into a
    small corner and junction with Odin. Ascend this to a small ledge
    and very large block belay.
3   25 m (4b). Traverse left for 3 metres and step into a V-shaped
    groove; climb this, move right at the top and go diagonally right
    to reach a slanting grass ledge. Traverse left round a corner and
    up another short corner to belay in a short V-corner by a large
    block to the right.
4   40 m (4a). Move up right onto the block, step right and climb a
    cracked slab (awkward) onto grass; scramble diagonally upwards
    to obvious flakes overlooking Walker's Gully.
5   40 m (4a). Climb up for a couple of metres and traverse an
    obvious flake to the right. Go up the corner on the right for 6
    metres and traverse right to gain the long corner. Climb it and
    step right to a block belay (this pitch can be split if desired).
6   25 m. Continue up the easy rock ridge to the top of the buttress.

Variation (pitches 2 and 3)   35 m   VS   1986
A more logical, direct and rewarding way to ascend Shamrock Tower.
2a (4c). From the first stance, climb the stepped corner on the left
    of the arête for 4 metres. Move up and right, round the arête, into
    the bottom of the V-groove. Climb the groove to its top and step
    right into a smaller groove; climb this to the obvious corner which
    is followed to the stance on pitch 3 of Shamrock Tower.

Odin   148 m   HVS   1960
The route follows the main Shamrock Ridge, and has some pleasant
pitches, but it is essentially a mountaineering route, and like all the
routes starting below the Great Heather Shelf it is split at half height.
The start of the route is about 6 metres to the right of Thanatos. 30
metres of scrambling leads to the left side of a bay with a spike belay.
1   18 m (4c). Step off the spike and go up steep rock and a shallow
    groove to a ledge and large block belay, junction with Shamrock
    Tower.
2   20 m (5b). Step off the block to a niche, then go to the right onto
    the nose, and up steep rock to reach a groove on the right. Climb
    this, then move back left across the steep wall to another grass
    ledge. A mantelshelf leads to a ledge and block belay.
3   40 m (4b). Climb over the bulge on the left (belay well back) or
    continue for 35 metres diagonally up and right to a massive
    upstanding flake.

4   45 m (4b). Go up 6 metres and traverse to the right, along a flake, to a short corner. Climb this, then a groove on the left. Continue up a long crack on good jams to a ledge.
5   25 m. Continue up the easy ridge above to the top.

Variation   80 m   HVS   1965
A better finish.
4a   20 m (4b). From the upstanding flake, move left and enter the obvious hanging groove, which is awkward to start. Climb the groove to a block belay just over the top on the right.
5a   25 m (4b). From the bottom of the block belay, step out right onto the steep buttress. Move up and right, then go straight up excellent rock to a good belay.
6a   35 m (5a). Go left across the ledge and gain the obvious groove, just right of the prominent little buttress, by climbing the steep wall on small holds. The smooth groove is difficult to start. After about 6 metres escape right and go up a wall, on sloping holds, to the obvious V-groove above. Go up this to the top.

★ **The Magic Rainbow**   70 m   E1   1972
A worthwhile route, giving a slightly harder alternative to Thanatos, to reach routes on the upper buttress e.g. Necromancer. Start 5 metres right of Odin at an obvious corner.
1   20 m (5b). Climb the corner, until it is possible to move across the steep left wall to a small stance below an impending groove. Climb the groove to a resting place on the right, and continue up the square groove above to a ledge and belay on the right; a sustained pitch.
2   30 m (5a). Above the belay is a very steep wall with a prominent gangway slanting right; traverse right, along the gangway, to a prominent crack. Gain the crack by an awkward move then pull up to a leftward-facing rake. Continue up a corner to a large ledge.
3   20 m. Climb the short wall, then easier rock leads to the terrace.

★ **Necromancer**   90 m   HVS   1968
The route is worth doing, but only for its upper pitches, which give fine slab climbing. It is best climbed in conjunction with either Thanatos or Magic Rainbow. The original start followed the left edge of Walker's Gully but it consists of 60 metres of grassy rock with a short, hard wall. From the right-hand end of the Great Heather Shelf scramble down into Walker's Gully to a block belay at the top of pitch 2 of Walker's Gully.

1   35 m (5a). Climb a grassy groove on the left into a wet cave. Exit right from the cave onto a steep slab and ascend it, keeping to the centre for the best climbing. Move up and right to a small stance and large block belay in a fine position overlooking the Gully.

2   30 m (5a). Climb the slab below the impressive final wall. Move to the left edge and climb the flake crack until it is possible to traverse right to the centre of the wall. Climb up to a small flake, then move right and continue up the slab to a ledge and block belay.

3   25 m. Climb the easy ridge above to finish at the top of the Shamrock.

Variation   Direct Start   12 m   E2   1986
Start from the block belay at the foot of the route at an obvious crack, just left of Walker's Gully.

1a (5c). Climb the crack with increasing difficulty until it fades out after 10 metres. Then move left, delicately, to join the original route.

The Eightfold Way   138 m   HVS   1968
The girdle traverse of Shamrock, which starts as for Photon. By combining this route with The Link and The Girdle Traverse it is possible to make a Greater Traverse (1969) of over 500 metres.

1   25 m (4a). Climb the steepening groove of Photon or, better, the first pitch of Eros.

2   30 m (4b). Walk along the grass ledge and stride across The Shamrock Chimneys to a large sloping hold. Step down and round the arête, and make an ascending traverse, delicate in places, passing a mossy streak, to a junction with Electron above the bulge of the first pitch; climb up the corner to a ledge.

3   10 m (4a). Traverse the short wall on the right to the top of a grassy groove. Follow an obvious pleasant traverse line across the steep exposed wall on the right. Just round the corner is a small stance with a natural thread belay, below the crux pitch of Lepton.

4   18 m. Traverse horizontally into the corner of Bosun. Leave this by an easy grass ledge on the right to a belay round the corner.

5   12 m (5a). From the right end of the ledge, step down and round the corner. Continue traversing to an undercut crack, which is descended until it is possible to step to the right to a ledge.

6   25 m (5a). Climb the V-groove to the overhang; then step to the right onto the wall and traverse (choice of levels) to a good jug round the corner. Mantelshelf on to this and traverse horizontally

into Odin below the steep section. Traverse horizontally past some wedged blocks into the corner of Shamrock Tower (poor stance).

7   18 m (4a). Gain a crack on the rib on the right and follow this for a short distance. Traverse to the right on to the steep wall and climb this on small holds. Near the top, step back to the right. Easier climbing leads to large belays.

The Link   72 m   HVS   1968

A high-level girdle traverse of the walls of Walker's Gully giving interesting climbing in exposed positions. This traverse links the girdle of Shamrock (The Eightfold Way) with the girdle of the main crag, making possible a 'Greater Traverse'. Start at the belay at the end of pitch 6 of The Eightfold Way.

1   12 m (4b). Gain a crack in the right-hand rib; descend this, and move down diagonally to a large pinnacle belay overlooking Walker's Gully. (First half of the last pitch of Necromancer in reverse). The belay can also be reached by an ascending diagonal traverse from a large flake at the top right end of the Great Heather Shelf.

2   15 m. Abseil down the impending wall into Walker's Gully.

3   18 m (4c). Follow a foot-traverse across the right wall and pull out onto the rib on the right. Ascend the waterworn groove until the grassy groove on the right can be gained. Continue up this to a small stance.

4   27 m (5a). Continue up the groove and mantelshelf on to the thin grass ledge on the right. Follow this to its end; then cross a small slab to gain a narrow mossy gangway. Descend this until it is possible to step to the right to better footholds and a good undercut handhold. Continue traversing round a prominent bulge and cross easier ground to a belay at the start of the final pitch of Grooved Wall.

★★ Walker's Gully   125 m   MVS   1899

The last pitch may be found harder by short people. One of the few good gully climbs of the district; it follows the deep cleft separating Shamrock from the North Face of Low Man. It is possible to gain access to a number of other routes on the right wall of the gully. The pitches may be split if necessary. Care to be taken to avoid rockfalls from above.

1   27 m. Climb a short chimney, easily, followed by scree, to the foot of a high, green chimney. Climb the right wall of the chimney and gain a sloping terrace.

2   40 m (4a). An exposed groove, with poor holds, is climbed until it is possible to step on to the first chockstone in the chimney.

Another chockstone just above is easily surmounted, followed by scrambling up the bed of the gully for 30 metres. Necromancer, and Walker's Gully wall routes start here.

3   18 m (4b). Climb rocks on the left of a chimney to a cave, which is usually wet. Climb up behind, then over, a chockstone; then bridge the gully until a sloping chockstone is reached. Another chockstone is very awkward.

4   25 m. A short scree slope, followed by an easy pitch, leads to a cave with a through route. This is strenuous but short. It can be avoided by climbing the left wall, outside the cave. An easy through route, or a staircase on the right wall, leads to two big boulders blocking the gully; these are climbed either on the right or the left.

5   15 m (4c). More large chockstones are encountered until the cave below the final pitch is reached. Move across the right wall on sloping holds to a recess under the final capstone. A tall man can then back-up with his back on the left wall. Otherwise continue climbing up the right wall. A thread runner may be found high up in the recess between the capstone and the exit wall, but it is strenuous to fix.

Variation   The Original Start   85 m   1898
This is not as good as the route described above and starts some metres to the left of the foot of the gully.
1a 15 m. Grassy ledges.
2a 20 m. Traverse left to a corner. Continue the traverse for 3 metres.
3a 15 m. The chimney, which has good holds.
4a 35 m. A walk over a grassy terrace to the right; then upwards to ' join the gully mid way up pitch 3.

Variation   Additional Finish   60 m   D   1909
The climb runs up the ridge on the left and its start is reached by crossing over the top of the capstone.
6   18 m. A crack is climbed to a block on the ridge. A steep wall is now ascended on good holds to a platform on the right.
7   12 m. Move onto a ledge on the right, in order to get onto a ridge on the left, as this provides the best climbing.
8   30 m. Easy scrambling, finishing near the 'Tea Table' block at the top of Shamrock Buttress.

Low Man

North Face of Low Man

The North Face is a large crag, up to 130 metres high, which offers a good variety of worthwhile climbs, and some not so worthwhile. On the left lie the modern style wall climbs, while on the centre and right-hand side, Difficults and Extremes lie side by side, many of which are among the best in the district. Due to an excess of grassy ledges, virtually all the routes become very unpleasant in wet conditions. All the climbs with the exception of Pedestal Wall, and the upper routes of Walker's Gully Wall, start from the Green Ledge, a very prominent feature, which crosses the cliff rightwards from the bottom of Walker's Gully.

The routes are described from left to right. The easiest descents are by The Old Wall Route (care needed in wet conditions), then by Shamrock Traverse, or by The Old West Route, then by the waterfall (great care needed in wet conditions) and then by Green Ledge.

Pedestal Wall 108 m S   1937
A rather grassy climb, which nevertheless offers good slab climbing in dry conditions. Seen from below Green Ledge, the climb follows a direct line ending at the foot of the Nor-Nor-West Climb, making possible 300 metres of continuous climbing to the top of High Man. Start almost at the lowest point of the crag by a shallow crack, or better, by the Variation Start.

1   30 m. Climb the shallow crack or groove straight up to a grass ledge (possible belay). Continue up the crest of a slabby rib to another ledge. Easy slabs lead to a big grass slope.
2   18 m. Almost straight ahead is a corner. Start up the easy slabby rocks on the right, and go straight up for about 10 metres to a block on the left edge of the slab. Above this a grass ledge is attained.
3   30 m. Continue up a ribbon of slabby rocks to a grass ledge, and climb a short wall on the left of a groove to a grass stance (possible belay). Either move to the right and climb a pleasant steep slab, or go straight up the chimney to a grass ledge.
4   30 m. Work up to the right, then break out left on to a fine slab, which leads to the left end of a long narrow ledge. Continue straight up, keeping well to the right for the last few metres.

Variation Start   1938
   Climb a thin crack 3 metres right of the original route. After a
   couple of metres, traverse to the right onto a light coloured bulge
   and continue up to a platform at the foot of a stepped groove. Go
   up this for a short distance and then move left to the last 12
   metres of pitch 1.

The next few routes start out of Walker's Gully from the small
amphitheatre at the top of pitch 2 and climb the right wall of the
Gully, with some steep climbing and fine situations.

Side Slip   57 m   VS   1976
The route follows a prominent line of grooves on the immediate right
(true left) of the top half of Walker's Gully. Start immediately out
right from the small amphitheatre. It can also be reached from the
Great Heather Shelf on Shamrock.
1   15 m (4b). Climb the cleaned groove on the right of the gully,
    moving right on to a large ledge.
2   15 m (4c). Follow the groove over a small overhang to a small
    stance.
3   27 m (4a). Continue up the left-hand groove to a large ledge and
    climb the corner to the top.

★ **Over the Hill**   50 m   E1   1987
A fine route with good situations, and very direct. Starts at the same
place as Soliton and is a harder companion to that route. Steep and
strenuous climbing with good protection make the route well
worthwhile.
1   25 m (5b). Traverse out of the gully, as for Soliton, for a couple
    of metres, then climb a short rock corner to a grassy rake, this
    point is level with and just to the left of the hand traverse into
    Soliton. Move up left into the leftwards facing diagonal crack and
    climb it until a long slanting overlap is reached. Move up and
    right into the continuation of the crack, and climb it steeply to a
    recess. Climb this and move right round a boss of rock to good
    belays and junction with the traverse of The Link.
2   25 m (5b). Move back left into the recess and climb a short
    delicate groove in a leftwards slanting gangway (The Link in
    reverse). When at the level of a grass ledge, climb straight up the
    wall into a large recess (Soliton moves right here). Make some
    bold, exhilarating moves straight up out of the recess, and climb
    steeply up the wall on widely spaced holds, which appear in all
    the right places, until forced to move right into a large corner
    recess. Climb this, moving right at the top.

Soliton   60 m   HVS   1972

The route follows a very prominent, narrow chimney-groove right of
Over the Hill and although somewhat marred by the wanderings of
its second pitch it contains some fine, steep climbing. Start
immediately right of Side Slip.

1   30 m (5a). Traverse out of the gully and move across mixed
    ground to the foot of an obvious crack and groove line on the
    right wall. The start of the crack is very steep and vegetated and
    is turned by a short scramble up on the left, followed by a
    horizontal traverse into the crack. Up this by steep jamming and
    bridging to a short chimney which leads to a good grass ledge
    and junction with Grooved Wall.

2   30 m (5a). Traverse left along a grass ledge, and continue round
    a bulge, junction with Over the Hill, and into a recess; climb a
    short, delicate groove in a leftward slanting gangway. When at
    the level of a grass ledge (the traverse of The Link in reverse),
    there is a large recess above. From a hand hold on the right edge
    of the recess, make a diagonal traverse rightwards across the wall
    to a good foot hold. Continue up the wall above to a groove,
    which leads to the top of the crag.

The Black Widow   100 m   E2   1968

Ascends the hanging groove in the black wall, high up to the left of
Sheol. The fierce second pitch is sustained and strenuous; it's a pity
the rest of the route does not live up to its early promise. Start in
Walker's Gully by scrambling 12 metres up to the foot of the steep
wall on the right of the gully.

1   25 m (5a). Follow a line of expanding flakes rightwards, across
    the wall, to join Grooved Wall. Climb the chimney and belay on
    top of a pinnacle.

2   25 m (5c). Climb up a little, and traverse right across a mossy
    wall to two sloping ledges. Pull round into a groove to reach the
    overhang. Climb the overhang with some difficulty, and up into
    a niche at the bottom of the groove. Follow the groove, on good
    holds at first, and then with difficulty to the final overhang.
    Traverse right to the arête, and pull onto a grass ledge.

3   30 m (5a). Traverse right for a couple of metres and climb a crack
    in the groove to a slab. Climb the slab to a small grass stance
    (possible belay), then by jamming up the overhanging twin cracks
    to a ledge.

4   20 m (4c). Climb the crack above and finish up the short groove.

★★★ **Tapestry**   70 m   E4   1980
Fit to hang on any wall! Climbs the wall and grooves, above and left
of The Black Widow. Excellent climbing in good situations, but with
a serious second pitch. Start at the same place as The Black Widow.
1   25 m (5b). Climb the centre of the huge pinnacle of The Black
    Widow pitch 1, and finish by its left edge (junction with Grooved
    Wall). Follow Grooved Wall to belay beneath the overhang at the
    end of pitch 1 of that climb.
2   20 m (6a). Climb the overhang of Grooved Wall and immediately
    step right to a shallow corner. Follow this almost to the top, then
    gain the wall on its left and climb it, moving right to finish on
    the belay ledge.
3   25 m (5b). Another very fine pitch. From the right end of the
    ledge, a cleaned groove in the arête leads to a soaring, leftward
    hand traverse. Follow this and then climb a crack back right to
    finish.

★★★ **Grooved Wall**   94 m   VS   1928
An excellent climb, taking the prominent series of difficult grooves
running up the right wall of Walker's Gully. Start immediately right
of the foot of the Gully and scramble 15 metres up grass. All
difficulties are well protected.
1   30 m. High grassy ledges lead up to a wide chimney. The
    chimney, which is in two sections, is followed to its top (the
    chimney is composed of a great flake for one of its sides). The
    first groove above is followed and a ledge on the right attained.
    Thread belay.
2   20 m (5a). Above the stance is an overhang, which is the crux
    of the climb. Gain the groove above and continue up it to a good
    belay.
3   20 m (4b). Continue up the groove, steeply at first, then more
    easily to belay by a corner on the side of the groove.
4   24 m (4c). The final groove above is not without interest, but
    ends after 12 metres. Continue up ledges to a stance. Shortly after
    this, a rock gateway opens onto the scree just above Walker's
    Gully.

★★★ **Cunning Stunts**   60 m   E2   1981
An aptly named climb, with three very different styles of climbing –
delicate, tricky and brutal. It takes the prominent corner and arête
between The Black Widow and Sheol. Start just left of Sheol below
a short grassy corner.
1   25 m (5b). The grassy corner leads to a steep, jamming crack
    forming the right side of a huge flake. Climb this and the

continuation ramp to a large detached block (thread). Step onto the right wall of the leaning groove (peg runner) and make an awkward move onto the next ramp; up this and the finger crack to a good ledge.

2   15 m (5c). Step left across the overhanging wall to gain a flake crack on the arête. Levitate strenuously onto the exposed ledge and up twin jamming cracks to belay below the final pitch of Tapestry.

3   20 m (5b). Climb the groove in the arête, as for Tapestry, to an overhanging, wide crack containing two chockstones. Climb this with grace to the top. Scramble 15 metres right over ledges to the descent path which traverses left to the top of Walker's Gully.

★ **Sheol**   86 m   E1   1965

The impressive, jagged soaring crack in the wall immediately right of Grooved Wall. An excellent first pitch on a route where the difficulties diminish rapidly, although the upper pitches are pleasant enough and on good rock. It is possible and very rewarding to combine the first pitch of Sheol with the last pitch of Tapestry, making an impressive way up the crag, by moving out left on the second pitch, up North-East Climb, then to the foot of the last pitch of Tapestry. Start by scrambling up grass to the foot of the crack.

1   22 m (5b). The crack, which is nearly vertical and tilts slightly to one side is followed in its entirety, to a good stance and chockstone belay.

2   22 m (5a). Up and to the right across the North-East Climb, are two grooves. Go up and climb the very steep, right groove by traversing in from the left and bridging up. Ledge and belay.

3   15 m (4c). Climb the deep groove on the left, moving to the right at the top to a ledge.

4   27 m (4c). Climb straight up and finish up the last pitch of Savage Gully, to belay on top of the nose of North Climb.

★ **North-East Climb**   126 m   MS   1912

A classic route, with atmosphere and good situations in the upper half. Much harder when wet. Start as for North Climb.

1   30 m. Pitches 1 and 2 of North Climb.

2   16 m. Climb a couple of metres up the Gully, then traverse 3 metres across the rib on the left. A 3 metre chimney leads to a small stance (possible belay). Move round the rib on the left on to a slab. Traverse the slab to grassy ledges.

3   23 m. A short chimney leads to a longer one with an awkward finish. Climb the short slab on the left, then walk left to a long V-groove on the wall of Walker's Gully.

4   24 m. Climb the groove to a corner with a belay.
5   18 m. A mossy wall on the right leads to a good ledge behind a
     big block (possible belay). A steep chimney is followed by easier
     climbing to a grassy corner.
6   15 m. Another steep chimney is followed by grassy ledges. From
     here a traverse can be made right to Low Man or left to the scree
     above Walker's Gully.

Savage Gully 98 m MVS   1901
Although a climb of some character, it is grassy in places and takes
time to dry. Start as for North Climb.
1   35 m. Follow North Climb to the foot of the twisting chimney.
2   25 m (4b). The Gully rises steeply above on the left. Climb the
     groove on the right for 12 metres and move left, round the rib,
     and make an awkward pull-up to a grass ledge. Regain the
     right-hand groove and climb it, passing the chockstone either right
     or left, to a good belay.
3   20 m (4a). A delicate step left leads to a rock nest. Climb the
     crack in the corner, then rounded rocks straight ahead lead to a
     stance.
4   18 m (4b). Climb bulging rock awkwardly for 4 metres, then
     climb the right wall on good holds to finish on a ledge level with
     the Nose of North Climb.

Variation Start   35 m   1968
This variation avoids some of the grass and starts at the top of Pitch
2 of North Climb.
2a (4c). Move left up slabs, to below a steep crack, which is climbed
     for 10 metres to a ledge, then move right to a groove. Climb the
     groove direct to a stance in a rock nest, midway up pitch 3 of
     Savage Gully.

★★★ **North Climb** 96 m S   1891
The route is a superb, classic Difficult with a Severe finish, which
has been the scene of many epics and should not be underrated by
novice parties. It is possible to avoid the last pitch by taking Savage
Gully exit, but this is not recommended. Starts from the left end of
Green Ledge at an obvious break.
1   10 m. An easy mantelshelf and short slab lead to a grassy ledge
     at the foot of Savage Gully.
2   20 m. A rectangular groove, with good holds on the left side,
     leads to a recess. A wall on the right is followed by a chimney
     in the Gully.

3   21 m. Savage Gully rises very steeply on the left at this point. An easy staircase on the right leads to a deep twisting chimney which is climbed to belay below a V-chimney.

4   14 m. Climb the V-chimney, which is followed by a short walk of 4 metres.

5   9 m. The Stomach Traverse. Climb a narrow chimney, which in its upper part bends to the right.

6   18 m. The cave pitch in the corner is climbed via a capstone on the left or right followed by a walk of 6 metres to the Split Blocks. These are climbed by the obvious chimney. Traverse to the left to a ledge below and to the right of the Nose. The first part of this traverse is known as The Strid.

7   5 m. The Nose. From the corner, work out left to stand on the tip of the projecting flake. A good side hold exists on the left round the Nose, with a good flat hold for the right-hand above. A bold move up and left can be made onto good but concealed holds (hard when wet). Move up without further difficulty to belay.

Variations

★ The Hand Traverse   8 m   HS   1892
The archetypal Hard Severe. Steep and hard on good holds. Recommended when the Nose is wet!

7a. From the right end of the ledge below the Nose, climb the steep wall for about 3 metres on good holds until the sharp edge of a flake is reached. Traverse boldly left to the top of the Nose.

Descent into Savage Gully   VD
Definitely not recommended as a finish to North Climb, but included for completeness.

7b. Arrange an abseil from below the Nose and descend 12 metres into Savage Gully. Traverse left 20 metres to the foot of a 12 metre chimney. Climb the chimney, followed by an easy upward traverse right for 20 metres into the easy upper part of Savage Gully (also known as Stony Gully).

Variation Starts
Two poor alternative starts exist. The first one The Intermediate Variation (50 m, D, 1921) starts 18 metres to the right and climbs mostly grass, parallel to the ordinary route, joining that route near the top of the twisting chimneys on pitch 3.

The second one starts 55 metres right of the ordinary route and is called The Westerly Variation (D, 1892). This takes a roughly diagonal line left across the North Face under an obvious square cut chimney, and taking the easiest line to the base of the large clean wall at its right-hand end. Follow grass leftwards to join the ordinary route at the Split Blocks on pitch 6.

Akhnaton   87 m   VS   1967
A direct route, which follows a series of grooves and is better than it appears at first sight. A highlight of the route is the Hand Traverse finish of North Climb. Starts 9 metres right of North Climb at a groove, on the right of a large pinnacle belay, in a grassy bay.
1   35 m (4c). Climb the groove, surmounting two bulges, to a grass ledge; continue a couple of metres to a belay on North Climb.
2   12 m. Follow North Climb above the stance to a block belay right of the continuation of the groove.
3   33 m (4c). Step left into the bottom of the groove, which is marked at half-height by a large pinnacle on the right. Continue up the groove; the last couple of metres of which overhang. Belay just left of The Strid on the North Climb.
4   7 m (4b). From the belay, step right and up the steep wall to hand traverse left and finish on the top of North Climb.

★ **Klingsor**   142 m   E2   1974
An eliminate style climb, which weaves its way up the face and contains some good steep climbing. Start at the foot of Akhnaton and climbs the groove system on the steep right wall, before breaking rightwards to the big wall of Scylla.
1   30 m (5a). Climb the groove and crack line throughout to belays on ledges above.
2   38 m. Move up right to a short corner leading to an easy rake. Follow this rightwards to emerge on a ledge below a very thin crack line in the steep wall, left of the crack of Scylla.
3   27 m (5c). Move up to a ledge with a perched block. Step off the block, and climb the wall, first right, then left of the crack line until a short hanging V-groove can be entered. Pull out right to gain a ledge above. Step left onto the steep wall and go straight up to a ledge.
4   25 m (5a). As for pitch 4 of Scylla; from the left end of the ledge, pull up an overhanging wall, and traverse left to the foot of a narrow crack, which is climbed to the top of a pinnacle. Climb straight up the short, narrow grooves above to a ledge.
5   22 m (5b). Step left to the toe of the buttress. Climb up and leftwards, across the steep slab, to a nut runner round the left edge, then traverse right to gain a prominent ledge. Enter a steep,

shallow groove on the right edge, go up this and the wall above to belay well back.

★ **Patriarch of the Pillarites**   65 m   E3   1988
An excellent climb, which ascends the bold hanging arête immediately right of pitch 1 of Klingsor and starts as for that route.
1   35 m (5c). Start as for Klingsor but pull onto the ramp on the right; follow this to a spike runner beneath an impending wall. Bridge up and make a hard pull round the arête on the left onto a steep wall. Climb this (bold) on small, spaced holds for 3 metres and step right into the thin corner which leads to the belay.
2   30 m (5c). Scramble 10 metres up Proton and climb the middle of three short corners. Move left to a small niche which is above an obvious crack. Climb the bulge above slightly right to a hollow flake and small pocket. Move delicately up to the overhang, and make hard moves right (crux) to a crack which leads to a finishing ledge covered in small debris. Move up to belay at the top of the Stomach Traverse on North Climb. A good way to finish the climb would be to ascend the upper pitches of Klingsor.

Proton   124 m   HVS   1966
A poor route, except for pitches 1 and 4. Start 18 metres right of North Climb at the foot of a long V-groove. The lower block is split by triple cracks.
1   33 m (5a). Climb the right-hand crack to a sloping shelf, and follow the corner crack above with difficulty, passing a large spike (possible belay). Move right, then back left into the corner, which is climbed to a grass ledge.
2   25 m. Climb up steep grass to join North Climb at the foot of the Stomach Traverse.
3   28 m. Climb the large corner above, passing three breaks to rejoin North Climb at 'The Strid'.
4   18 m (5a). A good pitch. Enter the V-groove on the left by a difficult rising traverse from the right. Continue up the groove to a block belay.
5   20 m. Move slightly left, then climb the cracked wall to a grass ledge. Easy climbing up a groove on the right leads to the top.

● **Hadrian's Wall**   126 m   MVS   1933
A Botanist's dream – a gigantic garden with a moss covered rockery at the top! Start 45 metres right of North Climb and 3 metres above Green Ledge.
1   18 m. Climb a short rib to grass, and traverse left under a small overhang. Follow a grassy corner to belay.

2   20 m. Trend left for 6 metres and up to a bilberry corner. Continue over grass to the foot of a small chimney.

3   20 m. The chimney is followed by more grass to a recess. Climb a deep V-chimney to a stance on the right.

4   25 m (4b). Another chimney with an overhanging chockstone leads to a long ledge at the foot of a huge wall taken by Scylla. Ascend the left edge of the wall for 6 metres to a series of ledges. Belay on a higher ledge.

5   25 m (4b). A staircase, trending left, leads to an exposed entrance to a chimney, which is smooth and strenuous but is short lived and more grass is encountered. Continue past a large spike to a V-chimney which is climbed for 6 metres. Move left onto the wall and climb this to a belay.

6   18 m. Follow the arête bounding Stony Gully to finish on the summit of Low Man.

★ **Scylla**   123 m   HVS   1963
A good route of a mountaineering character, which climbs the crack in the centre of the huge wall on the North Face of Low Man. Start between Nor'-Nor'-West Climb and Hadrian's Wall at the left side of a grassy bay.

1   25 m. Scramble into the corner to a small groove. Follow the groove, move right and go over grass ledges and a large chockstone to the foot of a very large chimney, directly below the centre of the huge wall.

2   25 m. Climb the chimney to belay below the wall.

3   30 m (4c). Climb the wall by a crack in the centre, which becomes a chimney-groove at 12 metres. Avoid a large loose block on the left and continue up the easier groove to belay on the highest grass ledge.

4   25 m (5a). From the left end of the ledge, pull up an overhanging wall. Traverse left to the foot of a narrow crack, which is climbed to the top of a pinnacle, from where a swing right leads to easier ground. Scramble right to a stance.

5   18 m (4c). Climb the arête on the right of a wide, dirty gully to the summit of Low Man.

Variation   Direct Finish   20 m   E2   1966
Ascends the overhanging crack above the stance on pitch 3 of Scylla. An exposed and strenuous pitch.

4a   (5c). Traverse across a water stained groove to start the crack. It is narrow at first, then wider, and is climbed by strenuous jamming. Move out at the top to the ledge and belay at the top of pitch 4 of Scylla.

★ **Puppet**   130 m   E2   1966
This route also ascends the large wall in the centre of the face. A
varied climb with difficult and exciting upper pitches. Start as for
Scylla.
1   26 m. Scrambling up grass leads to a ledge above a very large
    chockstone.
2   24 m (4c). Move to the right and climb a short corner for 6
    metres, then step back left above the overhang and go up a
    pleasant crack. Continue over ledges and an overhanging
    chockstone to below the crack of Scylla in the centre of the large
    wall.
3   18 m (5b). Ascend Scylla for 6 metres to a thread runner.
    Traverse across the wall on the right, ascending slightly to gain
    the deep groove. Climb this, or the arête on the right, to a small
    stance at the top.
4   18 m (4b). Continue up the corner and vague arête above, as for
    pitch 6 of Nor'-Nor'-West Climb, until a few moves to the right
    lead to a small stance.
5   20 m (5b). Climb the steep, shallow groove above and left; then
    continue up the steep wall, on improving holds, to a good ledge.
6   24 m. Move left and follow an easier ridge to the top of Low
    Man.

★ **Straits of Messina**   130 m   E4   1984
A fine eliminate route giving bold, delicate climbing up the wall
between Puppet and Scylla and the thin hanging crack above.
1   50 m. The first 2 pitches of Megaton, then up left to belay as for
    Scylla below the main wall.
2   33 m (6a). Climb the thin crack leading directly to the groove on
    Puppet (starting from the left). Up the groove a little, then pull
    out left onto an obvious square ledge. Move left across the wall
    for 2 metres. Climb up and continue up a thin crack-line in the
    slab to the rib. Up this to belay below a thin crack in the
    overhanging wall.
3   23 m (6a). Climb the crack curving leftwards to pull out onto a
    ledge above Scylla Direct.
4   24 m. Easily up the ridge on the left, as for Puppet.

★★ **Megaton**   120 m   HVS   1972
A varied and interesting route of some quality, which is sustained at
a good level, and contains a bold slab pitch. Start 12 metres right of
Scylla.

1   18 m (4c). Climb the short wall to a grass ledge. Climb a shallow
    groove on the left side of an easy-angled rib, or the rib itself, to
    another large grass ledge.

2   26 m (5a). From the lower end of the ledge, climb the delicate
    slab, moving left at 9 metres to a rightward-slanting fault beneath
    a steepening of the slab. Climb the fault until it finishes; then
    move right, back left, and up easier rock to a rock crevasse
    beneath the steep wall. Move left along grass ledges to belay
    beside a pile of blocks, below an obvious groove capped by an
    overhang.

3   36 m (5a). Step off the pile of blocks, and traverse to the right
    along two rock ledges to a groove. Climb this for 2 metres, then
    move left along a gangway to a thin corner-crack. Climb the
    crack, which climb widens after 4 metres, until the angle eases.
    Nor'-Nor'-West Climb crosses at this point. Move up to the right
    for 6 metres to a thread belay in a corner beside a detached block,
    midway between pitches 6 and 7 of North-West Climb.

4   20 m (4c). Make a difficult pull over the bulge above the block
    into the groove, which is climbed to a grass ledge (the last 3
    metres are difficult). Or, more easily, move left, round the rib,
    and up to the ledge. Move up to a smaller stance beneath a steep
    crack. (Nor'-Nor'-West Climb variation finish). Thread belay.

5   20 m. (4c). Climb the crack, which eases after 9 metres, to the
    top of Low Man.

Roraima   122 m   E1   1981
A poor climb whose only justification lies in pitch 2. The lower part
of the route takes a crack up the wall right of Nor'-Nor'-West Climb,
and the upper part lies between North-West Climb and Charybdis.

1   24 m. As for Nor'-Nor'-West Climb. Scramble to below a hand
    jam crack in the right wall.

2   32 m (5b). Climb the crack, which is sustained, and scramble to
    the terrace (junction with North-West Climb).

3   22 m (4b). Up the short groove behind the stance and then up
    the cracked, stepped arête above. Step left to belay below a
    cracked groove, just right of North-West Climb.

4   22 m (5a). Up the cracked groove to a ledge below another groove
    capped by an overhang. Avoid this by swinging onto the right
    arête, overlooking Goth. Follow the arête direct on good holds;
    belay as for Charybdis.

5   22 m (5a). As for Charybdis; follow the shallow groove until it
    is possible to step right to a leftward slanting crack, which is
    followed to the top.

★ **Nor'-Nor'-West Climb**   134 m   VS   1932

An excellent and pleasantly long climb with exposed and delicate climbing in its upper half. Start at the right side of a large grassy bay in the corner under the bounding buttress.

1   30 m. Go up the initial slab and continue up shallow slabs and ledges, first trending away from the wall of the impending buttress for 12 metres and then back to the shelter of it to a wide crack.

2   9 m. The large block ahead is reached and turned on the left. Thread belay.

3   12 m. Climb the slab, trending left to a bilberry ledge. Ascend the corner on the right to a ledge on top of the buttress and junction with North-West Climb.

4   9 m (4b). Climb a V-groove just left of the rock glacis.

5   15 m (4c). An exposed traverse left, first slightly down and then gradually rising, crosses the top of a thin crack near the finish and ends on a sloping ledge.

6   18 m (4c). Go up for 9 metres; then climb steep rock on the arête on the left until a few delicate moves to the right lead to a small stance. The latter part of the pitch is just to the left of Taylor's Chimney (North-West Climb).

7   10 m. An exposed traverse to the right crosses the top of Lamb's Chimney and leads to small ledges.

8   16 m. The 3 metre crack on the left is ascended; then a narrow ledge slants up and leftwards to a ledge.

9   15 m. The arête on the left leads to the top of the crag.

Variation Start   45 m   S   1936

The route goes up the lower north-west buttress to the point where the North-West and the Nor'-Nor'-West Climbs meet. Start just to the left of the ordinary start of the North-West Climb.

1a   16 m. Climb the wall at the left corner of the slab. Ascend the slab, using a thin crack, then step to the right to the top of the ordinary crack. Climb up the right wall, then ascend a slab to a belay on the left of the buttress. Continue, passing a crack, to a large block lying against the buttress. Just beyond, a large pinnacle provides a belay.

2a   14 m. Climb the left-hand crack, using the pinnacle, to a cave (thread runner). Climb out of the cave, facing left and go over the chockstone. Step on to a large platform on the right and ascend on the left to a large belay and stance directly above the chockstone.

3a   15 m. Go straight up for 6 metres to join North-West Climb on the top of the lower buttress 10 metres from a belay.

Variation Finish   20 m   VS   1954
9a (4c). The overhanging black chimney on the left of
Oppenheimer's Chimney looks formidable but offers an
interesting final pitch. It is strenuous for 6 metres, then leads,
more easily, in a direct line to the summit of Low Man.

★ **Ximenes**   50 m   HVS   1968
A good approach to several routes on the West Face (e.g. Goth),
which takes the front of the buttress leaning against Low Man. Start
between Nor'-Nor'-West Climb and North-West Climb at a small
corner below a crack.
1   18 m (5a). Climb into the crack, which is followed on good jams.
    Move left and climb the slab to a belay at the foot of a crack in
    the wall above.
2   15 m (5b). Climb the obvious crack above which is awkward and
    strenuous, but well protected, and leads to a ledge.
3   18 m. Follow easy slabs to the terrace below the routes on the
    West Face of Low Man.

★★★ **North-West Climb**   130 m   MVS   1906
A fine route, giving varied climbing and good situations. Start at the
right-hand end of Green Ledge at an obvious rightwards slanting,
short gangway.
1   20 m. Climb the gangway to a ledge, and follow a chimney for
    10 metres, then make a short traverse left across a slab, beneath
    a rock shield.
2   36 m (4a). The chimney is taken direct to finish in a corner
    (possible belay). A short buttress on the left is succeeded by a
    crack, after which the angle eases. Cross the large platform to a
    large glacis-slab about 9 metres to the right.
3   25 m (4b). Ascend a slab, and the corner above, and make a
    leftwards traverse to a good ledge. Continue the traverse round a
    corner on the left, then climb over a bulge into a recess. Climb
    up the back of the recess to make an awkward landing on a grassy
    ledge; belay on a higher ledge.
4   25 m (4a). Climb the corner, then traverse to the left to a nose
    of rock, which leads to a Block Ledge. Above is Lamb's
    Chimney. Step left, and climb straight up ledges to a short
    V-chimney. A long stride back across the top of the chimney
    leads to mossy rocks, above which are small grassy ledges.
5   24 m (4b). Traverse right, then ascend to the foot of the final
    chimney (Oppenheimer's Chimney). After an awkward start it
    becomes more reasonable and easy scrambling then leads to the
    top.

Variations
Variation Start   Kirkstile Variation   60 m   S   1937
A rather pointless variation on an otherwise fine route which starts
about 10 metres right of the ordinary start.

1a. Climb a gangway leftwards and traverse left below the first
    chimney of North-West Climb to a scoop, which is climbed.
    Continue up a buttress, make for a chimney up on the right and
    ascend this. On the right is a steep wall which is followed to a
    pyramid of rock, which is climbed by a crack.

Variation Original pitch   1906
4a. 15 metres from the block ledge a short traverse left is made to
    an open chimney which is climbed for about 10 metres, when a
    traverse is made back right to the small grassy ledge at the top
    of the more direct pitch.

Variation Finish   30 m   1913
    Avoids Oppenheimer's Chimney by traversing lower down and to
    the right round the corner. Climb an exposed steep wall on the
    right, which leads to an easier wall which can be climbed on the
    right or left.

★ **Charybdis**   129 m   HVS   1964
A good climb, which follows slabs, then a series of grooves in the
arête between the North and West Faces of Low Man. Start from the
Green Ledge as for North-West Climb.

1   15 m. Ascend pitch 1 of the North-West Climb; then go up the
    10 metre chimney to a stance and belay.
2   30 m (4c). Continue up the same chimney; then ascend a wall
    split by cracks to a large grassy platform.
3   20 m (4c). Move to the right to a glacis. Ascend this and go up
    the corner. Belay below the obvious deep overhanging groove.
4   15 m (5a). Climb into the groove (chockstone runner). Descend
    a little and climb the left wall, by layback, up a big flake. Return
    along an awkward gangway to the top of the groove and go over
    a loose block to a sloping stance and thread belay. (The main
    groove can be climbed direct).
5   12 m (5a). Climb the green groove above, moving left at the top
    to a ledge.
6   15 m (4b). Climb the groove on the right, or the fine arête on
    the right of the groove, to a large block belay and junction with
    Goth.
7   22 m (5a). Climb the shallow groove above, 6 metres to the right
    of Oppenheimer's Chimney. Move to the right over the bulge;
    then follow a slanting crack back left up the wall to the top.

West Face of Low Man

This is one of the best faces of Pillar Rock with a considerable choice of wall climbs of all grades. The rock is excellent and, since there are few grass ledges, it dries quickly after rain. As it faces west the routes catch the afternoon sun. The climbs are reached by crossing grassy ledges, leftwards, from the top of the waterfall (care needed). The climbs are described from left to right beginning with the obvious corner of Goth. Easiest descent is by The Old West Route.

★★ **Goth**   75 m   E1   1959

The route follows the obvious curving groove on the North-West side of Low Man. A fine, intimidating climb with the crux pitch in a good position. The best approach is via pitches 1 and 2 of Charybdis, or alternatively, by traversing leftwards, across grass ledges, from the chockstone at the head of the waterfall, to the foot of the groove below the huge sloping overhang.

1   20 m (4c). Climb the groove to a stance beneath the overhang. Small chockstone belay.
2   35 m (5b). Traverse left for 2 metres to the foot of a groove leading up to the roof of the overhang. This is climbed until a dubious block in the roof of a small overhang is reached; then break out left across a small slab to an arête and runners. Climb the overhanging wall above to a narrow sloping ledge. Traverse to the right along the ledge (strenuous) to the corner above the overhang and continue up this until a small overhang bars the way. Traverse left across the wall to a stance.
3   20 m (4a). Climb up to a short, curving crack on the right. Ascend this and finish up rough slabs.

Gaul   73 m   HVS   1974

Takes a line between Goth and The Hun. Start 4 metres right of Goth.

1   20 m (4c). Climb a short crack to a sloping grass ledge, then continue up the rough slab and groove to a stance on Goth.
2   35 m (5a). A good pitch. Above the slab, on the right, is a groove. Climb this and the wall above direct to the stance at the top of pitch 3 of The Appian Way.
3   18 m. Ascend the crack on the left, as for pitch 4 of The Appian Way.

★ **The Hun**   60 m   VS   1966

The route ascends the bottomless chimney just right of the overhang of Goth. The climbing is exhilarating and exposed although the route has good holds and is well-protected. Start by a large block on a terrace reached by scrambling across from the chockstone at the head of the waterfall.

1   30 m (4c). Ascend the small wall on the right; then climb the steep layback-crack above for 6 metres. Move left to a large block below the bottomless chimney. Climb into this; then go up the right wall to the stance at the top of pitch 2 of The Appian Way.
2   30 m (4b). Continue up pitches 3 and 4 of The Appian Way.

The Terrorist   55 m   E2   1988
Although only containing 12 metres of original climbing, it makes possible a direct ascent of the great wall between The Hun and The Appian Way, and provides steep and fingery climbing.

1   48 m (5c). Follow The Hun as far as the pinnacle above a layback flake. Climb the steep crack-line above to an overlap, and pull out right to reach good holds, on the traverse of The Appian Way. Climb the wall directly to finish just left of a mossy streaked corner.
2   7 m. Climb the wall behind to the top.

★★ **The Appian Way**   65 m   HS   1923
A very pleasant and exposed route with delicate wall climbing and good situations. Start at the same point as The Hun.

1   20 m. Avoid the mossy open chimney by climbing up on the left for 4 metres and traversing to the right across the top of the chimney; then go up the corner to a stance with a flake belay.
2   15 m. Climb the thin crack in the corner and, from the top of this, traverse delicately left across the imposing wall to a fine spike of rock on the skyline. This fine wall may also be climbed direct. Stance and belay on spike.
3   12 m. Move left and ascend a series of steep ledges straight ahead to a grassy terrace, where will be found a large block leaning against the wall. Thread belay.
4   18 m. The slightly overhanging crack on the left of the block is followed by slabs. The overhanging crack may be avoided by traversing ledges from the right end of the terrace. The climb finishes at the cairn at the top of North-West Climb.

Triton   62 m   VS   1974
Eliminate style variations on The Appian Way and Attila. Start as for The Appian Way.

1   20 m. Pitch 1 of The Appian Way.
2   16 m (4c). Step round the corner on the right and climb up the grooves in the arête to a ledge and flake belay.

3   26 m (4b). Climb up rightwards from the belay to the front of
     the hanging corner. Climb this to a grass ledge, then up the short
     groove above.

Attila 64 m HVS   1967
Start 4 metres to the right of The Appian Way and follow a fine
looking line up the centre of the curved wall. Unfortunately the
climbing is not as good as the line it follows.
1   20 m. Ascend a fault in the wall to a spike at 4 metres. Move to
     the right; then trend back left to the belay at the top of pitch 1
     of The Appian Way.
2   18 m (4c). The corner-crack leads to an overhang, which is
     climbed on the left (awkward) to a belay on the arête, directly
     below the second overhang.
3   20 m (5a). Step left and climb leftwards, under the overhang, to
     a V-groove, which leads to a large flake belay.
4   7 m. Step left from the flake and ascend the crack and slabs
     above.

Variation 18 m MVS   1975
2a   (4b). From the ledge beneath the first overhang, move right and
     climb a groove until an open corner is reached. Climb this for a
     short distance until it is possible to move left on to the slab. Belay
     at the top of pitch 2.

★ **Nook and Wall Climb** 76 m S   1920
A meandering climb, which nevertheless contains some interesting
and historic climbing. It has largely been superseded by The Devil's
Entrance. Start 25 metres left of, and at the same level as the top of
the waterfall, and 3 metres left of Thor.
1   13 m. Step left onto a wall and move left into a chimney. Move
     right and climb slabs to a grass terrace.
2   15 m. A rock staircase on the left leads to steep rocks. Climb for
     a couple of metres, then traverse right to a grassy corner. Follow
     the rib ahead to a grassy shelf. (The first nook is on the left).
3   15 m. The rectangular corner is climbed to a rock ledge, then
     traverse left along a flake and climb up to the second nook. This
     situation can also be identified by the mossy wall on the left.
4   24 m. A rock staircase leads to The Bad Corner. (This is the
     hanging groove above, which can be climbed at Very Severe,
     (4c). The ordinary route avoids it). Move one step down to the
     right and boldly cross the wall with the aid of a flake to a corner.
     Avoid the ledge on the right, and go up the corner, then climb
     the wall to a rock glacis. Ascend this to a grassy ledge and

tremendous belay. Care is needed with protection and rope management to avoid drag.

5   9 m. A short easy chimney finishes on a grassy terrace.

The Devil's Entrance   60 m   MVS   1972
The climb starts as for Thor, and is a direct version of Nook and Wall Climb.

1   9 m (4a). Climb the crack of Thor and move out left at the top to belay.

2   15 m (4a). Climb the wall behind the belay, and follow a crack to the right edge of the first nook of Nook and Wall Climb.

3   24 m (4b). Climb the groove; then move out left at the top to belay on a glacis.

4   12 m. Step back to the right into the groove, and move up to another glacis with perched blocks. Climb easily up the corner to the top.

★ Thor   62 m   MVS   1967
An enjoyable climb with good situations. Start just right of Nook and Wall Climb at the foot of a short crack.

1   27 m (4a). Climb the crack on good jams, moving slightly right at the top to ascend a slab, using a flake on the left. Continue straight up steeper rock and move to the right, past a large flake, to a small rock ledge and flake belay.

2   35 m (4b). Climb a steep crack above to a small overhang. Turn this on the left; then step back to the right and continue, moving to the right, across the wall above, to a grass ledge and belay.

Err   75 m   MVS   1970
Start as for Thor.

1   35 m (4a). Climb the jamming crack of Thor; then traverse to the right, across the broken slabs, to a perched block, and continue rightwards to a rock glacis.

2   40 m (4b). Climb the groove behind the belay; then move left and climb the short wall for a couple of metres. Pull round the rib into a groove, climb this to an overhang, and continue across the slab on the right. Climb over ledges to the top of the crag.

Variation   40 m

2a. Climb the groove behind the belay, then swing right to gain a shallow groove below a slab. Climb the slab direct.

Ledge and Groove Climb 78 m   S   1933

An inferior but slightly harder variation on West Wall Climb, but if followed by The Pulpit Route it gives 150 metres of climbing from Low Man to High Man. Start 6 metres left and down from West Wall Climb.

1   7 m. Climb a staircase leading right to below a V-groove on West Wall Climb.

2   15 m. Traverse delicately left along a ledge (The Ledge) to its end, and ascend slabby rocks to a stance at the top of pitch 3 of West Wall Climb.

3   20 m. Step down and cross a little wall on the left. Grassy rocks lead to a crack with loose flakes. Follow this, until it is possible to move out right (possible stance). Climb a slab which leads to a belay at the end of pitch 6 of West Wall Climb.

4   12 m. Reverse the traverse of West Wall Climb to a good ledge with a block belay.

5   24 m. The steep, mossy groove above is hard to attain, but once entered, the holds improved, towards the exit on the right. Cross grass to the right and go up a short, easy crack behind a block, beyond which a staircase leads to the Old West Route. A step across the Old West Route leads to the start of The Pulpit Route.

★ **West Wall Climb** 65 m   VD   1919

A good climb on sound rock, which starts about 12 metres above the level of the top of the waterfall, at a platform below a 3 metre wall.

1   15 m. An easy mantelshelf leads to a grass ledge. Follow a V-shaped chimney and steep rocks straight ahead to a sloping ledge (flake belay up on the left).

2   15 m. Make a short traverse to the right; steep rocks then lead to a rock glacis. A crack on the right wall leads to a good ledge.

3   15 m. Make an upward traverse to the left to belay at a pile of blocks.

4   20 m. From the top of the blocks climb a short awkward groove, which is followed by easier rock which leads to near the top of Low Man.

The Devil's Exit 52 m   HVS   1974

Starts as West Wall Climb.

1   15 m. Pitch 1 of West Wall Climb.

2   12 m (5a). Climb the crack directly above to an awkward landing.

3   25 m (4c). Climb straight up into the hanging groove and continue to the top.

★ **Strider**   200 m   VS   1974
A girdle of the West Face of Low Man, which takes in most of the
best pitches. Start up North-West Climb.

1-2 56 m. Climb the first 2 pitches of North-West Climb. Belay just
left of the glacis.

3   26 m (4b). Climb the groove left of the glacis; then continue up
the rib on the right to a junction with Charybdis. Follow
Charybdis to belay at the top of pitch 5 of that climb.

4   12 m. Traverse to the right, along easy ledges, to a belay on Goth,
at the top of pitch 1.

5   26 m (4c). Gain the slab on the right, and cross it to a steep rib;
then pull round this, and swing across to the chimney of The Hun.
Continue up The Hun to the stance at the top of pitch 1.

6   20 m (4a). Reverse the traverse of pitch 2 of The Appian Way
to a ledge below the overhang of Attila. Climb the crack on the
right, and traverse the flake to a ledge and belay at the first Nook
on Nook and Wall Climb.

7   20 m (4a). Climb the groove of The Devil's Entrance for 6
metres, then traverse right, crossing the groove of Thor below the
overhang. Stance and belay round the corner.

8   40 m. Make a descending traverse to join the last pitch of Err.

High Man

West Face of High Man

The 90 metre wall on the west side of High Man is the most
impressive face of Pillar Rock and is also the quickest to dry. It is
here that several superb slab routes on excellent rhyolite are to be
found. The easiest line is the tremendous, classic New West Climb
and the other obvious lines are the big groove of Gomorrah on the
left, and the smooth slabs of South-West Climb on the right. Climbing
in the afternoon or especially on sunny evenings gives an added
dimension to the character of the face.

The climbs are easily reached from the western scree or by
scrambling up The Old West Route. The routes are described from
left to right. Easiest descent – Slab and Notch Climb followed by the
western scree, or The Old West Route. Great care is needed not to
dislodge scree whilst descending the Western Gully below the West
Face. A large rock fall at the top of the gully has made the place
rather unstable!

The Crumb   57 m   HS   †   1974
Start at a deeply cut chimney, half-way up The Old West Route.
1   15 m. Climb the chimney and groove above.
2   12 m. Cross the grassy gully and climb straight up to a grass ledge below a groove.
3   30 m. Climb the crack above and move right into the groove. Follow this to the summit of High Man.

The Pulpit Route   68 m   VD   1934
An aptly named route. After a dismal start, the route provides varied and interesting climbing to the left of the great nose of rock upon which Gondor lies. Start high on The Old West Route where the latter crosses the top of a gully (good spike belay), about 30 metres left of Gomorrah.
1   15 m. Climb a mossy wall to the right of a large ill-defined pinnacle, to a sloping grassy terrace. Traverse right to belay in a large grassy gully.
2   22 m. Cross the gully and climb a wall to a ledge with blocks. Climb a groove running up left and transfer into another one, 1 metre to the left, which leads up into 'The Pulpit'.
3   22 m. Step up left and traverse a wall for 2 metres. Climb a clean rock rib to a large ledge (possible belay). Ascend the chimney above or the wide groove on the right, then traverse right across a wall to join the main buttress. Belay by a dubious block.
4   9 m. A nose of rock, which can be avoided, ends the climb near the top of High Man.

★★ Gondor   75 m   E2   1967
An impressive and exposed climb, which is both strenuous and delicate. The route follows the bulging arête on the left of the prominent groove of Gomorrah. Start at the base of the ridge left of Gomorrah. A must for any visiting party.
1   30 m (4a). The easy lower section of the ridge (pitch 1 and part of pitch 2 of Gomorrah) leads to a ledge and block belays.
2   18 m (5b). Climb the groove in the arête to the bulge. Above on the left is a large triangular hold. Pull up, and move boldly up right until the angle eases. Belay in a small corner below a grass ledge.
3   27 m (5c). Climb down from the stance for 2 metres and traverse delicately right, round the nose onto the wall. Climb up and left to easier climbing, following a groove to a large ledge and block belay. An alternative way to start this pitch (the original route) is to climb the overhanging arête on the right wall for 2 metres (very bold), then move onto the wall and continue up as above.

New West Climb, Pillar Rock

★ **Gomorrah** 80 m VS   1919
A good climb with no great difficulties, which ascends the big groove
on the left side of the West Face of High Man. Start about 6 metres
left of Vandal, and 6 metres above The Old West Route.
1   25 m. Ascend a rib for 8 metres, then climb a slab to a green
     shelf. Turn a nose of rock on the left and ascend a wall and a
     short slab to a ledge and block belays.
2   20 m (4b). Step to the right and traverse round the corner to a
     block below the big groove. Gain the groove by climbing either
     the short crack or the wall on the right. Ascend the groove to a
     stance below a roof.
3   20 m (4b). Continue up the chimney to a sentry box. Move up
     the left wall; then step to the right into the crack. Climb the crack
     for 6 metres until a traverse to the right can be made to a small
     stance and flake belays on the rib.
4   15 m (4b). Either return to the chimney and ascend this, or climb
     the rib behind the belay on good holds to the top of High Man.

Variation Direct Start 30 m MVS   1967
1a As for Vandal, the grassy corner to a stance beneath the roof
    (possible belay). Move left across a slab and ascend the groove
    over a slight bulge. Continue to belay on blocks on pitch 2.

Variation Finish 30 m VS   1967
A good alternative.
3a 20 m (4b). From the belay, traverse left, with difficulty, to gain
    the foot of a steep crack. Climb this, and pull into a square
    groove. Exit left into another groove, which leads to a good ledge.
4a 10 m. Easy climbing leads to the top of High Man.

★★ **Vandal** 80 m HVS   1959
A fine route, steep and well protected; low in the grade. It follows
the line of cracks rising from the right side of the large triangular
overhang of the West Face. Start directly below the triangular roof.
1   25 m (4c). Climb the grassy corner to about 5 metres below the
     roof. Cross the wall on the right and go up to a small ledge; then
     climb the short steep crack on the right to a good stance.
2   35 m (5a). A fine pitch. Climb the obvious crack on the right to
     another overhang at 12 metres. Continue up the corner or make
     a long step left to gain the rock rib on the left. Continue up a
     fine slab, then move to the right and up to a grass stance (poor
     belay); it is best to continue for 6 metres and move left to belay
     on the rib of Gomorrah.

3   20 m (4a). Traverse diagonally to the right across slabs to the arête, and finish up the last few metres of Sodom. Alternatively, climb diagonally left, and climb a ridge to the top of High Man.

Sodom   88 m   VS   1919
Provides enjoyable friction climbing up the arête on the immediate right of Vandal. Start 12 metres along The Old West Route on a ledge 3 metres above it.
1   20 m. An easy slab is climbed for 12 metres, then the route trends to the right up a groove. Steep rock leads to a grassy niche with a belay above on the left.
2   20 m (4a). Move 3 metres to the right to a corner with a crack above it. Ascend this (often wet) to a shelf on the right. Go up a wide staircase with big sloping steps for a short distance, then move left to a grassy corner. Belay high up on the rib on the left.
3   28 m (4b). Ascend the rib via two small sloping ledges to a larger one. Gain this and continue past a small corner on sloping holds to another corner with poor belays. Traverse to the right, over slabs, to the top of the chimney on New West Climb. Small belay high on the left wall. (The rib has now been recrossed.)
4   20 m (4b). The chimney, which narrows at the top, is climbed to a sentry box. Continue up the chimney and groove above to a large belay near the top of High Man.

Cheekwooly   85 m   S   1974
A combination of variations which provide the most independent route to the top of High Man. Although sandwiched between superior climbs, it does follow a fine line. Start to the right of Sodom in the back of an obvious corner groove, 5 metres left of Rib and Slab Climb.
1   45 m. Climb the groove line which trends slightly to the right, to belay on the traverse on pitch 3 of New West Climb (the pitch can be split if necessary).
2   40 m. Climb the steep groove above, 4 metres right of a chimney on New West Climb, to where it opens out (part of South-West by West Climb). Climb the rib on the left to the top, just right of the top pitch of Sodom.

Variation   40 m   VS
Start immediately right of the chimney of New West Climb, below an overhung V-groove.
2a   (4c). Move left round a rib to beneath an overhung V-groove. Climb this over a bulge and continue up the original route.

★★★ **Rib and Slab Climb**   90 m   HS   1919
At its grade, one of the best climbs on Pillar Rock. An extremely enjoyable way to the summit of the rock. Start level with the foot of New West Climb, and about 12 metres to its left.
1   26 m. Climb easy rocks and ledges, working slightly left to a grassy ledge. Step right onto a steep rib, and climb it to break out left at a small ledge. Climb a slab with a groove on its left side, or the rib on the right to a ledge.
2   20 m. The groove above is hard to start (crux) but the difficulties soon ease. Climb the steep rib on the left of the groove of New West Climb to a stance at the top.
3   20 m. Traverse right onto a superb rough slab; climb it, keeping to the centre for the best climbing, though easier on the right, to the belay blocks of New West Climb.
4   24 m. Follow New West Climb for about 3 metres then go up the blistered slab on the left to finish within a couple of metres of the summit of High Man.

★★★ **New West Climb**   87 m   VD   1901
A fine climb, which finds its way through areas of rock usually reserved for harder climbs. The situations are superb, making it one of the best routes of this standard in the Lake District. Start just below a big embedded block a little lower than South-West Climb.
1   20 m. Follow easy rocks, trending slightly to the left, to a rib which leads to a small corner. Follow a steep staircase to belay on a good ledge.
2   10 m. Climb a wide, shallow chimney which leads to a small platform, and traverse left for about 4 metres to a good belay.
3   17 m. Climb the obvious groove to slabs, followed by a traverse left to the foot of a chimney.
4   20 m. The imposing chimney above is climbed or thrutched, depending on ability or girth, to an obvious chockstone at 9 metres (possible belay). Traverse right and surmount a pile of blocks which form a magnificent belay.
5   20 m. Climb the slab above to finish in the same place as Rib and Slab Climb.

The South-West by West Climb   80 m   VS   1938
A contrived but worthwhile climb. Start a few metres to the right of New West Climb.
1   18 m. Traverse left on loose rock to the rib, which bounds New West Climb on the right, and follow it to belay on that climb.
2   25 m (4c). A smooth rectangular slab on the right leads to a horizontal ledge below another larger slab. Climb this until the

rock steepens, then step left to a good foothold before making a few hard moves up to a stance half-way up pitch 3 of Rib and Slab Climb.

3   15 m. Traverse left into an easy groove and climb this to the traverse of New West Climb. A more difficult alternative can be made by traversing right, climbing between Rib and Slab Climb and South-West Climb and reversing the upper New West traverse.

4   22 m (4a). Traverse left and climb the groove above to the overhang; turn this on the right and continue up the arête on the right to the top.

★★★ **South-West Climb**   70 m   MVS   1911
Delectable climbing on small but positive holds. A justly popular route. The start is at the bottom and just to the left of West Jordan Gully.

1   30 m (4b). Easy climbing leads to a grassy ledge on the left of a slab. Climb the slab to a deep-cut hold. Move awkwardly right and continue up the slab to where it steepens. Good holds lead to a small ledge (possible belay). Continue up the slab on the edge of the gully to the second ledge.

2   22 m (4b). Traverse left for 4 metres, then climb the slab, keeping to the right. Traverse right towards Jordan Gap, under a large block, to a stance.

3   18 m (4b). Return under the block and climb up a steep rib, joining the Far West Jordan Climb, to the summit of High Man.

Variation   Original Route   19 m   1911
2a From the belay on pitch 1, traverse left and ascend a grassy slab to a wide V-chimney (usually wet), which leads to the final pitch of New West Climb.

Boot Strap   104 m   VS   1967
A mini-girdle taking in only the West Face of High Man. A sustained route which contains some good if not original climbing. Start as for South-West Climb.

1   22 m (4b). Follow South-West Climb for about 20 metres to a sitting belay about 3 metres above the overlap.

2   24 m (4a). Traverse left onto South West by West Climb, cross this and traverse round the corner to gain the belay at the top of pitch 3 of New West Climb.

3   16 m (4b). Follow the traverse of New West Climb and continue past the chimney to attain the small sloping ledge on the rib of pitch 3 of Sodom. Climb this to a small ledge.

4   12 m (4a). Step down and left, and traverse to the rib overlooking Gomorrah. Make a long step onto this climb and go up to a belay beneath an overhang.

5   20 m (4b). A good pitch. From the belay, traverse left and ascend a crack on good holds. Continue over a small overlap into another groove and climb up to a good ledge and large belay.

6   10 m. Easy climbing leads to the top.

West Jordan Gully   30 m   S   1898
This is the prominent cleft separating Pisgah from High Man. An interesting climb, deep inside the mountain.

The way is obvious and the capstone can be surmounted either on the left or on the right. It is also possible to climb a crack on the left wall at the start of the climb which leads to a niche on the left-hand capstone route.

The Girdle Traverse   432 m   VS   1931
A classic expedition, combining many fine pitches. The route described is practically the reverse of the original girdle, with the advantage that most pitches are now ascended rather than descended. The main difficulties are found on Grooved Wall; the rest of the route being easier. As is common with other long mountain crag traverses some prior knowledge will be an advantage. By combining this route with The Eightfold Way and The Link a greater traverse of Alpine proportions may be climbed.

1   70 m (5a). Pitches 1 to 3 of Grooved Wall.

2   30 m. A mossy wall on the right leads to a good ledge behind a big block, as North-East Climb, pitch 5. Follow horizontal grass ledges rightwards to Savage Gully; block belay.

3   18 m. Cross the gully and ascend the crack leading to the ledge beneath the nose on North Climb.

4   9 m. Cross the Strid, and descend the Split Blocks. Go down the ledge on the right to a long ledge beneath the left edge of a huge wall (taken by Scylla).

5   20 m (4b). Ascend the left edge of the wall for 6 metres, then traverse right to the highest ledge to belay on Scylla.

6   25 m (4a). Cross the waterstained groove at a low level and go round the arête on the right to the small stance on Nor'-Nor'-West Climb. Continue the traverse rightwards, to small ledges.

7   24 m. An easy traverse, round the corner past the foot of Oppenheimer's Chimney, leads to the stance above pitch 3 of The Appian Way. Belay on a large flake leaning against the wall.

8   20 m. A horizontal traverse rightwards leads to a belay on Nook and Wall Climb.

9   30 m (4a). Continue to traverse, taking the easiest line to belay
    at the top of Ledge and Groove Climb.
10 24 m. Scrambling across The Old West Route to the start of
    Gomorrah.
11 25 m. Climb pitch 1 of Gomorrah.
12 40 m (4b). Continue up pitches 2 and 3 of Gomorrah.
13 15 m (4a). Traverse to the right, round a corner, and cross Vandal
    to the small stance on pitch 3 of Sodom.
14 12 m. Descend the sloping ledges below and traverse to the right
    to belay at the foot of the chimney of New West Climb.
15 30 m. Traverse right and climb the slab of pitch 3 of Rib and
    Slab Climb for 12 metres. From here a horizontal traverse to the
    right, across a V-groove, leads to the top of pitch 1 of South-West
    Climb.
16 40 m (4b). Continue up pitches 2 and 3 of South-West Climb.

Pisgah

West Face of Pisgah

Pisgah West Ridge   40 m   MS   1909
A pleasant climb, which starts just to the right of West Jordan Gully
by a corner. It is possible to split the pitch if necessary.
    Ascend the wall immediately right of the corner to a small
pedestal ledge. Climb the broken arête above to a large crack;
follow this, trending right to a grassy groove. Traverse left onto
a slabby buttress and follow the crest to easier slabs which lead
to the top of the Pisgah.

Variation   25 m   S   1909
    At the top of the large crack, level with the base of the grassy
groove, an exposed traverse left is made to a corner with a grassy
stance. A grassy crack is awkward to enter. As soon as it widens,
climb the buttress on the right which leads to the upper part of
the original route.

Sentinel   55 m   E1   1967
The route contains a hard first pitch and then is much easier. It takes
a direct line up the steep crack above the start of Pisgah West Ridge,
starting immediately right of West Jordan Gully at a blunt arête below
the crack.

1   20 m (5b). Climb the arête to runners below the crack. Surmount the overhang, with difficulty, and follow the crack more easily to a stance.
2   35 m. Continue up the easier crack above for 6 metres, then move out left and make a short traverse to a V-groove, which is climbed to the easy-angled slabs of Pisgah West Ridge. Continue up these to the top.

Great Doup   (Pillar Cove)   Alt. 750 m   North Facing

Of a similar nature to West Cove, only an indication and brief description will be given. Route finding is left to the skill of the mountaineers wishing to climb here. The Cove would repay a visit in a good winter.

Great Doup Buttress (D, 1900) is situated at the head of Great Doup, the cove east of Pillar Rock. Although the Buttress presents such an imposing appearance, the climbing is only of a moderate nature. The climb starts at the lowest point of the buttress and trends right to follow the right-hand side of the buttress.

Great Doup Pinnacle (40 m, S, 1927) is situated on the immediate left of, and about 75 metres higher than the start of Great Doup Buttress. A difficult rib is followed by a grassy scoop between two ribs and leads to a rock platform. A well defined crack leads to a steep wall which is followed to the top.

Western Buttress   30 m   S   1943
The climb starts at the toe of a small buttress on the west side of Great Doup.
   Follow a corner into a groove, continue up the groove and follow a crack in a slab on the left. Move left into a grassy groove which leads to the summit rocks.

Hind Cove   (178 122)   Alt. 600 m   North East Facing

Hind Cove also provides routes of an exploratory nature. It is the spacious hollow, which is crossed by the High Level Route, just before the ascent to Robinson's Cairn. All the climbs except Rib and Gully Climb, are situated high up the combe, on its right side, about 90 metres above the path. They are easily located by a conspicuous black cleft.

Hind Cove Gully (1897) is the black cleft just mentioned, which provides an easy route. The main feature of the place is the depth that the fissure penetrates the hill side.

Hind Cove Buttress (80 m, VD, 1923) forms the left wall of the gully. The route is fairly obvious.

The Slab Climbs are situated on the right side of the gully, and are:

Route 1 (60 m, VD, 1923) forms the right wall of the gully, the route being fairly obvious.

Route 2 (40 m, VD, 1923) starts 9 metres to the right of Route 1, and keeps to its right, the finish being a couple of metres right of and below the finish of Route 1.

Rib and Gully Climb (60 m, VD, 1925) is situated on a prominent outcrop of rock high up on the left of the cove, and about the same level as the right-hand crag. A scree gully bounds it on the left. Starting from the foot of the crag, the rib is followed for about 25 metres, and leads to a grassy gully with a small cave pitch (10 metres). The gully is followed to the ridge of Pillar Fell.

Raven Crag   (178 124)   Alt. 350 m   North Facing

Raven Crag lies on the Pillar side of the River Liza and may be recognized as the lowest crag above the forestry fence on this side of the valley.

The crag is the third to the east from the beck and small waterfall, which comes down from the combe below Pillar Rock.

It is a fairly long crag sloping back at a deceptively easy angle, forming a broad backbone of rock. To the left (eastern side) of the crag is a short, very steep wall of good rock, about 25 metres high. The obvious central corner has been climbed at Very Severe but nothing else has been reported!

On the easier-angled front of the crag, two other routes have been recorded, neither of which is very good. Above the crag are some slabs about 60 metres high which would give continuation to the routes.

Centipede (100 m, S, 1937) starts at the lowest point of the crag and aims to follow the crest of the buttress. Variations are possible almost at will, so no attempt has been made to describe the route.

Scarab (80 m, VD, 1937) starts about 45 metres up and right of Centipede, and keeps more or less to the right of it.

It is possible to climb almost anywhere on the front face of this buttress, with the combination of the upper slabs and the routes in Hind Cove (or Pillar Rock) a good mountaineering style day can be had.

Proud Knott (183 120) Alt. 400 m   North Facing

This prominent crag is heavily vegetated, and although a few routes in the easier grades have been recorded, it is perhaps best left to the wilder inhabitants of the valley.

MOSEDALE

Mosedale is the valley lying Nor'-Nor'-West of Wasdale, and its head, known as Blackem (Black Comb) Head, runs into the ridge connecting Pillar and Red Pike.

There is a great deal of rock in this valley but unfortunately it does not form good climbing crags, with the possible exception of Elliptical Crag and the Mosedale Buttresses.

Routes of a mountaineering interest can be worked out on the crags below the summit of Red Pike, while shorter, more continuous climbs can be found on Elliptical Crag and Mosedale Buttress.

Neither of the above crags are at all popular and they are more of historical interest than of real climbing interest.

Mosedale Buttresses (176 115) Alt. 500 m   South Facing

Another obscure crag, it can reputedly be seen from a yard of the Wasdale Head Hotel, and appears as a small, dark patch on the southern slope of Pillar Fell (along with many others).

The climbing is on three tiers. The Lower Buttress is vegetated, but the climbing is fairly clean.

The Middle and Upper Buttresses give short pitches but no definite routes.

To reach the crag, follow Mosedale Beck as for Wind Gap, then when below what you believe to be the crag, strike up the unpleasant hill side.

Route 1 47 m S   1921
Start on the left side of the lower buttress.
1   20 m. Climb easy rock to the right-hand of two corners, ascend the corner and a difficult groove above to a grassy stance. Block belay up and left.
2   15 m. Climb a rib directly above the block to a ledge in a corner. Step left and ascend a continuation of the rib to a good terrace.
3   12 m. Two short sections of easy rock lead to the top.

Route 2 59 m S   1921
Start on the right-hand side of the lower buttress.

1   20 m. A wall is climbed to a narrow heather ledge in a corner.
Make a difficult step round the steep rib on the left to gain a
sloping stance. Move up and right, then go up a broken groove
to a large platform.

2   27 m. Move left and climb a groove, then take to the right edge
of a small buttress and follow it to a ledge. From the right-hand
edge of the ledge, climb the face above to a vertical wall.
Traverse diagonally left to ascend an open corner to a large
terrace.

3   12 m. As for Route 1.

Routes 3 and **4** (1921) are short, Difficult in standard and found on
the left and right sides of the Middle Buttress respectively.

Route 5 (35 m, D, 1921) follows a line on the right-hand side of the
Upper Buttress, while **Route 6** (45 m, D, 1921) follows a line left
of Route 5 and rejoins Route 5 near the top.

There is also a traverse of the Upper Buttress called **Easter Traverse**
(66 m, S, 1924). It starts at the extreme right end by ascending to a
square corner, about 2 metres up, and then follows the best line across
the buttress.

Elliptical Crag   (171 116)   Alt. 600 m   South Facing

This obscure, chameleon like crag stands about 150 metres below
Wind Gap. As this path is not very popular, especially in ascent,
neither is the crag. It also does not help that the crag stands in the
way of the main drainage path of this side of the fell and even though
it faces south, it will often be found wet.

The crag is nearly 60 metres high, and the rock is of good quality.
As the lines are obvious a detailed description will not be given. The
climbs will be described briefly from left to right.

Easter Crack   50 m   VD   1910
An enjoyable combination of crack, slab and mantelshelf climbing
which lies on the left side of the crag, the line being obvious.

Left Face Route 60 m D 1910

Start to the right of Easter Crack and takes a diagonal line to the central ledge. It then breaks back left to finish near Easter Crack, or follows a series of corners to finish near Right Face Route.

Right Face Route 60 m S 1910

Climb a line to the left of the obvious Black Crack. Follow slabs to the central ledge, climb a corner on the right to another ledge, and move right again to climb a crack on good holds.

Black Crack/Black Corner 60 m 1910

Moderate climbing for 30 metres leads to the Black Corner. The Black Crack overhead is, as it looks, repulsive, even when there is no water spouting from its lip. (Quote) Circa 1935 'It will go if the rock is dry and free from moss; if not there is nothing to be done but retrace ones steps!'

Directrix 50 m MVS 1967

(4b). Start halfway between Black Crack and Small Chimney. Climb a corner at the left end of the wall, move right onto a slab, and over heather to a steep crack which is followed to easy slabs and the top.

Small Chimney 30 m M 1910

A short climb with a few moderate pitches.

Slab Climb 20 m D 1913

Take a line between Small Chimney and Small Crack and is of little merit.

Small Crack 20 m M 1910

A short, uninteresting climb of moderate difficulty.

Boulders

'Y' Boulder is of historical interest as well as providing passing amusement. It is to be found about $1\frac{1}{2}$ km above Ritson's Force and is easily recognized by the Y-shaped crack. Another moderately-sized boulder lies a short distance further up the valley.

KIRK FELL

Black Sail Buttress (194 111) Alt. 620 m   North Facing

Another remote dark and heavily vegetated crag high on the Ennerdale side of Kirk Fell with few rewards for such a long approach. The easiest way of identifying the climbing area from the surrounding broken fellside is by the large square overhang at half-height.

When approaching from Wasdale Head, follow the good track up Mosedale for 1½ km then bear off right on the Gatherstone Beck track up to Black Sail Pass (1½ km). From Black Sail Pass turn south onto the track up the northern spur of Kirk Fell for about 300 metres then contour left following a poor sheep track for 200 metres to the base of the crag. Approximately 1¼ hrs from Wasdale Head (the easiest and shortest approach.)

The routes are described from right to left. The descent is by scrambling to the top of the buttress, then going north to meet the Kirk Fell northern spur track. Follow the track down to the sheep track used on the approach.

Three Blind Mice 75 m MVS   1969
A route that makes the most of the relatively clean arête on the right-hand side of the crag. Start directly below the arête.
1   25 m (4a). Straight up the arête to a stance.
2   25 m (4b). Climb the wall just right of the arête to gain a leftwards sloping recess that leads up over a bulge to a large terrace.
3   25 m (4b). Step off the block on the left, traverse delicately left across the slab to the arête then climb the shallow groove to a ledge. Move left round a bulge and up the arête to the top.

The Cat Run 75 m MVS   1969
A climb spoiled by the vegetation but still with an interesting second pitch. The route aims for the large overhang in the centre of the crag then avoids it by a long traverse left. Start below the centre of the shallow vegetated groove above 6 metres left of the obvious arête climbed by Three Blind Mice.
1   45 m (4a). Climb over ledges to the bottom of a break leading through the overlaps. Follow the steep break on good holds for

15 metres then go up diagonally left over easier ground to a large terrace. Good belay below the large block.

2   30 (4b). Climb the grassy groove just left of the large block, make an awkward step left onto the slab and continue up to the large overhang. Traverse left on good holds to the extreme left arête, then climb up over easy but grassy rocks to ledges.

Kirk Fell Ghyll   Alt. 675 m   North Facing

Kirk Fell Ghyll (1944) is the huge cleft passed on the right when approaching Boat Howe Crags from Black Sail Pass. It consists of about 150 metres of scrambling and has three waterfall pitches, the hardest being the top one (Mild Severe), depending on the amount of water flowing down it. All difficulties can be avoided by scrambling up the ghyll walls either right or left at will. During a hard winter the ghyll gives good snow and ice practice.

Boat Howe Crags   (199 110)   Alt. 700 m   North Facing

Boat Howe Crags is the name given to the area of broken crags and central pillar of rock (The Boat) high on the Ennerdale side of Kirk Fell.

A dark and remote north facing crag which requires a considerable spell of dry and warm weather to come into condition. The main climbing area is on the very steep, compact central pillar of The Boat, where the rock is solid, very rough, but unfortunately, also very dirty. The rock on either side of The Boat tends to be broken and is also very dirty.

When approaching from Beck Head the first prominent arête seen is Longshoreman's Arête but the climbing in this area is broken and poor. Further right is a deep cut square gully with Custom House Arête on its right-hand side. This marks the start of the East Buttress. The East Buttress comprises a wide expanse of broken rock with the recorded scramble of Esplanade Climb running up its centre and is bounded on its right-hand side by Sea Wall Arête. Just right of Sea Wall Arête are the obvious and pleasant Breakwater Slabs which mark the start of the real climbing. Further right again is the very steep central pillar of The Boat where the route grades and character change with the hardest lines taking the front face of the pillar. The descent gully is up and right from the base of this pillar.

From Wasdale follow the Gable Crag track to Beck Head then bear left up the east shoulder of Kirk Fell for approximately 100 metres where an indistinct traverse line may be picked up crossing the Ennerdale face of Kirk Fell to Boat Howe Crags. Alternatively follow the track from Beck Head to Black Sail Pass until directly below the obvious compact buttress of Boat Howe Crags and then strike off directly up the fellside to the crag, (longer and very hard work).

The best approach, once being able to establish the top of the descent gully, is to continue up the east shoulder of Kirk Fell until just beyond the top of the steep section, then to bear off north-west to the top of the crag, where an easy descent brings you round to the foot of Boat Howe Crags.

The climbs are described from left to right, in line with the normal approach, and the best descent is on the right via an easy gully.

Coastguard Climb   40 m   VD   1926
Start about 70 metres up the scree gully at the left end of the crag, at the bottom of a steep crack reached by an easy 15 metres rightwards traverse from the gully. Broken and not recommended.
1   8 m. Climb the crack to a ledge.
2   20 m. Follow ledges and grooves up left to a broken ledge.
3   12 m. Climb the slab on the right to the ridge.

Sea Wall Arête – East Buttress   70 m   D   1925
An interesting route which generally follows the right edge of the East Buttress.
1   15 m. Scramble up to a ledge below a wall with a crack in it. Climb the strenuous crack to a rock stance.
2   13 m. The right edge of the slabs above leads to a stance.
3   17 m. Ascend a few metres then go up the corner on the right followed by slabs to below a large corner.
4   25 m. Climb the left wall of the corner and the slabs above to the top.

Variation   23 m   VD
3a Climb the arête on the left to join pitch 4 below the slabs.

The following three routes, which share the same finish up the 'Lighthouse' are all situated on Breakwater Slabs, where the rock is good and dries quickly. Worth a visit.

Moss Slab   62 m   HS   1939

A good climb taking the left edge of Breakwater Slabs.

1   27 m. Climb the arête to a spike and continue up the slab on the
     left until it steepens into a wall. Make an awkward traverse left,
     then go up and back right. Finish straight up the arête.

2   15 m. As pitch 2 of Breakwater Slabs and Lighthouse.

3   20 m. As pitch 3 of Breakwater Slabs and Lighthouse.

Breakwater Slabs and Lighthouse   65 m   S   1925

Start below the obvious crack in the centre of the slabs.

1   30 m. Climb directly up the crack to a large grass ledge.

2   15 m. Up the grass trending right to below some broken slabs.

3   20 m. Climb the broken slabs after which the climb steepens at
     the 'Lighthouse' but the holds remain good to the top.

★ **Breakwater Slabs, Grooved Arête**   50 m   MVS   1928

An excellent pitch up the right-hand arête of the slabs.

1   30 m (4a). Make an awkward step onto the arête from the right
     and climb it to a junction with Breakwater Slabs and Lighthouse
     below the broken slabs.

2   20 m. As pitch 3 of Breakwater Slabs and Lighthouse.

Up and left of the central pillar of the boat is a small buttress called
the Larboard Fender which has a short easy crack up the front.
Between this and the boat is a small chimney called The Hatchway
and marks the start of the following route.

Hatchway and Rigging   40 m   VD   1925

A poor and disjointed route.

1   8 m. Climb the chimney via its right wall to a large ledge.

2   7 m. Scramble right to the bottom of a crack in a wall.

3   17 m. The Rigging. Climb the wall to a spike on the left. Step
     across right into a groove and up the crack to the top of a tower.

4   8 m. Easy scrambling leads to the top.

Larboard Arête   43 m   S   1925

Start at the foot of the left arête of the boat, below and right of The
Hatchway.

1   20 m. Climb the arête to a ledge at 12 metres and continue up
     to another ledge.

2   15 m. The groove to the left leads up to the top of the tower on
     Hatchway and Rigging.

3   8 m. Easy scrambling to the top.

★ **The Prow of the Boat**   55 m   HVS   1940

A good climb giving two worthwhile pitches in spite of their dirty appearance. Start below an easy rib that leads up to an obvious V-groove running up just left of the front of the boat.

1   25 m (5a). Climb the easy rib and continue up the V-groove until a small resting ledge can be gained on the left. Traverse right across steep rock then up to good ledges. Good belay at the far right-hand end of the ledge.

2   30 m (5a). Traverse delicately right for 4 metres to gain the bottom of a left-facing corner. Climb this corner passing a doubtful flake, over a bulge then go diagonally left to a ledge below an overlap. Pull over the overlap and up the delicate slab above to the top. A poorer alternative is to traverse right from below the overlap to a rib which is followed to the top.

★ **Numenor**   53 m   E1   1969

Steep and strenuous climbing up the thin ragged crackline and bulges 7 metres right of The Prow of the Boat. Unfortunately, the climbing is spoiled by the moss and dirt. Start below a shallow leaning corner.

1   23 m (5b). Climb the awkward leaning corner up to a bulge. Pull out right onto the steep wall, move up to the foot of the sharp crack and climb it over a bulge up to the next bulge. Move left for 3 metres and go up steeply to a small stance.

2   30 m (5b). Climb up to join The Prow of the Boat at the bottom of the left-facing corner on pitch 2 and continue up this climb to finish.

Fanghorn   50 m   E2   †   1969

Climbs The Prow of the Boat directly, starting at the toe of the blunt arête on the right.

1   20 m (5b). Climb the little corner on the right of a rib, step left and pass a little overhang to enter a shallow groove. Continue up the arête then make a delicate move up and right using a sling for aid. The shallow corner above leads up to a stance on the right of the arête.

2   30 m (5a). Straight up the wide open groove above, then left to a shallow corner and up this to the top.

Starboard Arête Direct   52 m   MS   1940

A poor route that zig-zags its way up the left wall of Starboard Chimney on rock that is dirty with loose holds.

1   16 m. As pitch 1 of Starboard Chimney.

2   16 m. Step out of the vegetation from its lowest point and follow
     a line of holds diagonally left across the wall to a groove. Climb
     the groove to a ledge and junction with Starboard Arête.
3   20 m. Traverse the ledges right, then move up diagonally right to
     where the wall steepens, level with the top of Starboard Chimney.
     Step round to the right and go straight up the shallow groove to
     the top.

Starboard Chimney   30 m   VD   1925
The chimney right of The Boat, which divides it from the Starboard
Fender buttress. The steep vegetation on the first pitch and unstable
stones in and above the second pitch render the route dangerous.
1   16 m. Climb the cave pitch followed by 7 metres of steep
     vegetation.
2   14 m. The loose rock and unpleasant chimney. Exit on the right
     near the top. Care required not to shower the second with stones.

Starboard Arête   63 m   MS   1926
Pleasant climbing on relatively clean rock. Start as for Starboard
Fender.
1   10 m. As pitch 1 of Starboard Fender to the grass ledge.
2   12 m. Using the top of a large leaf of rock, go up and left into
     a corner. Make a descending traverse left into Starboard Chimney
     to the belay at the top of pitch 1.
3   13 m. Climb the wall on the left to a ledge and traverse it left
     until it is possible to step down to a stance (on this pitch there
     used to be a thin flake of rock called the 'Clinker', but it has
     long since disappeared).
4   13 m. Up the wall on the left then make an ascending traverse
     left over ledges to a large belay block (the 'Capstan').
5   15 m. From the Capstan climb the slabs above direct, or traverse
     right into a groove and up this to the top.

On the right of The Boat is the small Starboard Fender buttress,
which is bounded on its left by the unpleasant Starboard Chimney.

Starboard Fender   35 m   VD   1935
A poor route.
1   20 m. Climb to a grass ledge up either, the crack near the right
     corner of the buttress, or the short corner further right. Continue
     up over broken rocks, step right onto a slab and climb this to a
     large ledge.
2   15 m. Traverse right and ascend easily to the top.

Variation Direct Finish   15 m   HVS
An interesting but much harder variation finish.
2a (4c). Climb the steep wall on the left to a recess, then finish up
    the left rib. Poorly protection.

Stern Girdle Traverse   98 m   S   1926
A girdle of The Boat starting up Larboard Arête and descending
Starboard Arête. It can be climbed in either direction. Reasonable
climbing with only the centre section being new.
1   20 m. As pitch 1 of Larboard Arête.
2   15 m. As pitch 2 of Larboard Arête.
3   15 m. Descend slightly and traverse right to a grass ledge.
     Continue traversing right and down to a large belay ledge (the
     'Capstan').
4   13 m. Reverse pitch 4 of Starboard Arête.
5   13 m. Reverse pitch 3 of Starboard Arête.
6   12 m. Reverse pitch 2 of Starboard Arête.
7   10 m. Reverse pitch 1 of Starboard Fender from the grass ledge.

Right of The Boat across a large open scree gully lies the West
Buttress. It is large, broken and very dirty, with its two recorded
routes being of similar character – good winter potential.

Landlubber   68 m   HVS   1969
A route that follows the shallow groove left of the large sweep of
slabs in the centre of the buttress. Start 10 metres down and right of
the point where the crag meets the large scree gully. The better of
the two routes, but very dirty.
1   20 m (4c). The short ramp leads up to the foot of a groove. Climb
     the groove then the flake crack above to a stance.
2   18 m (4c). Climb up the break diagonally right to a grass ledge,
     then up a crack to a large stance.
3   30 m (4b). Gain the prominent corner up and right, step left to a
     narrow mantelshelf, then continue left below a bulge to a large
     sloping ledge in a corner. Climb the left wall to the top.

Horizon Climb   97 m   HS   1926
A disjointed and poor route starting in a corner left of a small buttress
and at the right-hand end of the large sweep of slabs.
1   20 m. Climb the corner to a grass ledge, make an ascending
     traverse right then up steeply to ledges.
2   16 m. The broken loose rocks above lead with care to a large
     sloping grass ledge. Poor belays.

3   18 m. Either traverse diagonally left and up over rocks and grass ledges to a broken corner, or step right from the sloping grass ledge and climb the arête.
4   25 m. Scramble up and traverse right along a grass ledge, passing en route the site of the 'Cleet' (a scar remaining where once stood a curious pointed rock, believed to have been struck by lightning in the summer of 1967).
5   The easy ridge to the top.

GREAT GABLE

The climbing on Great Gable is some of the most easily accessible in the district, the Napes Ridges being about 1 to $1\frac{1}{2}$ hours easy walking from either Wasdale Head or Seathwaite in Borrowdale.

Unfortunately access restrictions in Ennerdale valley make approaches to the Gable Crags from there impractical unless you wish to spend the majority of the day walking.

Wasdale is the most popular starting point for access to the majority of the crags when approaching from the west, with ample parking available on the triangle of land just before the hotel. Limited parking is also available at the road end but is generally taken by the campers or insomniacs. Roadside parking at Seathwaite is used by those approaching from Borrowdale and walking to Sty Head, whilst parking at the top of Honister Pass is a useful starting point for the crags on the north side of Gable.

The climbing ground may be divided into three main areas. The Napes Ridges/Tophet Wall group and Kern Knotts both lie on the Wasdale side of Great Gable, overlooking the path to Sty Head Pass; while Gable Crag lies just below the summit of Great Gable, facing north to the head of the Ennerdale valley.

In addition to these three main groups, there is the less frequented Green Gable Crags, which are situated on the Ennerdale side of Green Gable.

Access around the Gable Crags area is made relatively easy by following the well-marked paths which encircle the mountain known as the Climbers' or Gable Traverse. See relief drawing page 119 and end paper maps.

From the summit of Sty Head Pass the Gable Traverse runs across the south side of Great Gable, under Kern Knotts then rises to cross the reddish scree of Great Hell Gate which is bounded on its left-hand side by the imposing Tophet Wall. After crossing great Hell Gate the main track contours west, well below the Napes Ridges, then goes round the south-west corner of Great Gable until rising up to reach Beck Head. (The gap between Great Gable and Kirk Fell). The track then descends slightly before striking off east below Gable Crag and up to Windy Gap. (The gap between Great Gable and Green Gable). By descending the path down Aaron Slack the Sty Head track is regained at Sty Head Tarn.

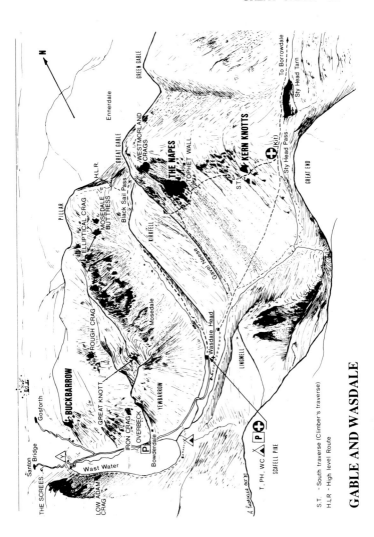

N

GREEN GABLE

To Borrowdale

Ennerdale

Sty Head Tarn

H.L.R.

WESTMORLAND
CRAGS

GREAT GABLE

THE NAPES

KERN KNOTTS

PILLAR

ELLIPTICAL CRAG

MOSEDALE
BUTTRESS

Black Sail Pass

TOPHET WALL

S.T.

Sty Head Pass

GREAT END

ROUGH CRAG

KIRKFELL

Gavel Neese

Mosedale

BUCKBARROW

Gosforth

GREAT KNOTT

YEWBARROW

Wasdale Head

LINGMELL

Santon
Bridge

IRON CRAG

OVERBECK

Bowderdale

West Water

THE SCREES

LOW ADAM
CRAG

SCAFELL PIKE

T, PH, WC

S.T. - South traverse (Climber's traverse)

H.LR. - High level Route

GABLE AND WASDALE

Gable Crag   (213 105)   Alt. 800 m   North Facing

Gable Crag is the name given to the crags near the summit of Great Gable, on the Ennerdale side. It is made up of a number of isolated buttresses, separated by stretches of very steep grass or wide scree gullies.

Approaching from Windy Gap, the track below the crags is followed past the foot of a wide scree gully, to a point just below the lowest part of the crag. From here, the conspicuous Bottle-Shaped Pinnacle will be seen high up on the right. At the same level as the Bottle-Shaped Pinnacle, a short distance to the left, rises a steep buttress containing Mallory's Climbs. Passing the ridge containing the Bottle-Shaped Pinnacle, a wide expanse of rock, split by a conspicuous chimney, Engineer's Chimney, will be seen at approximately the same level as the Pinnacle. The routes in the vicinity of Engineer's Slabs (to the right of the Chimney) are best approached by Sledgate Ridge, which starts near the path below the crag. Continuing along the base of the crags, the foot of the wide Central Gully is passed; a short distance beyond, the small buttress split by Smuggler's Chimney rises above the track. The most westerly buttress is Prayer Mat Buttress. It is separated from the main crag by a wide scree gully.

Due to its north facing location, and altitude and hence its relatively short season for development, or even climbing, this mountain crag has suffered over the years from lack of attention. Recently however some excellent climbs have been established on its central wall (Engineer's Slabs area) to bring the crag the attention it deserves as a traditional crag with modern routes.

The routes are of high quality with classics such as Engineer's Slabs, The Tomb, and Sarcophagus, to name but a few. The routes are steep (the term slab should be viewed with caution), sustained but generally well protected and follow natural lines on sound rock, although care should be taken at the top of the routes due to the presence of loose, unstable blocks.

As the crag has a northerly aspect the sun only falls on the crag late in the day and this can result in cold conditions on all but the calmest of days, with the natural lines holding water well into a dry spell but this can be a positive asset in winter when a number of excellent lines can form.

From Wasdale follow the approach as if going to the Napes via Gavel Neese but instead of turning off right at Moses Finger continue

(*opposite*)   Dream Twister, Gable Crag
(*next page*)   Snicker Snack, Gable Crag

straight up until the obvious traverse line off left is reached. Follow this stoney track up to Beck Head Tarn, then the cairned track up the north-west shoulder of Great Gable, until a narrow track leads off left (the North Traverse) under Gable Crag. (Approximately. 1¼ hrs).

Alternatively, from Borrowdale, follow the Sty Head track from Seathwaite up to Sty Head Tarn then turn north up Aaron Slack to Windy Gap, the col between Gable and Green Gable. From here a short descent brings you down onto the North Traverse that leads across west under the crag (approximately 1½ hrs).

When approaching from the north, Honister Pass in Buttermere is a good starting point. From the top of the pass follow the old quarry road west for 1 km then turn south onto a well marked track that runs down the west side of Grey Knotts and Brandreth, eventually leading into Stone Cove below Gable Crag.

The best descents are by going the long way round, either via Windy Gap for routes east of Oblique Chimney, or via the west ridge and under Prayer Mat Buttress for routes west of Oblique Chimney. A descent is possible down the buttress left of Engineer's Slabs for routes in this area, though it requires great care.

The routes are described from left to right.

Windy Ridge 37 m S   1944
The climb lies on the isolated buttress nearest to Windy Gap, with a wide scree gully on its left and a narrow scree gully on the right. Start at the right-hand side of the buttress.
1   23 m. Climb the open, grassy groove, followed by a steep wall to a sloping ledge. The steep groove above is followed, using some loose holds, to a large grass ledge.
2   14 m. The slabs above are climbed from left to right, then follow a groove on the right to the top. An easy rake leads off right into the gully.

The climbs which lie in the region of Mallory's Routes and The Slant are situated on the buttress above and right of the wide scree gully, which is a few metres west of Windy Gap. The best approach is by steep scrambling from either the top of Windy Ridge or from the Windy Gap to Gable summit tourist path.

Aaron's Slab 39 m HS   1959
Start at the foot of a clean slab, 5 metres left of the start of Mallory's Left-Hand Route. Worth the effort of finding it.

Engineer's Slab, Gable Crag   (*previous page*)
Central Climb South Face, Kern Knotts   (*opposite*)

1   27 m. Climb the slab, firstly in its centre, then by its right-hand edge to a small grass ledge. Follow the slab above to a large ledge.
2   12 m. Traverse left and climb either the steep crack or the steep left edge of the wall.

Mallory's Left-Hand Route   30 m   VD   1908
Starts at the left-hand edge of the buttress by a detached block. Not recommended.

A leaf of rock is followed to a ledge. Step left and climb the slab for 12 metres, where a short difficult traverse right to a large block leads to easier rocks and a good ledge. Scramble to the top.

The Serpent   32 m   E1   1970
A vicious little route that sees few ascents, due to its position on the crag and the quality of its neighbours. Start at the curving crack between The Slant and Mallory's Left-Hand Route.
1   20 m (5b). The crack which is both awkward and strenuous is followed, trending right into the niche above. It is possible to gain the niche by traversing in from The Slant.
2   12 m (5a). Climb the crack above the slab through the overhang to the top.

★ Vindolanda   35 m   E3   1974
Above the start of The Slant is a prominent, steep crack line giving sustained and difficult climbing.

(6a). Climb up to a small ledge beneath the crack, as for The Slant. Difficult moves up to and past a nasty peg runner lead to a slab; follow this to a belay and easy ground.

★ The Slant   45 m   E1   1968
A fine route, climbing the obvious gangway and groove on good rock with a technically interesting crux. Start below the bulging wall, 12 metres left of Mallory's Right-Hand Route.
1   30 m (5b). Climb the bulging wall, pull onto the bottom of the sloping gangway, and follow this to a flake crack below an obvious V-groove. Enter the groove, which is often wet, (crux) and climb it to a large stance on the right.
2   15 m (5a). Traverse 3 metres left to the groove. Climb it to the top, passing an overhang at half height.

Mallory's Right-Hand Route   37 m   MVS   1908
A poor and dirty route, starting at the right-hand end of the buttress below a steep crack.

1   30 m (4a). Easy rocks on the right lead to the bottom of a crack. Climb the crack to a ledge and loose rocks.
2   7 m. The loose easy chimney leads to the top.

Variation Start   30 m   MVS   1968
A much needed improved start to the first pitch.
1a (4a). Climb a slab on the left by an upward diagonal traverse to a flake crack on the right. Follow this to the main crack.

The Bandersnatch   47 m   HVS   1970
An interesting route that wanders up steep, clean rock to the right-hand side of Mallory's Right-Hand Route. Start 10 metres right of Mallory's Right-Hand Route below a steep groove.
1   22 m (5a). Enter the groove from the right (long reach). Climb the groove, exiting right, then diagonally right up steep slabs to the edge of the buttress. Traverse left below the overhang, then straight up to a grass ledge.
2   25 m (4c). The arête above is climbed, first on the right then on the left via a huge block to the top.

Potheen   40 m   MVS   1970
Worth a visit for its second pitch. Start at an open grassy chimney, 10 metres above and right of The Bandersnatch.
1   10 m. Climb the easy grassy chimney and crack to belay as pitch 1 of The Bandersnatch.
2   30 m (4b). Descend 2 metres, traverse right across slabs to an arête and climb straight up to below a steep crack. Climb it and the short groove above to the top.

Bottle-Shaped Pinnacle Ridge
The first definite ridge (from Windy Gap), easily identified by the bottle-shaped pinnacle high up the ridge and the oblique chimney on its right. The ridge is a loose scramble and is not recommended.

Barney Buttress   150 m   VD   1939
The crest of the ridge is followed throughout with numerous stances.

Oblique Chimney   23 m   VD   1892
Climbs the chimney situated high on the crag to the right of the Bottle-Shaped Pinnacle and Ridge. A depressing traditional chimney.
    Climb the right wall of the chimney passing two caves to exit right at the top onto scree. Belay well back.

On the right wall of Oblique Chimney is a huge rock-fall scar. The following route starts just right of this from approximately the same height as the base of the Bottle-Shaped Pinnacle.

Corkscrew Slabs   53 m   VS   1958
Interesting and open climbing.
1   18 m. Easy rocks right of the rock slab lead to a grass ledge with a crack on the left. Climb the crack to another ledge.
2   35 m (4b). Traverse left, climb the groove, then make a delicate ascending traverse across slabs on the right to a small ledge below the bulge, which is passed on the right to steep but easier ground.

Moonshiner   40 m   HS   1958
Climbs the short, steep wall between Oblique Chimney and Engineer's Chimney, starting approximately 7 metres left of a large block below a rib.
1   15 m. Climb the rib to a grass ledge.
2   25 m. Step onto the rib above from the right, and climb directly up to a small grass ledge below a crack. Step left onto a small ledge, then climb up trending right to the top.

The following two routes start below a broken buttress that runs up from just above the path to below and left of the main central wall. Each provides an excellent way to the base of that wall but of contrasting grade and seriousness.

The Slay Ride   75 m   E3   1988
Start 3 metres left of the obvious crack of Sledgate Ridge. The bold crux start, giving poorly protected technical climbing, leads to pleasant but still difficult climbing above.
1   25 m (5c). Gain a small ledge, move right to a hollow flake, then climb the steep wall above to a ledge. Climb the diagonal crack above which leads to a large ledge and belay in a little bay on the right (junction with Sledgate Ridge).
2   20 m (5c). The thin crack leads, with a very long reach, to an easy arête which runs to a large grass ledge.
3   30 m (5b). A small ramp leads to the left-hand crack which is followed to a horizontal break. Climb the arête above to where it ends, then cross a square groove on the right to a belay.

Scramble across right and descend a short gully to the foot of Engineer's Slabs.

★ **Sledgate Ridge**   73 m   HS   1958

Good climbing that is unfortunately broken. Start at the obvious crack in the steep, little wall.

1   20 m. The difficult crack can be avoided by an easy chimney on the right – but you would only feel guilty! The water worn grooves on the right are followed for 10 metres, then the wall on the left to a large ledge.

2   18 m. From the left end of the ledge, climb the wall, then the slabs on the right to a large grass platform.

3   35 m. Climb the wall above to a ledge below three vertical cracks. The centre crack leads to the top.

The following routes are all situated on the main, central wall/slab that starts about half way up the crag, with the dark cleft of Engineer's Chimney at its left-hand end and the sharp arête of Unfinished Arête on its right. The majority of the routes are of high quality, sustained and generally on sound rock, giving some of the best high mountain crag climbing in the area.

The best approaches are via Sledgate Ridge or The Slay Ride, to suit your mood or ability. Alternatively, scramble up steep broken ground to the right of a broken buttress directly below the wall.

It is possible to descend from the top of the routes in the Engineer's Slab area by traversing left over grass ledges then scrambling down steep broken ground on the left of Engineer's Chimney to the top of a short gully that leads down and right to the base of Engineer's Slabs.

Engineer's Chimney   36 m   VS   1899

This dark, uninviting cleft, which is often wet, gives difficult traditional chimney climbing, and a difficult route in winter.

1   16 m. Easy climbing leads to where the chimney divides.

2   20 m (4a). Climb the left-hand branch of the chimney, using the left wall as required, until a strenuous pull through the narrows takes one into the wider chimney above. Traditional tactics lead past a chockstone to a crack in the left wall which is followed to the top. The narrow section of the chimney can be avoided on the left wall by an ascending traverse to a large flake and back again above the crux.

★★ Powder Finger   45 m   E3   1987

An excellent single pitch route that climbs the slim technical groove just right of Engineer's Chimney. Start 4 metres right of Engineer's Chimney from a grass ledge.

(6a) Easy rocks lead to a ledge and loose blocks. An awkward pull into the groove on the left is followed by sustained climbing up to the overhang, then step right onto the arête and rest point (thin tape on spike can be arranged). Move up to a poor flake (another thin tape here, but difficult to arrange), then make some committing and strenuous moves rightwards over the bulge to a good hold on Dream Twister. From a standing position on this hold, traverse back left and up to a crack (junction with Spirit Level), then continue left into a shallow groove which leads to the top (beware rope drag).

★★ Dream Twister   45 m   E3   1987

A good, well protected, natural line, with an overhang and crack above providing a sustained crux section. Start as for Powder Finger.

(5c). Easy rocks lead to a ledge and loose blocks. Pull into the groove on the left, exiting right at the top onto the wall and a good ledge. Climb the wall direct to the overhang. Pull over this using the crack above, moving left at its top into a wider crack curving rightwards to a good ledge. The short crack above leads to a large grass ledge and thread belay.

★★ Spirit Level   92 m   E1   1971

A traverse line across the main wall of Engineer's Slab, providing a fine route of contrasting pitches on excellent rock. The first pitch, which climbs Engineer's Chimney, is unpleasant, often wet and is best avoided by climbing the excellent and well protected pitch of Dream Twister up to a junction with the Spirit Level traverse line. Pitches three and four require care in protecting the second.

1 22 m (4a). Climb Engineer's Chimney, moving out left to a ledge and peg belay.

2 13 m (5b). Difficult moves lead across the overhang on the right to the edge. Climb the crack above for 6 metres, then traverse right, crossing Dream Twister, to a stance on The Troll (above the block overhang).

3 10 m (5a). Traverse horizontally right, crossing The Angel of Mercy, then continue diagonally right to join Interceptor at the short traverse on pitch 2. Reverse the traverse and groove down to the sentry box belay.

4 10 m (5b). Traverse right crossing Engineer's Slabs onto a blank section of the wall above the overlap. Delicate and worrying

moves now lead to Sarcophagus, followed by easier climbing to a stance on pitch 2 of The Tomb.

5   12 m. Easy climbing right and up leads to the sloping ledge on The Jabberwock.

6   25 m (4c). As pitch 3 of The Jabberwock.

★ **The Troll**   60 m   HVS   1967

To the right of Dream Twister is a block overhang about 25 metres up the face. The wall up to this block and to its right provides good open climbing. Start directly below the block.

1   28 m (5b). Climb the wall on small but good holds to the block overhang. The crack on its right leads with difficulty to a ledge.

2   32 m (5a). Step right and climb the steep slabs for 12 metres to a break, then traverse right, making awkward moves into the flake line of Snicker Snack. Follow this, then step right into a groove just left of Interceptor that leads to the top.

★★ **The Angel of Mercy**   60 m   E1   1979

To the right and above the roof of The Troll is a steep wall split by a crack, which provides the crux pitch of this fine route. Start as for The Troll.

1   25 m (5a). As pitch 1 of The Troll, but stop at the peg and nut belays below the roof.

2   35 m (5b). Move up and make difficult moves across the sandwiched slab on the right to gain the crack. Follow the crack, which gives excellent climbing at its grade to where the angle eases, then climb the ramp up and right to below an overhanging crack splitting the headwall. Difficult moves lead up the crack to the top (large Friend useful).

★ **Interceptor**   65 m   VS   1967

An excellent companion climb to Engineer's Slabs and of a similar grade. It works its way through the overhangs between Snicker Snack and Engineer's Slabs, starting about 5 metres left of the combined start for these two routes.

1   30 m (4c). An awkward pitch with difficult route finding. Climb diagonally left to the left end of a grass ledge, then straight up to another grass ledge at its right end. An ascending traverse right on small holds leads to the twin cracks of Engineer's Slabs and the sentry box. (Care should be taken to protect the second.)

2   15 m (4c). Climb straight up the groove line above to the overhangs, traverse left into two parallel cracks (Snicker Snack) and climb these to a stance by a huge flake.

3 20 m (4c). Layback the flake, traverse right to a groove and climb it until a prominent spike on the right can be reached. Climb the rib to the top.

★★★ **Snicker Snack**   57 m   E3   1986
A superb, modern classic taking the obvious cleaned crack line up the steep wall between The Angel of Mercy and Engineer's Slabs. The climbing, which is both difficult and sustained, gives one of the best routes on the crag. Start in the middle of the wall, as for Engineer's Slabs.
1 45 m (5c). Climb the wall of Engineer's Slabs for 12 metres, then continue straight up the thin crack line above to belay at the huge flake of Interceptor.
2 12 m (5b). Climb the flake and traverse right, surmount a small overhang to gain a thin crack (about 3 metres left of the finishing groove of Interceptor) and follow this to an awkward finish.

★★★ **Engineer's Slabs**   60 m   VS   1934
A magnificent climb of great character, taking the obvious crack and groove line up the centre of the wall. The last pitch, which is often damp, can prove to be a little intimidating but this does not detract in any way from the quality and varied climbing below. Start just left of a groove in the middle of the face.
1 26 m (4c). The wall leads past a small pinnacle to the foot of a crack. Climb the crack for 5 metres to twin cracks on the right which lead to a chimney and sentry box.
2 34 m (4c). Traverse right for 2 metres into a crack, and climb this for 8 metres to a ledge, followed by a layback crack to a good ledge. The chimney above gives access to a groove that leads to the top.
Alternatively, if the final groove is wet, it can be avoided by following the jagged crack on the left wall which leads to the arête and a junction with Interceptor at the spike, then up the ridge above.

Mome Rath   58 m   E2   1989
The route climbs the broken crackline running down from the final groove of Engineer's Slabs, then it breaks out left into the obvious overhanging groove between Engineer's Slabs and Interceptor. A bit contrived in its lower section, but it has an interesting and very exposed top pitch. Start just right of Engineer's Slabs.
1 33 m (5b). Climb the poorly protected wall onto easier ground that leads over ledges to the base of the crackline. Follow the crack above over some doubtful blocks to the overhang, pull over

strenuously and follow the crack above to a junction with Engineer's Slabs to belay at the foot of the layback crack.
2   25 m (5c). Step left and climb the overhanging groove in a superb position, exiting left at the top. Follow the break line above over flakes to a junction with Interceptor which is followed to the top.

★ **The Tombstone**   64 m   E3   1988
Bold and serious climbing, with the second and third pitch taking the steep wall just left of The Jabberwock. Start 2 metres right of Engineer's Slabs.
1   15 m (5b). Climb diagonally right to gain a sloping ledge. Stand on this to gain a line of good holds which lead up and right, crossing The Tomb, to the large flake belay on Sarcophagus. (A poorly protected pitch.)
2   22 m (5c). Climb on top of the flake and continue to the overlap (runners). Pull over this on small holds and make a difficult move up (sky hook runner) to gain a flake, just left of the crack and below the big ledge of The Jabberwock. Move up to the big ledge, then traverse left to a shallow groove which leads to a good belay on The Tomb.
3   27 m (5b). Climb the wide crack above for 10 metres, step right and climb the flake to a bottomless, black sentry box. Pull out right onto 'The Tombstone' to join the top pitch of The Jabberwock; traverse left immediately utilizing a doubtful block to finish up a crack.

★★★ **The Tomb**   68 m   E2   1966
A superb route that was the first of the more difficult routes to be forced up the face. The climbing is never too hard, but the crux pitch requires a confident approach, with widely spaced but good protection. Start 6 metres right of Engineer's Slabs.
1   18 m (4c). Traverse right and up to gain the obvious sentry box. Climb this and the wall above, leftwards to a ledge, then step left to belay below a break.
2   20 m (5b). The wall on the left is climbed on small holds for 6 metres to a rest point (protection slot above). Move right under the overlap to its end, where protection can be strenuous to place. Pull through the overlap onto a small ledge, and traverse right into a steep crack which leads to a good stance. The overlap can be avoided by climbing the left wall until it is possible to traverse back right above it.
3   30 m (5a). Climb the groove above to the overhang, and step left into the open groove which leads to the top.

★★★ **Sarcophagus**   64 m   E3   1977
A technically absorbing face route, climbing the blank wall below the
traverse of The Tomb, then the overhang and break above. The route
requires steady nerves on its poorly protected second pitch but the
quality is there all the way. Start as for The Tomb.
1   18 m (4c). As pitch 1 of The Tomb to the sentry box. Climb up,
     stepping right from the wall above to a large flake.
2   18 m (5c). Step up left to a small block at the right end of a
     grass ledge. Step off the block and make a series of committing
     moves up the wall to join The Tomb at the end of the traverse.
     Move left to a thin crack, climb up to the overlap (good runners),
     and pull over strenuously, stepping right onto a narrow ledge.
     Small nut belays. An exciting pitch.
3   28 m (5b). Move up and left into a groove/crack line. Follow this,
     and jam the crack above to finish up a groove, left of the groove
     on The Tomb.

Engineer's Slabs – Unfinished Arête   63 m   VS   1934
Interesting climbing up the obvious arête that marks the right edge
of the face. Start just right of The Tomb where the grass ledge begins
to fall away to the right.
1   15 m (4b). Traverse right to below a sentry box. Climb up and
     right to a small groove that leads to a grass ledge below the arête.
2   23 m (4c). Climb the arête to a small overlap. Traverse right, then
     up to a grass ledge. Continue up the arête to a sloping ledge with
     shattered blocks (junction with The Jabberwock.)
3   25 m (4c). As pitch 3 of The Jabberwock.

★★ **The Jabberwock**   75 m   HVS   1970
The obvious steep crack and grooved headwall at the right end of the
face provide a route of high quality with a sensational top pitch. Start
from the lowest point.
1   22m (4c). Climb the cracked wall to ledges on the right of a large
     flake.
2   28 m (5a). Climb the crack, passing a large ledge at 18 metres,
     to a sloping ledge and shattered blocks. (Junction with Unfinished
     Arête.)
3   25 m (4c). The short slab on the left leads to a very exposed
     groove which is climbed to the top on good holds.

In the upper left-hand side of Central Gully is a large pinnacle with
a crack in its upper west face.

Access to the pinnacle is from the top of the Engineer's Slabs face
by scrambling up and right for 50 metres until above and right of the
pinnacle, which is easily identified by having several blocks perched
on its top. Abseil down the gully on its right-hand side to a grass
terrace situated just below and right of the crack.

The Short Crack   12 m   HVS   1988
A good bit of contrived fun.
   (5b). Traverse left on sloping holds to gain the crack, and up this
   to the top on excellent jams.

Trundle Ridge   75 m   VS   1970
A pleasant climb that runs up the left bounding rib of Central Gully.
Start a few metres up and left of the lowest rocks of the ridge in a
grassy corner below a steep wall split by a thin crack.
1   15 m (4b). Climb the wall just right of the crack to a grass saddle.
2   25 m (4b). Behind the saddle is a slab. Climb the slab, then
    continue up a steep crack to the top of a pinnacle. (Rock requires
    care.)
3   10 m. Descend a few metres and cross a chimney by a jammed
    block, then scramble up to a grass ledge and block belay on the
    left.
4   25 m (4b). From the right end of the stance, step right and gain
    the arête. Climb the arête for 2 metres, and move left onto the
    cracked slabs. These are followed until moves back right regain
    the arête, which leads to a large stance.
    The top of the crag is reached after 60 metres of scrambling.

The Central Gully, (Direct Finish)   70 m   VD   1896
This is the large broken gully right of Engineer's Slabs which
provides an easy scramble to the top of the crags. There are a few
pitches of Difficult standard and the top crack, if climbed direct is
Very Difficult, but all difficulties can be avoided on the left. In winter
the route is transformed to star quality status.

Heinz Route   170 m   S   1947
   A route that staggers its way up the broken north containing
   buttress of Central Gully. In its lower section the route takes in
   a large pinnacle before bearing off left, following a series of
   ledges and chimneys to the top. Not recommended.

Nothing to Declare 50 m E2   1988
Although the climbing is a little disjointed, each pitch has something
to offer. Start just left of Smuggler's Chimney at the base of a clean
slab.

1   10 m (5a). Climb the slab, trending left to gain a crack on the
    left edge at mid height (runners); step right and continue
    delicately to a large ledge.
2   25 m (5b). From the right-hand side of the ledge, step right and
    climb a thin crack for 5 metres, then pull out right on the wall
    to gain a good ledge. From the right-hand side of the ledge make
    a very long stretch up to a flake which leads back left to another
    ledge on the bulging wall. The short pillar on the left leads to a
    large terrace. Belay a long way back.
3   15 m (5a). From the foot of a small gully (the true continuation
    to Smuggler's Chimney), climb up and right to stand on a cluster
    of spikes. Step up and swing back left round the rib, then continue
    up a cracked wall, passing a niche to a block belay.

★ **Smuggler's Chimney** 37m VS   1909
(Struggler's Chimney to those who know.) An absolute must for the
masochist or the unswerving traditionalist, with the climbing being
both difficult and very strenuous and ideally suited to the small
person. Start below the deep, narrow cleft.

1   10 m (4a). Climb to the foot of the chimney, either by the flake
    on the right, or a crack on the left.
2   27 m (4c). The narrow chimney is climbed with difficulty to a
    large terrace.

American Dream 82 m S   1988
Start at the foot of the ridge 10 metres right of Smuggler's Chimney.

1   30 m. Climb the pleasant ridge to a large sloping grassy recess
    below a steep wall.
2   32 m. Climb the wall by a crack on the left, then, just below a
    grass ledge, swing left on good holds to regain the ridge. Continue
    up the ridge to belay below a small square shaped buttress with
    a chimney on its right.
3   20 m. From the right, climb a ramp to gain a flat pinnacle below
    the chimney. From the pinnacle, either climb the chimney direct,
    or step right round a bulge to a good ledge and easy ground.

★ **Smaug** 63 m HVS   1988
Start about 30 metres right of Smuggler's Chimney, just right of a
steep, dirty, green corner. Very good and varied climbing, the last
pitch taking the wide crack high up.

1   40 m (5a). Scramble up to the base of a V-groove, move left and climb the obvious crack in the slab on the left to its top. Belay below the rib.
2   15 m (5b). Step right and climb the thin crack just right of the rib to below a steep crack.
3   8 m (4c). Climb the excellent, overhanging, off-width, jam crack to the top (big Friends useful).

Sundowner 50 m S   1958
Starts right of Smaug below a steep, prominent slab with a chimney on its right and wanders up the buttress left of the scree gully that separates Prayer Mat Buttress from the rest of the crag.
1   30 m. Climb the left end of the slab to a grassy groove that splits the slab diagonally. Follow the groove right, step across the top of a chimney and up to a grass ledge below a crack. Traverse up and left round a corner, then climb directly up to a grass ledge.
2   20 m. The slab above leads to a rake trending left. Leave the rake on the right and climb to a corner below an open chimney. Climb the corner cracks exiting right.

Doctor's Chimney 30 m D   1896
Between Prayer Mat Buttress and the main crag there is a steep scree gully. Approximately 40 metres up this on the left lies the chimney.
    Easy rocks lead to a detached block, then climb the right wall to a pinnacle. The chimney above is climbed facing left to gain a small ledge on the arête, followed by easier chimney climbing above.

Strike While It's Hot 22 m E1   1988
Left from Doctor's Chimney is a very steep corner capped by a large roof, access to the bottom being over steep grass and connecting ledges. This single pitch route provides an entertaining problem with a strenuous crux roof.
    (5b). Climb the overhanging corner to the roof. Strenuous moves on good jams lead through the roof until a step left can be made onto easier ground and into the break line above.

★ **Prayer Mat Buttress** 30 m MVS   1926
The most westerly buttress on Gable Crag. Pleasant climbing starting from the lowest point of the buttress, below an arête, just left of an iron spike.
    (4b). Climb the arête to a small ledge at 10 metres. Awkward moves left lead to a sloping ledge, followed by an arête to a small rectangular ledge at 10 metres (the Prayer Mat). The overhanging

corner on the right leads to a pleasant slab and the top (it is possible to go left from the Prayer Mat but this is not recommended).

The Gable End   25 m   VS   1988
Start at the iron spike just right of Prayer Mat Buttress. Nice open climbing.
   (4b). Climb directly up to, and enter, a short square cut groove. Climb the groove, step right to a ledge, then up the slab above direct to the top.

Green Gable Crags   (214 106)   Alt. 750 m   West Facing

These seldom visited crags are situated on the Ennerdale side of Green Gable, near the summit of the mountain. They provide an excellent, remote and scenic venue for the lower grade climber on sound rock that, due to its westerly aspect, dries quickly. Recent attention has nearly doubled the number of routes available, and these are generally at similar grades to the earlier ascents.

The crag can be approached from various directions, each having its own advantages and drawbacks, but all resulting in approximately $1\frac{1}{2}$ hours of hard work from the point of departure.

From the Sty Head track take the steep path up Aaron Slack passing over to the Ennerdale side of Windy Gap, then traverse north across the scree to a ledge at the foot of a small buttress and the start of Alpha. ($\frac{3}{4}$ hr from Sty Head.)

A more direct route from Wasdale is to take the Great Gable track to Beck Head via Gavel Neese and Moses' Trod, then follow the cairned track up the north-west shoulder of Great Gable until a narrow track leads off left, The North Traverse, under Gable Crag to Windy Gap. Continue as above. ($1\frac{1}{2}$ hrs.)

Alternatively, approach the col between Gillercombe and Green Gable from the top of Honister Pass via the Brandreth track or via the Gillercombe track from Borrowdale. From the col climb towards the summit of Green Gable and drop over the ridge onto its westerly flank 50 metres below the summit ($1\frac{1}{2}$ hrs).

See relief drawing on page 119.

The descents are on the left side of the crag, except from the Alpha Buttress. The routes are described from right to left i.e. from Windy Gap.

Alpha   30 m   VD   1927
Start at the right-hand side of the first buttress.
1   20 m. Climb the broken wall to a ledge and continue up to a
     platform. Belays on the right.
2   10 m. Retrace your steps for 2 metres and climb the steep wall
     on small but good holds followed by easy climbing to the top.

Calculus   32 m   S   1988
5 metres left of Alpha is a thin crack.
     Climb the crack with difficulty to easier ground which is followed
     direct to the top, finishing just left of Alpha.

Omega   32 m   VD   1988
Start at the left-hand edge of the buttress.
     Follow the edge of the buttress, moving right below a broken
     overhang. The shallow groove above is climbed to a small
     overhang which is passed on the right to a ledge. Easy climbing
     to finish.

★ **Abacus**   35 m   HVS   1988
A good route taking an impressive line on excellent rock, starting just
left of Omega at a slab below a large overhang.
1   15 m (5a). Climb the slab to the overhang, move right and pull
     round a rib to the bottom of a groove.
2   20 m. Climb the arête.

Beta   50 m   VD   1927
From Alpha, walk along the scree at the base of the crag. The start
is on the left of a deeply cut chimney at the lowest point. The route
is broken and of poor quality.
1   30 m. Climb the broken rib and then scramble to the foot of a
     steep buttress.
2   20 m. Steep rock is climbed to a small overhang, which is passed
     on the left to a good ledge. Climb the wall on the left of the
     small overhang to finish.

Variation   20 m   S
2a From the ledge on pitch 2 climb the wall on the right.

★ **Gamma**   20 m   D   1927
The climb lies 18 metres left from the top of Beta on a narrow rib
of steep rock, which is also accessible via the grassy gully. An
excellent little route.

Climb the rib to a ledge at 10 metres. Continue up the ridge to finish.

Delta   13 m   VS   1928
(4b). This steep, exposed and unprotected route takes the slab left of Gamma. A good pitch.

The following three routes are to be found by traversing left across the scree at the base of a wide grassy gully to the mass of slabs. The first route starts at a mossy slab just right of the first continuous slab.

Timshel   80 m   VD   1988
An interesting expedition finishing on the summit of the mountain.
1   30 m. Climb the mossy slab to gain the groove below the steep wall. Follow the groove, step right onto a slab and then back left to a pinnacle. Traverse right for 3 metres to a flake and climb the wall to a grass ledge.
2   10 m. Walk 10 metres up and right to belays near a smooth wall below a prominent buttress with an obvious central crack.
3   27 m. Climb the smooth wall on its left to reach the buttress. Climb the centre of the buttress on excellent rock and the fine crack to finish. Belay well back on the left.
4   13 m. A broken wall above is climbed at its centre.

★ **Epsilon**   67 m   MS   1927
A good route with fine situations, starting at the foot of the continuous slab.
1   27 m. Climb the broken wall for 7 metres to a grass ledge. The slab above is climbed using a crack on the right to a small grass ledge.
2   27 m. After an awkward start, the slab above leads to a grass ledge. Continue up broken rocks to below a rough wall.
3   13 m. From a small spike climb the wall on good holds.

Epsilon Chimney   57 m   D   1928
The cleft immediately left of Epsilon provides traditional chimney climbing.
1   22 m. Scramble up mossy rocks to the foot of the chimney. Climb the chimney past a chockstone to a good stance.
2   22 m. Continue up the chimney past yet another chockstone to a ledge. The chimney, now having finished with you, allows the clean rib on the right to be climbed to the foot of a rough wall.
3   13 m. As pitch 3 of Epsilon.

8 metres left and below the foot of Epsilon Chimney is a small detached buttress, taken by Aaron. 3 metres right of this is a broken wall where the following route starts.

Caleb   43 m   VD   1988
1   18 m. Climb the wall to a grassy ledge. Traverse 6 metres right to the obvious corner crack.
2   25 m. Step right and climb the steep wall immediately left of Epsilon Chimney.

Aaron   47 m   VS   1925
A good route demanding committing moves with little protection. Start at the middle of the small buttress.
1   12 m (4a). Climb straight up, stepping left to finish up the edge to a grass ledge. Belay on the left wall.
2   35 m (4a). Climb the wall above on good holds until an awkward move leads to a mantelshelf. Continue directly above to a ledge and by easier climbing to the ridge.

Eta   40 m   MS   1927
Start 6 metres left of Aaron below a series of short broken ribs.
1   10 m. Climb the rib in the centre to a large grassy recess.
2   20 m. Climb a rib on the right of the corner and up a rough slab, step left onto a small rib and continue up until a traverse right is made onto a rock ledge.
3   10 m. Climb the slab to finish.

East of Eden   53 m   S   1988
Start at a wall just left of the broken ribs of Eta.
1   10 m. Climb the wall, breaking out left at the top. Continue up to a large grassy recess on the right.
2   20 m. Climb the mossy slab above, followed by a short steep wall on the right to a wide ledge on the front of the buttress. Go up to the overhang, step right into a chimney, then back left onto the ridge and up to a pinnacle.
3   23 m. Climb the broken arête easily.

12 metres left of the ribs containing Eta and East of Eden are broken slabs bounded by steep grass on the right. The first slab marks the start of the next route.

Green Peace   45 m   S   1988
Start just right of centre of the slab. Worthwhile for its second pitch.
1   15 m. Climb the slab to a grass ledge. Move 5 metres right to
    below a broken rib.
2   30 m. Move up right and climb the wide crack, passing left of
    the square overhang; step right onto its top and climb the blunt
    arête on small holds to the top.

★★ **Fie**   45 m   VS   1933
An excellent climb on good rock. Start as for Green Peace.
1   15 m. As pitch 1 of Green Peace.
2   30 m (4b). Climb the slab on the left of the moss to an overhang
    at 6 metres. Pass the overhang with the aid of a small crack on
    the left and continue up the slab, trending to the right of a short
    arête. Finish up the right side of the arête.

Theta   48 m   D   1927
A pleasant route up the slab, starting at its centre, just left of Green
Peace.
1   18 m. Climb the broken slab to a ledge. Continue up the slab on
    the left (crowned by a loose block) to a good stance.
2   30 m. Follow the middle of the large broken slab to an overhang,
    which may be passed on either side, to a ledge. A short wall leads
    to the top.

Arjuna   43 m   D   1988
Start round the corner from Fie and 10 metres up, at a broken wall,
3 metres below a small detached triangular spike.
1   30 m. Climb the steep wall using a small flake at 3 metres.
    Follow broken rocks to the foot of an obvious corner groove on
    the right and continue up to the grassy corner below the
    overhanging chockstone.
2   13 m. Pull up awkwardly on the chockstone to gain the good rock
    on the left wall. Finish up the arête.

North Face   27 m   D   1925
7 metres above and left of Arjuna is a small steep buttress, about
level with the top of pitch 1 of Theta and 3 metres right of a grassy
gully. The major difficulties lie in finding the route.
1   15 m. Climb the buttress to a niche. Move right and continue to
    a large grass ledge.
2   12 m. Climb the mossy rib on the left wall of the large square
    overhang.

Girdle Traverse   190 m   VS or S

A traverse of the crag has been recorded going from right to left, finishing up Fie or Theta. The route is broken and scrappy involving several abseils and would be a waste of time and effort for anyone visiting the crag.

Kern Knotts   (215 096)   Alt. 520 m   South West Facing

This very steep, compact crag provides climbing of high quality and character, predominantly within the Very Severe and Extreme grades, on sound, rough rock. Due to its position the rock dries quickly, this being particularly useful when the higher crags are out of condition, and even on windy days it is possible to find sheltered routes on its steep walls and corners.

The routes range from the traditional, to the more modern athletic variety and provide many classic lines. The older routes should not be considered as soft options, with the polished nature of some of these classics providing additional spice.

The main feature of the crag is a steep wall at its right-hand end, set at right angles to the rest of the crag. This wall has produced two of the best known crack climbs from the early days of Lake District exploration: Kern Knotts Crack and Innominate Crack, both routes being of quality. The buttresses to the left and right of this wall provide some very steep, hard problems.

The crag is conveniently situated next to the track that runs from the summit of Sty Head to the Napes Ridges and holds a commanding position overlooking the upper Wasdale Valley and Scafell Range. Five minutes walk from the pass brings you to the crag. ($^3/_4$ hr from Wasdale or Borrowdale.)

It should be noted that following a rock fall, in which a huge block came away to the right of Innominate Crack, some routes are no longer available in their original form. The block, which had a crack on each side, provided the first pitch to The Cenotaph and Sepulchre (the classic layback pitch). An alternative start to The Cenotaph has been established but sadly Sepulchre has been lost.

Descents are possible from both ends of the crag but the one on the left is easier. The routes are described from left to right.

Pyfo   55 m   VD   1962
Starting at a small buttress at the extreme left end of the crag, the route climbs the buttress and then takes a traverse line right avoiding the top of the crag for as long as it takes to produce a route. Pointless.

Feline Crack   33 m   VS   1979
Climbs the first thin crack line on the wall, about 17 metres right of Pyfo, at some light bands of rock.
(4c). Climb easy rocks and the steep crack above to a sloping ledge and continue direct to the top.

Flake Climb   30 m   VS   1919
Start just right of Feline Crack at the obvious broken crack and chimney line. Good value.
(4c). Easy rocks lead to the base of a steep crack. Climb the crack to a sloping ledge (The Cat Walk) which is followed to the foot of a short chimney. Up the chimney to the top.

12 metres right of Flake Climb is a conspicuous opening taken by Kern Knotts West Chimney. Just left of this feature is a very steep, blunt arête giving the following route.

★ **Sylvester**   25 m   E2   1981
A very good pitch that requires a bold approach.
(5c). Easy rocks lead to a good spike runner; step right onto the cracked wall to gain a ledge on the arête (runners up and right of here – get them while you can). Now climb the shallow groove above using sloping holds and with poor protection.

★ **Pussy**   40 m   E4   1989
A rising traverse linking Sylvester and the top of Feline Crack. Good sustained climbing. Start as for Sylvester.
1   30 m (6a). Easy rocks lead to a good spike runner; step right onto the cracked wall to gain a ledge on the arête (as for Sylvester). Step left beneath the overhang and pull into a groove with difficulty, then continue leftwards to reach a good flake line. Follow this to a good hold, then slide gently left to reach a good flake, followed by a delicate sloping finish onto the ledge above Feline Crack.
2   10 m (4b). Climb the rounded rib on the left of the corner above, to the top.

Moggy Traveller   20 m   E4   1990
Although being a direct finish on Pussy the end result is a good
fingery pitch on clean rock finishing up the shallow groove left of
Sylvester. Start as for Sylvester.

   (6a). Follow Sylvester to the ledge on the arête, step out left
   below the overhang as for Pussy and pull up into the groove,
   climb this directly to the top. (Pussy continues left from the base
   of the groove.)

★ **Fat Freddie's Cat**   20 m   E3   1990
Another good fingery route, well protected and surprisingly
independent from its neighbours. Start just left of Kern Knotts West
Chimney.

   (5c). Climb easy rocks to reach an awkward crack 2 metres right
   of the arête. Climb the crack to a ledge and continue up the
   right-hand one of two shallow grooves.

Kern Knotts West Chimney   32 m   VD   1897
Traditional climbing, starting below the conspicuous opening.
1   16 m. Easy rocks lead to the chimney, which is followed using
    traditional techniques to a platform.
2   16 m. Climb the crack above to a ledge at 8 metres, followed by
    easier rocks to the top.

★ **Kern Knotts West Buttress**   33 m   MVS   1912
Climbs the steep buttress to the right of Kern Knotts West Chimney,
giving good, open situations. Start to its left.
1   16 m (4b). Easy rocks are followed by a short steep section to a
    spike. Climb the V-groove above, swing left at the top and
    continue steeply to a large ledge.
2   17 m. The easier rocks on the left are followed to the top.

The Kraken   35 m   E1   1974
The next obvious feature on the crag is a steep corner, right of Kern
Knotts West Buttress and 10 metres left of Kern Knotts Chimney.
The Kraken starts at this corner and gives good climbing with pitches
of contrasting style.
1   15 m (5b). Climb the short corner, move right and pull
    strenuously over a bulge on flat holds. Climb the groove to a
    small ledge.
2   20 m (5a). Climb the green corner above, step delicately left at
    3 metres onto the rib and follow this and the corner to the top.

Variation   19 m   HVS
2a (5a). Climb the corner direct to the top.

★★ The Crysalid   30 m   E2   1976
An excellent exercise in steep, fingery climbing, with the crux at the
top. Start 4 metres right of the corner of The Kraken at a blunt arête.
1   15 m (5a). Climb the arête to below a faint crack in the steep
    slab. Follow this and a short mossy wall to a small stance (left
    of the final groove).
2   15 m (5c). Step right and climb the steep groove to a good but
    doubtful flake. Step left onto a slab and follow this to the top.

★ Central Climb South Face   37 m   MVS   1919
Start 4 metres left of Kern Knotts Chimney, just right of a grassy
crack.
1   25 m (4b). Easy rocks lead up right to a pinnacle. Climb steeply
    above for 12 metres, then traverse left to belay as pitch 1 of
    Crysalid.
2   12 m (4b). Continue left to the base of a steep scoop which is
    climbed with a good finishing hold.

Variations
Variation Start   10 m   VS   1933
A better although more difficult start.
1a (5a). A few metres right of the original start is an obvious, steep,
    thin crack. Climb it, followed by easier rocks to the pinnacle on
    pitch 1.

Variation Start   20 m   VS   1956
1b (4b). Start just right of Crysalid at an obvious groove. Climb the
    groove and slabs to the belay on pitch 1.

The Triffid routes take the two very steep crack lines just left of Kern
Knotts Chimney, that join to form an inverted 'V' in the upper section
of the crag. They provide two good pitches, both being very
strenuous, with no easy solutions. Start at the foot of the chimney.

★ Triffid   30 m   E2   1978
(5c). A steep crack leads to a pinnacle (as pitch 1a Central Climb
South Face). Climb up to a bulge and take the steep crack on the
left to easier ground.

★ **Triffid Right-Hand Finish**   30 m   E3   1981
   (6a). As Triffid to the bulge, then take the steep crack on the right
   to easier ground.

★★ **Kern Knotts Chimney**   60 m   HS   1893
This is the prominent chimney on the Wasdale (west) side of the
buttress. A classic which has become a victim of its own popularity,
now being very polished, especially on its second pitch which should
be approached with care.
1   30 m. Easy rocks lead to a large platform. Climb the chimney,
     passing a chockstone en route. Pass under a block to belay on the
     other side of the buttress.
2   30 m. Step from the top of the block onto the slab using hideously
     polished, sloping holds. Easier rocks then lead to the top. (The
     slab may be avoided by going left but that would spoil the fun.)

The following seven routes all finish at the top of the same buttress
and share pitch 2 of Kern Knotts Chimney as a means of reaching
the top of the crag.

Kern Knotts Buttress   29 m   HVS   1919
A contrived route with a technically difficult move on the second
pitch. Start just right of Kern Knotts Chimney at a steep crack on the
front of the buttress.
1   12 m (4b). The steep crack leads to a large platform.
2   17 m (5b). Make a very difficult move from the right end of the
     platform onto the front of the buttress using tiny finger holds and
     a small sloping foothold and continue via a niche, trending right
     to the top of the buttress, to finish on sloping holds.

★★ **The Buttonhook Route**   30 m   HVS   1934
A very steep, exposed and classic climb that threads its way up the
corner of the prominent buttress giving two excellent pitches of
contrasting character. Start at the foot of the buttress.
1   10 m (5a). Climb a short, cracked slab to the overhang. Pull out
     right to reach a good jug and climb the steep rock above to a
     stance. This point can be reached more easily by a traverse left
     from the bottom of Kern Knotts Crack.
2   20 m (5a). Traverse left to a small ledge at 5 metres, then climb
     the very steep rock above, trending left. The angle eases after 7
     metres. Trend right to a pinnacle on the right edge of the buttress,
     then direct to the top on sloping holds.

★ Misfit   30 m   E2   1981

An eliminate line on The Buttonhook Route, taking the thin crack line directly through the overhangs, followed by the steep rib on the right. Strenuous.

(5c). Climb the first 3 metres of The Buttonhook Route to below the bulge. Pull over this using the thin crack (strenuous), then out right at the top on good holds. Step back left (as The Buttonhook Route), up the groove, then step right onto the rib, which is followed to a flake. The thin crack on the left of the rib leads to the top.

★ Close to the Wind   25 m   E1   1988

An excellent pitch, although it competes with The Buttonhook Route and Misfit for the available space in the upper section. Start at a groove just left of Kern Knotts Crack.

(5b). Climb the right-hand side of the groove to a good hold and runners; move up left awkwardly to the stance on pitch 1 of The Buttonhook Route. Gain the ledge up and right, below an obvious steep groove capped by an overhang. Difficult moves up the groove lead to a sloping ledge on the right. Follow the wall and vague groove to the top.

★ Kern Knotts Crack   22 m   VS   1897

Takes the first obvious break in the right-facing wall. A route of great character, its grade being set by the mirror finish of the crux sentry box.

(4b). Climb the crack to a sentry box at 8 metres. Either climb the sentry box direct by some very precarious antics, or bypass it on the right wall using small holds followed by a long step back left. The upper section of the crack is easier.

★★ Innominate Crack   20 m   VS   1921

The best single-pitch crack climb of its grade in the valley. It follows the thin cracks in the centre of the wall.

(4b). Follow the twin cracks until forced into the right-hand one, which is followed to the top, passing a sloping ledge at 15 metres.

★ Sepulchre Direct   22 m   E3   1981

A good pitch, replacing the lost Sepulchre, although considerably harder than the original route. Start below the obvious corner.

(6a). Climb the easy-angled groove to the roof. The next few moves left and up the steep wall to a resting foothold are thin. Continue left to the foot of the corner and up this to the top.

(*opposite*)   Innominate Crack, Kern Knotts
(*next page*)   Sepulchre Direct, Kern Knotts

★ **Cenotaph Left-Hand**   34 m   E3   1981
An intimidating route up the steep rock to the right of the large
corner. Start in the back of the cave.

   (6a). The wall on the right leads to the overhangs; then climb
   carefully into the groove above over unstable blocks. Follow the
   flake out left to a roof, where an aggressive pull leftwards round
   the beak (peg runner) leads to a straight crack; step left to finish
   on larger holds.

The Cenotaph   34 m   HVS   1955
The original Cenotaph route, breaking out right into the obvious
groove. Sustained.

   (4c). As Cenotaph Left-Hand to the groove above the unstable
   blocks, but then continue up the steep groove to the overhang
   (good protection). A committing move right leads into the obvious
   steep finishing groove.

El Vino   34 m   E2   1974
Climbs the steep groove line through the overhang, 3 metres right of
The Cenotaph. Steep but safe.
1   9 m. Climb the short wall to a broad ledge.
2   25 m (5c). The hanging groove above is followed to the roof;
    pull round on the right and make a very strenuous move into the
    corner above. Up this to the top.

★ **Kern Knotts Chain**   134 m   HVS   1928
A good 'fun route' even though in its early stages it does wander
embarrassingly close to the top and bottom of the crag before finally
establishing itself on a mid height line. This left to right girdle, which
can be reversed, is guaranteed to create havoc on a busy day due to
its use of existing popular pitches. Start at the top of Flake Climb.
1   25 m (4c). Reverse Flake Climb to the bottom of the steep crack.
2   23 m. Traverse slightly down and right over easy rocks to a
    corner which is followed up into West Chimney. Climb the
    chimney to the top of pitch 1.
3   25 m (4b). Traverse easily rightwards to join Central Climb which
    is reversed to the pinnacle on pitch 1. (Care needed to protect
    second.)
4   5 m. Traverse right onto a large platform in the Chimney. (Top
    of pitch 1 of Kern Knotts Buttress.)
5   12 m (5b). As pitch 2 of Kern Knotts Buttress, but making an
    upward traverse right after the crux to a pinnacle on the edge of
    the buttress.

Sacrifiicial Crack, Tophet Wall   (*previous page*)
The Viking, Tophet Wall   (*opposite*)

6   14 m (5a). Traverse the steep wall on the right into Kern Knotts Crack at the height of the pinnacle, then traverse into, and finish up, Innominate Crack.
7   30 m (4a). Pitch 2 of Kern Knotts Chimney.

To the right is the East Buttress, this being separated from the main crag by steep broken ground. The obvious leaning corner is climbed by Kern Knotts Corner.

Eastern Bloc   47 m   MS   1989
Start just left of Kern Knotts Corner.
1   27 m. Climb up and left to a dirty groove, then pull up and right onto the arête, passing a large block to reach a large ledge. Climb up onto a second large ledge.
2   20 m. Walk left below the upper rib to a cave, then climb the wall on the left to a rounded finish.

Kern Knotts Corner   35 m   VS   1932
1   27 m. Pleasant climbing up the corner and slabs leads to a large jammed block; over this and onto a ledge on the left. Easy climbing leads to a good ledge.
2   8 m (4c). The strenuous undercut crack on the left is climbed.

The East Buttress   40 m   HS   1924
Starts below a rough, clean wall 10 metres right of Kern Knotts Corner.
1   30 m. Either make strenuous moves on small holds up the wall, or climb the shallow groove on the left, followed by easy rocks to a grass ledge at the foot of a buttress on the left. Starting at the right-hand end of a wall of light grey rock, traverse left to a sloping ledge, then straight up a small crack to a ledge.
2   10 m. Choose any one of the three finishes.
   (a). The left corner of the chimney.
   (b). The chimney.
   (c). The right corner of the chimney.

Lower Kern Knotts   (214 096)   Alt. 470 m   South West
                                                            Facing

Directly below Kern Knotts lies the small outcrop of Lower Kern Knotts, and at the same level but 100 metres west is the larger outcrop of Lower Kern Knotts West. Both of these outcrops contain routes as listed below but far superior routes are available on the main crag just above.

The West Route (M, 1924) Left of the crack up easy rocks. **The Crack** (D) The obvious crack in the middle. **The Slab Climb** (S, 1920) The wall right of the crack.

Lower Kern Knotts West   (214 095)   Alt. 470 m
South West Facing

The Buttress (S, 1921) The slab and groove in the centre of the buttress. **Slab and Chimney Route** (D). The slab and crack about 10 metres right of The Buttress.

The Napes   (210 101)   Alt. 700 m   South West Facing

The birthplace of English rock climbing. This excellent crag, although rather broken, provides climbing of all grades in superb surroundings with its unique ridges and steep walls overlooking the upper Wasdale Valley and the Scafell Range.

The majority of the crag is fast drying and holds the sun late into the day.

The Napes is quite distinctive with its classic ridge climbs and of course The Napes Needle. Its relatively easy access and fine climbs has resulted in this being a popular stamping ground for the lower grade climber and beginner. As a bonus it also has Tophet Wall, with an atmosphere quite different to the rest of the crag. It is steep, unnerving and tends to be cold, with the sun being a morning visitor only. Recently many hard climbs have been added, these are among the hardest and best in the area.

Although most of the climbs are on sound rock, care should be taken when on the ridges as any stonefall will rake the gullies and their walls, eventually crossing the busy path at the bottom. Also this path is now very polished and loose in places and requires care.

From Wasdale follow the track to Burnthwaite (³/₄ km) then take the Sty Head path situated on the north side of Lingmell Beck which, after crossing the new footbridge at Gable Beck, gradually steepens up to a wall and gate. Beyond the gate the path steepens, traversing the scree slopes well below the Napes Ridge until just below the summit of Sty Head Pass, Kern Knotts will be seen above on the left.

THE NAPES (FROM THE SOUTH-EAST).

A   Hell Gate Pillar
B   Tophet Wall
C   Lucifer Ridge
D   Needle Ridge
E   Napes Needle
F   The Dress Circle
G   Eagle's Nest Ridge
H   Abbey Buttress
I   Arrowhead Ridge
J   Scimitar Ridge
K   Rainbow Ridge
L   Sphinx Ridge
M   The White Napes
N   Westmorland Crags
O   Westmorland's Cairn
P   Path from Sty Head
Q   Path up Gavel Neese
R   Traverse to Beck Head
S   The Sphinx Rock
T   The Napes Traverse

1   Great Hell Gate
2   Needle Gully
3   Eagle's Nest Gully
4   Arrowhead Gully
5   Little Hell Gate

A track now leads off left over scree and boulders past Lower Kern Knotts to join the Gable Traverse at the foot of Kern Knotts. A more direct and a 'little' steeper alternative route is to leave the Sty Head Pass path on the left, just after the bridge over Gable Beck and follow the path (Moses Trod) up the steep south-west shoulder of Great Gable (Gavel Neese). Continue up the scree past a conspicuous boulder (Moses' Finger) to join the Gable Traverse path then traverse right and up to the base of the Napes Ridges (approximately 1 hr).

From Borrowdale follow the Sty Head track from Seathwaite up to Sty Head Tarn and a junction with the 'Climbers' or 'Gable Traverse'. Continue west along this excellent track to the base of the Napes Ridges (approximately 1¼).

When approaching the Napes from Sty Head, the first feature of any significance is Tophet Wall which forms the west side of Great Hell Gate. This wall gives magnificent climbing with Lakeland Classics such as Tophet Wall and Supernatural. From the left-hand end of Tophet Wall a path runs along the base of the Napes Ridges giving access for climbing. The first obvious line is Lucifer Crack which climbs a ragged crack line up the steep left wall of a large corner round to the left from Tophet Wall. Beyond this the rocks become very broken with the climbing being in tiers, the lowest, Chantry Buttress, is reached either via steep grass or by descent from behind The Needle.

The track continues left until directly below the characteristic shape of Napes Needle that stands directly below the classic ridge climb of Needle Ridge. At this point the path splits and you can either continue into Needle Gully which is followed for a short distance before breaking out left onto the Dress Circle platform or, one can follow the broken path up the right-hand side of The Needle, then pass between it and Needle Ridge and down into Needle Gully to join up with the other path. This is known as 'Threading The Needle' and is very popular with walkers. Unfortunately it is very polished with some suspect holds.

The steep wall above the Dress Circle is split by the prominent line of Crocodile Crack with the imposing Eagles' Nest Ridge a few metres to its left. The track then continues left, under the distinctive chimney of Eagles' Nest Ordinary Route, before descending a short broken gully into Eagles' Nest Gully just below the start to Abbey Buttress. From here the crack crosses broken ground to below Arrowhead Ridge, another excellent ridge climb, with its distinctive arrow formation at the top of the steep section. The track then continues its way to Sphinx Rock and the last of the climbing.

Descents from Tophet Wall, Needle Ridge and Eagle's Nest Ridge are by scrambling up to a junction with, then going down, Great Hell Gate. This scree descent is worn and requires caution. Descents from Arrowhead Ridge and routes west of it, are by scrambling up, then going west to meet the top of the steep, rocky path that leads down towards the Sphynx Ridge. It then bears off slightly east over loose ground, to join the path that crosses the base of the crag. Alternatively, scramble up to a junction with Little Hell Gate and follow this down to the base of Sphynx Ridge. The general descents described are lengthy, but alternative and shorter descents do exist from certain areas, and these are described within the text. On no account try to ascend or descend the gullies, as they are loose and dangerous.

As the normal approach to The Napes is along the 'climbers' traverse from Sty Head, the climbs are described from right to left starting high up Great Hell Gate at Hell Gate Pillar.

Hell Gate Pillar

Above and right of Tophet Wall is a ridge that divides Great Hell Gate. The lower end of this ridge forms a steep little buttress containing the following two routes, both suffering from loose rock.

Hell Gate Pillar   30 m   MVS   1934
Start about 7 metres above the foot of the ridge on the Tophet Wall side.
(4a). Climb the slab to the overhang, then cross the slab on the right using small holds to a corner. Step down and round the corner on the right to a scoop, which is climbed, followed by a short wall on the right to a ledge. The corner on the left leads to an easy arête. (Rope drag can be a problem).

Hell Bent   25 m   E4   1987
A serious and poorly protected problem, climbing the steep arête on the Tophet Wall side of the pillar.
(5c). Climb the steep arête direct to the top, passing a small overhang at 15 metres, after which the difficulties end and the protection appears.

Tophet Wall

From the top of the routes on the Tophet Wall area it is possible to descend via an easy but loose rake that leads down into Great Hell Gate, starting a short distance above the finish of Tophet Wall Climb.

Back of the Napes   37 m   MS   1942
The climb lies on the right side of Tophet Ridge on a wall facing Hell Gate Pillar. It is steep, damp, loose and thoroughly unpleasant. Start 8 metres up the scree from the foot of Tophet Ridge, where the wall is grooved.
1   10 m. The broken wall leads to a ledge. Belay at the foot of a steep groove.
2   15 m. Traverse right and climb the steep wall by an awkward traverse right followed by a traverse back left into a short crack that leads to a corner. Belay as pitch 2 of Tophet Ridge.
3   12 m. As pitch 3 of Tophet Ridge.

Tophet Ridge   42 m   MVS   1932
Start at the foot of the ridge that forms the right edge of Tophet Wall.
1   15 m. Climb the ridge to a grassy corner right of a large overhang.
2   15 m (4b). Make a long reach above the overhang to a small hold and pull over to good holds that lead to. a rocky corner.
3   12 m. Traverse right to broken rocks and climb these to the top, or alternatively traverse left onto Tophet Wall at the foot of pitch 4 and finish up this.

The Tartarus Trip   52 m   E1   1987
Climbs the bulging wall left of Tophet Ridge, finishing up the obvious square pillar. An interesting second pitch. Start below a V-groove directly above the old start to Tophet Wall, and reached by easy scrambling.
1   15 m (4b). Climb the V-groove to block belays below the bulging wall.
2   25 m (5b). Make a bold pull over the bulge, after finding the hidden holds, onto easier ground. Traverse right to the arête (Tophet Ridge) and climb the front of the square pillar above in an exposed position.
3   12 m. Easy climbing to the top.

★ **Demon Wall**   76 m   VS   1945
Contrived in its lower section, but worth doing for its fine position when traversing the 'Great Slab' on pitch 3. Start about 4 metres right of the direct start to Tophet Wall at a rightwards slanting groove.

1   18 m (5a). Climb the groove to a good spike, then make a difficult pull out left onto the steep wall which is followed up to a ledge and belay as pitch 1 of Tophet Wall.
2   18 m (4b). Step right round a bulging corner into a grassy recess. Climb its left wall on small holds to a ledge which is followed back left to a junction with Tophet Wall below a large corner.
3   20 m (4c). The Great Slab. Ascend Tophet Wall until a line of good flake holds encourage a break out left onto the open slab from the relative security of the corner. A rising traverse is made across the slab in a superb position to a spike belay on the edge.
4   20 m. Traverse left, crossing Tophet Groove, then step left round a corner onto easy ground. Follow the pock-marked slab to the finish.

Variation   The Upper Traverse   27 m   HVS   1974
A recommended alternative.
3a (5a). Climb the corner on pitch 2 of Tophet Wall to gain the obvious leftward-rising hand traverse line, directly below the overhanging wall. Follow this and at its end climb a mossy groove into a slabby recess (junction with Tophet Grooves). Pull over to easy ground.

★ **Sacrificial Crack**   66 m   E4   1978
The top overhanging section of Tophet Wall is split by a large, but often wet crack, which provides the very intimidating crux pitch of this powerful route. Start as for Demon Wall.
1   18 m (5a). As pitch 1 of Demon Wall.
2   25 m (5b). A poorly protected pitch. Climb the rib just left of Demon Wall pitch 2 to a broken ledge, then pull over a bulge above into the right-hand of two short grooves (directly in line with the crack on pitch 3). Climb the groove to a belay just right of the crack at a shattered pinnacle.
3   23 m (6a). Climb the crack with a difficult move left at half height, followed by a long reach to a perfect jam below the recess. A strenuous pull now leads into the recess and possible rest, then climb the crack above direct to the top. A very impressive and sustained pitch.

★★★ **Tophet Wall**   75 m   HS   1923
A true classic, winding its way through some very impressive rock architecture. It is one of the best climbs of its grade in the Lake District. Start right of an overhanging crack in the centre of the wall.
1   20 m. Climb the wall just right of the crack, until a step left can be made into the crack, which is followed to a ledge. An

ascending traverse right leads to a ledge at the foot of a wall. (The original route joins the climb at this point along easy grass ledges from the right.)

2   17 m. The wall above is climbed to a broken ledge and corner on the left. Climb the crack in the corner followed by the right wall, to a slab that leads to a corner.

3   15 m. Semi-hand traverse 10 metres right in a sensational position, to a corner. Climb the rib on the right to a ledge.

4   23 m. Ascend the small pinnacle on the right, then step left into the crack which is followed to a rock ledge. Easy climbing leads to the top of the ridge.

Left of Tophet Wall climb is an area of steep walls and slabs which contains the two magnificent test pieces of Supernatural and Incantations.

★★★ **Supernatural**   82 m   E5   1977

A serious and intricate line through the walls and bulges left of Tophet Wall. Start at a groove just right of Tophet Grooves.

1   25 m (5c). Climb the groove, moving right at the top onto the wall and protection. Move up and make a difficult pull left onto the rib, which is followed to a large ledge and pinnacle. Belay at its right-hand end.

2   32 m (6a). Climb the steep wall above to a bulge and protection (small wires under the break), then traverse the hanging slab on the left to a steep groove which is climbed to a good spike and resting place. Step right and climb a rib and groove that lead to good holds on the Great Slab above. Step left and climb the slab to join the lower traverse on Demon Wall which is followed to a spike belay.

3   25 m (5b). Climb the rib directly above the belay to a ledge on the right, then up the mossy slab on the left to a sloping ledge. Traverse right along the ledge then move up and right round the rib to better holds. Easy climbing up a wall and short groove lead to the top.

★★ Variation   Direct Finish   30 m   E5   1984

An alternative, but much harder, final pitch taking in the overhanging headwall, making the route even more demanding.

3a (6b). Reverse Demon Wall lower traverse for 5 metres then climb directly up to below the overhanging wall. Worrying moves are made up past a peg runner to below a small overhang, then climb the thin crack and pull into the base of a large groove. Follow the right wall of the groove and the continuation groove above to the top.

★★★ **Incantations**   87 m   E6   1984
Extremely powerful, serious and sustained climbing up an improbable crack line just left of Supernatural. Start below the nose as for Tophet Grooves.
1   22 m (5b). As pitch 1 of Tophet Grooves but belay further right.
2   35 m (6b). Climb the crack above to good holds on the left (nest of good runners). Difficult and bold moves lead up to and past a poor peg runner, (good wires out left from the peg but difficult to place) then up the overhanging wall, past a hollow flake, to reach a thin right-slanting crack in the steep slab above. Follow the crack to ledges, continue rightwards over a bulge and step up right onto the Great Slab. Climb up to the Demon Wall lower traverse then move off left to belays.
3   30 m (6b). Climb the rib above the belay, then step right to below a thin right-slanting crack in the overhanging wall, just left of Supernatural Direct Finish. Follow the thin crack by a sequence of very strenuous moves (peg runner high on the left but difficult to clip) to a junction with Supernatural Direct Finish and a rest in the groove above. The groove and right-hand branch lead to the top.

Tophet Grooves   79 m   HVS   1940
An interesting route that climbs the big open groove on the left of the main buttress but unfortunately it is often wet, very dirty and pitch 4 has some suspect rock. Start below a nose about 10 metres left and down from the start to Tophet Wall.
1   17 m (5b). Climb the nose direct, stepping left into a groove that leads easily rightwards to a large sloping ledge.
2   12 m (4a). Descend the groove slightly then climb the crack to a large pedestal. Traverse easily left crossing The Vikings to a ledge and belays below a groove.
3   15 m (5a). Climb the groove, passing doubtful blocks to the overhang, then traverse right across a very mossy scoop onto a rib. Move up the rib, then step left back into the groove (small belays).
4   20 m (4c). Step right and climb the mossy wall to a ledge, then ascend the grassy crack on the right to a large pedestal belay.
5   15 m (4b). Continue up the crack and groove above to the top.

Variation   Direct Start   17 m   HVS   1968
1a (5a). Climb the groove directly up to the bottom of the groove
on pitch 3.

★ **The Satanic Traverses**   30 m   E5   1989
A sustained and very thin traverse line on the extreme lip of the
central overhanging wall climbed by Incantations and Supernatural
providing a serious undertaking with widely spaced protection, not
for the faint hearted. Start from the left end of the belay ledge at the
top of pitch 1 of Tophet Wall.
   (6a). Step left onto the steep wall then climb up, using a small
pocket, to place a crucial but hidden rock 4 in a slot, then reverse
back down to the belay ledge. Traverse leftwards just above the
overhang to a spike, then down to the jug on pitch 2 of
Supernatural, continue leftwards with your feet on the very lip of
the overhanging wall to a junction with Incantations' reasonable
holds and good protection. Continue the traverse to finish on
Tophet Grooves, then go up this to a spike belay which will
protect anyone wanting to follow.

★★ **The Viking**   57 m   E3   1969
A superb route of magnetic attraction which climbs the obvious,
overhanging crack line between Tophet Groove and Incantations. Start
directly below the crack.
1   15 m (5b). Climb the crack until it steepens, then step right into
    another crack, which is followed to a junction with Tophet
    Grooves. Stance and belay on the left.
2   27 m (5c). The extremely strenuous and overhanging crack above
    is climbed passing an awkward flared niche at the top. Easier
    ground is followed to a belay on Tophet Grooves.
3   15 m (4b). As pitch 5 of Tophet Grooves.

★ **Golden Calf**   42 m   E4   1978
To the left of Tophet Grooves Direct Start are two conspicuous thin,
offset cracks up the leaning buttress, topped by a thin crack up an
overhanging wall. Start at the foot of the first crack. A quality route
deceptively difficult, with a vicious last pitch.
1   17 m (6a). Climb the crack direct to a belay well back in the
    corner.
2   8 m (4a). Traverse easily right to belay below the groove on
    Tophet Grooves.
3   17 m (6b). Climb the groove until it is possible to bridge up
    beneath the thin crack . Difficult and fingery moves lead up the
    crack to the top.

Brimstone Buttress   69 m   MVS   1938
Round the edge of the buttress, left of Golden Calf and just right of
Tophet Bastion is a steep, right-angled corner. After the initial hard
start up the corner, the climb deteriorates with loose and vegetated
rock. Not recommended.
1   20 m (4b). Climb the crack into the corner, then step out onto
    the right wall, where small holds lead up until the crack can be
    rejoined near the top. Scramble up to a belay below a sweep of
    slabs.
2   17 m. The slabs above are climbed, trending right to the edge,
    then directly up, finishing via a shallow scoop.
3   32 m. Follow the ridge to a large ledge, then move up the arête,
    first on the left, then on the right, to the top.

★ **Tophet Bastion**   66 m   VD   1919
Pleasant but polished climbing up the left arête of the Tophet Wall
area. A good, all weather route. Start at the bottom of a broken arête.
1   20 m. Easily up the arête to a grass ledge, then climb the steep
    corner on the right to a rocky platform. It is possible to avoid the
    corner by the steep wall on the right, followed by easier ground
    to the rocky platform.
2   17 m. Climb the slab above for 8 metres to a ledge, then step
    left round the corner and up the arête to a stance.
3   12 m. Step right and climb straight up to the bottom of a groove
    at 7 metres. The groove above leads direct to the top or can be
    avoided by the easier crack on the left. From the belay, scramble
    up steep grass to the obvious feature of the "Shark's Fin" high
    on the left.
4   17 m. Starting from the right, climb the edge of the rib to the
    foot of a crack, which is climbed on its left wall, exiting left at
    its top.

★ **Tophet Girdle**   117 m   VS   1945
A left to right traverse of the Tophet Wall face incorporating Tophet
Bastion, a traverse of the Great Slab and the upper pitches of Tophet
Wall. An interesting outing. Start as for Tophet Bastion.
1   20 m. As pitch 1 of Tophet Bastion.
2   18 m (4a). Traverse right to the top of pitch 1 of Brimstone
    Buttress, then work up and right to the edge which leads via a
    shallow scoop to belays (rock requires care).
3   16 m. Climb easy slabs above to the edge of a gully then follow
    the grass ledges to the pedestal belay at the top of pitch 4 of
    Tophet Grooves.

4   23 m (4c). Traverse the Great Slab by reversing pitch 3 of Demon Wall into a corner and a junction with pitch 2 of Tophet Wall, which is then followed to its belay (care should be taken in protecting the second).
5   15 m (4a). As pitch 3 of Tophet Wall.
6   25 m (4a). As pitch 4 of Tophet Wall until a break leads off right, crossing the Tartarus Trip, round a rib into a corner. The shattered ridge on the right is climbed, then easy scrambling to the top.

The Napes Ridges – East

The following routes lie east of The Needle.

To the left of Tophet Bastion is an area of loose, vegetated rock ending at a steep vegetated corner, this marking the right wall of Lucifer Ridge. The following two routes start at the bottom of this corner from a point where a grassy ledge breaks out left.

★ Hell Raiser   26 m   E2   1987
A fine little test piece.
1   12 m (5c). Climb the thin crack in the wall directly to the belay ledge.
2   14 m (5b). Climb the bold little wall between pitch 2 of Lucifer Crack and Lucifer Ridge to sloping pockets. Pull up to good holds, step right and finish directly up a thin crack just left of the big flake.

★ Lucifer Crack   30 m   S   1925
A pleasant little route.
1   13 m. Traverse the grass ledge left to a crack about 6 metres above its start. Climb the niche and crack to a large ledge.
2   17 m. Climb the cracked wall above the ledge. (Some holds require care.)

Lucifer Ridge   43 m   VD   1934
Start at the foot of the ridge.
1   12 m. Moderate climbing leads to a stance at the side of the steep arête.
2   16 m. Descend a little, then climb the face on the left of the arête to the top of the pinnacle. Alternatively, climb up the corner above the belay. Step across the gap and climb the arête, on good holds, to the ledge above pitch 1 of Lucifer Crack.
3   15 m. Follow the arête direct, on good holds, to the top.

Jaga   123 m   VD   1951
A broken route, climbing the grassy looking rock on the left wall of
Lucifer Ridge. Start below and right of the sentry box in the wall
above.
1   18 m. Climb the wall until level with the sentry box, then traverse
    left into it.
2   18 m. Leave the sentry box on the right and climb the wall above,
    trending right to a large grass ledge.
3   30 m. Traverse left for 7 metres, climb the ridge ahead until it
    finishes under a nose of rock, then hand traverse left on good
    holds finishing up a nose of rock at its end.
4   20 m. Climb easy slabs and then the prominent rock tower.
5   12 m. Climb the slabs immediately behind the tower, trending
    right to a stance.
6   25 m. Continue up the slabs and small rock wall to a small ledge.
    Climb the rocks under the overhang, working first right then left
    to the top.

Scrimshanker   30 m   VS   1965
The obvious leaning corner about 30 metres left of the top of Lucifer
Crack. Start at the bottom of a V-groove. More difficult than it looks.
    (4c). Climb the groove for 6 metres to the base of a crack. Follow
    the awkward crack past a chockstone and exit left at the top onto
    easy ground. Finish up Belfry Buttress.

To the left of Scrimshanker is a broken slab with steep grass below.
The routes on this wall are better than their appearance would suggest
and are best climbed combined with Chantry Buttress and Belfry
Crack or Buttress Route. The result gives a worthwhile outing that
ends on Needle Ridge.

Buzzard Wall   23 m   D   1922
Start at the right-hand end of the broken slab.
    Climb the wall, trending right to a grassy corner at 7 metres, then
    follow the clean slab on the right up to a large ledge. The short
    wall above leads to a grass finish.

Zeta Climb   43 m   VD   1924
Start midway across the slab just right of a grass groove.
1   18 m. Ascend the rocks just right of the groove to a grass niche,
    then make an ascending traverse left to a grass ledge.
2   25 m. Climb up the slabs on the left to a ledge and large block.
    A short wall on the left then leads to a large ledge, followed by
    easy slabs and steep grass.

Belfry Buttress   18 m   HS   1968
The small clean buttress above Zeta Climb. Good open climbing that
can be used as a last pitch to Scrimshanker. Start 2 metres right of
the obvious Belfry Crack.

Climb the awkward groove to the top of a pedestal, then go
straight up the wall to a large ledge. The short slab above leads
onto Needle Ridge.

★ **Belfry Crack**   20 m   MVS   1925
A little gem that climbs the obvious crack up the centre of the
buttress. Strenuous.

(4b). Either ascend easy rocks on the right of the crack, then step
left onto a ledge at the base of the crack, or climb direct to the
same point. The crack above is best climbed facing right until a
ledge on the left is gained. Make a difficult step back right into
the crack, then up to a platform followed by easy rocks to Needle
Ridge.

Chantry Buttress   30 m   MS   1921
This is the independent, little buttress about 30 metres right of The
Needle. A good little route that deserves more attention. Start at the
lowest point of the buttress.

Easy rocks lead to a grass ledge. The slab on the right, followed
by a clean crack, lead to a ledge. Traverse left round a corner,
ascend the groove, then make an awkward step right onto a ledge.
Easy rocks to the top.

Salome   80 m   VD   1954
A poor and disjointed route. Start from the foot of a crack in the
slabs, 7 metres down and right from the Needle Gap.

1   18 m. Climb the crack, then traverse left along the rising ledge
    to a platform. Continue up until a swing right round a nose is
    made onto a slab that leads on small holds to a large block. Step
    right to a ledge.

2   28 m. Make an awkward step right to gain a crack, which is
    climbed to a large ledge. Continue up the corner crack, then bear
    left up the face of a pinnacle on small holds to a large ledge.
    Easy rocks lead up to a belay behind a large block.

3   24 m. The wall behind the block is climbed with difficulty, then
    bear right to the foot of an obvious chimney that leads to a rock
    ledge. Climb the crack on the right to a large ledge.

4   10 m. From the left-hand end of the ledge move up to the break
    in the ridge.

★★ **Needle Ridge**   99 m   VD   1884

The classic and justifiably popular Needle Ridge is frequently used, both as a beginners' introductory route and as a mountaineering route to the summit of Great Gable. The route provides excellent and safe climbing in superb surroundings on good though polished rock. Start from the gap directly behind the Needle.

1   12 m. Climb the very polished slab above to a chimney that trends left to a stance below a steep wall. Alternatively, start from Needle Gully at the lowest point of the ridge and follow the arête on good holds to the stance.

2   15 m. The steep wall above, followed by easier rocks, leads to a broken wall. Climb the wall, then traverse 7 metres right to the rib.

3   25 m. Follow the rib above, then easy rocks to a corner, which is climbed on the right.

4   12 m. Climb the groove on the left. Alternatively, climb the groove for 3 metres, then traverse right, under the overhang and finish straight up.

5   35 m. Easy scrambling to the top.

The Needle

This detached pinnacle of unique character is one of the most recognizable features in The Lake District and justifiably attracts many climbing and photographic parties. The inexplicable desire for climbers to sit, stand, pose and perform on the flat, but small, top of the pinnacle and the fact that nearly all the climbs meet at the shoulder and use a common final pitch for both ascent and descent results in inevitable queues. The majority of the routes are now very polished, with the section from the shoulder to the top requiring particular care, this section of climbing setting the grade for all routes using this passage. The climbs are described from left to right starting from the gap.

★ **The Wasdale Crack**   17 m   HS   1886

The most popular way to the top, with contrasting pitches, both very polished. The climb starts from the ledge just right of the gap.

1   13 m. Climb the crack, left, then right to its finish; then ascend an easy slab to the shoulder.

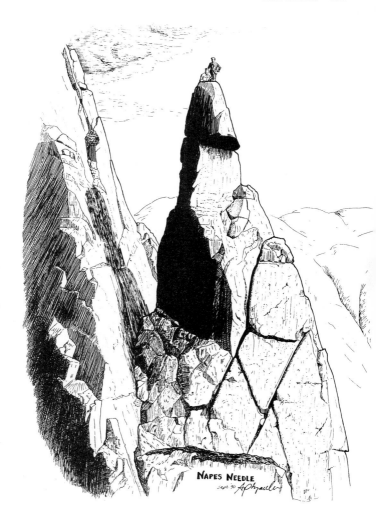

NAPES NEEDLE

2   4 m. The highly polished and notorious top block (crux). Mantelshelf onto the ledge below the top block. (It is easier from the right-hand corner but it can be climbed by the left-hand corner.) Traverse left onto the face of the top block and up to the top. Belay round and under the overhanging nose of the top block. Care should be taken on the descent and, if in doubt, a safety rope should be arranged over the top block, under the nose and back to the shoulder.

★ The Arête 20 m   HS   1894
Start at the bottom of The Wasdale Crack.
1   16 m. Traverse delicately right until a pull round onto the arête can be made. Climb the arête to the shoulder.
2   4 m. Pitch 2 of The Wasdale Crack.

★ The Crowley Route 22 m   HS   1893
1   18 m. Climb the slab between the arête and The Lingmell Crack, crossing The Lingmell Crack en route to the shoulder.
2   4 m. Pitch 2 of The Wasdale Crack.

★ The Lingmell Crack 22 m   HS   1892
Climbs the obvious crack on the side facing Lingmell.
1   18 m. Climb the crack over a small overhang to a ledge, then up to the shoulder.
2   4 m. Pitch 2 of The Wasdale Crack.

★ The Obverse Route 22 m   HS   1912
An independent route to the top, starting right of The Lingmell Crack.
1   18 m. Climb the steep slab to a platform and then the wall above to the shoulder.
2   4 m. Using the mantelshelf as a handhold, traverse right, to the corner nearest Needle Ridge; go up this to the top.

Direct Obverse from the Gap 13 m   HVS   1928
A serious little route with a nasty landing, starting from the gap.
    (5a). Difficult and unprotected moves up a crack line lead to the shoulder, and a junction with The Obverse Route, which is followed to the top.

Girdle Traverses
It is possible to girdle the Needle at two heights which, although possessing a certain attraction would, due to congestion, result in an exercise in diplomacy and rope management of nightmare proportions. **The Higher Needle Girdle** (S) traverses from the

shoulder under the nose and back to the shoulder. **The Needle Perimeter** (VS, 1941) starts and finishes at the gap. From the Wasdale Crack traverse right to the arête, then cross a slab past a large flake to a platform and belay on pitch 1 of The Obverse Route. Traverse horizontally right for 3 metres to a crack (strenuous) that leads back to the gap.

The Napes Ridges – West

The following routes lie west of The Needle

Eagle's Corner   70 m   MVS   1924
Basically a poor route with an interesting third pitch of Mild Very Severe, but even this can be avoided. The climb lies across Needle Gully on the east face of Eagle's Nest Ridge, and starts below broken ground at the foot of a grassy chimney at about the same height as the base of The Needle.
1   25 m. Scramble up to a grass ledge at the foot of the chimney which is climbed to grass ledges above.
2   15 m. Scramble up left, cross an incipient chimney, and climb the corner of the buttress on good holds to a stance and junction with Tricouni Rib.
3   15 m (4a). Traverse left along a ledge for 5 metres to a corner. Step round the corner and continue traversing left on small holds, crossing The Cayman, to a wide crack and a junction with Crocodile Crack, above the crux on pitch 1. Climb the crack to a large grass ledge.
    This pitch may be avoided by climbing the slab above the ledge or the crack at its left-hand end.
4   15 m. The grassy chimney on the right is followed by a similar chimney to the ridge.

★ **Amos Moses**   60 m   E1   1987
An excellent climb taking a direct line up the buttress right of Alligator Crawl. Start at the bottom of the large subsidiary buttress below the right-hand end of the Dress Circle.
1   25 m (5a). The buttress is split by a corner crack. Enter this from the left using a small rib, and climb the corner past two bulges to a slab. Climb up to grass ledges and the top of the pinnacle.
2   35 m (5b). The wall above is split by a prominent thin crack. Climb the crack to a small ledge (traverse line of Eagle's Corner), then move up and left to the foot of an obvious groove in the wall above. Enter this and climb it to a junction with the upper

section of Eagle's Nest Ridge. (This pitch can be split at the top of the thin crack at 15 metres.)

Up to the left of the subsidiary buttress marking the start of Amos Moses is the Dress Circle. This flat area of ground offers a convenient place for changing when climbing in the Crocodile Crack area and also provides a comfortable sunbathing, lunch platform with fine views of Napes Needle.

Tricouni Rib   65 m   MVS   1925
The subsidiary buttress is separated from the main face by a crack. The easy rocks just right of this crack mark the start. Not recommended.
1   20 m. Climb the easy rocks to a large grass ledge then up to the top of the pinnacle.
2   15 m (4b). Step off the pinnacle and traverse right on small holds to the edge of the buttress. Climb the edge, then the face above to a ledge and junction with Eagle's Corner.
3   20 m (4a). Climb up and right to the edge of a gully. Move up, then step across the gully to an undercut rock on the right. Awkward moves up its left edge are followed by a frightening finish on steep grass. Belay in a corner higher up.
4   10 m (4a). Climb easy rocks right of the belay, then traverse left into a broken chimney, which leads to Eagle's Nest Ridge.

Alligator Crawl   57 m   HS   1960
Start below the chimney between Crocodile Crack and Tricouni Rib.
1   15 m. Climb the chimney to a ledge.
2   27 m. From the top of the block step onto the wall and climb the crack to the traverse line on Eagle's Corner. The corner above leads to a large grass ledge and belay on Eagle's Corner pitch 3.
4   15 m. Pitch 4 of Eagle's Corner.

★ **Crocodile Crack**   58 m   HVS   1960
Directly above the Dress Circle is an obvious crack line running through an overhang to the top of the buttress. The climbing is good, hard and sustained. Start at the bottom of a flake crack to the right of the main crack above.
1   43 m (5a). Climb the flake crack for 8 metres (protection), then make a long step left into the main crack, which is climbed to an overhang at 15 metres. Continue up the widening crack, past a small ledge on the left, to join Eagle's Corner at the traverse. Up the crack to a large grass ledge.
2   15 m. Pitch 4 of Eagle's Corner.

★★ The Cayman   59 m   E2   1977

An eliminate line up the centre of the slender face between Crocodile Crack and Alligator Crawl producing one of the best pitches on The Napes. Start just left of Crocodile Crack below an overhang.

1   45 m (5b). Climb the overhang and crack above to where Crocodile Crack crosses the face. Step right, then follow the wall above to an overhang which is climbed via a thin crack above. Continue up the wall above to the next overhang, pull over, then move up and right to a ledge on the arête. Climb the arête to the top of the pinnacle.

2   14 m. Pitch 4 of Eagle's Corner.

Eagle's Crack   62 m   VS   1940

Midway between Crocodile Crack and Eagle's Nest Ridge Direct is an obvious slab capped by an overhang with a crack system above. Good climbing, but the loose flake on pitch 2 requires care. Start below the slab.

1   20 m (4c). Climb the slab to the overhang, step right to the rib and continue up the crack above for 7 metres to belays on the left wall.

2   30 m (4c). Follow the crack over the loose flake until a bold mantelshelf move is made onto an obvious ledge on the right undercut rib. Climb up and left to regain the crack above the overhang; then follow the crack to a thread belay.

3   12 m. Climb the crack and mossy slab above to a grass ledge. The short crack just left of pitch 4 of Eagle's Corner leads to the ridge.

★★ Eagle's Nest Ridge Direct   37 m   MVS   1892

Delightful open and delicate climbing up the steep arête at the left end of the Dress Circle. Small wires have made all the difference to this once, very bold lead. Start directly below the arête.

(4a). Steep rocks with good holds are climbed, bearing right, to a ledge overlooking the Dress Circle. Climb up and left to the arête, using two parallel cracks, then step up to a small platform (The Eagle's Nest), followed by another platform (The Crow's Nest) after a further 5 metres. Delicate moves, on sloping and polished holds, are made from the platform onto the slab above, which leads to Eagle's Nest Ordinary Route.

The pitch can be split at 25 metres.

Ling Chimney   40 m   VD   1899

The narrow grassy chimney on the left of Eagle's Nest Ridge Direct. Better than it looks.

Up easy rocks for 3 metres to the bottom of the left-hand of two cracks, then climb the crack to a chimney which is followed to a junction with the Ordinary Route. (The pitch can be split at the bottom of the chimney.)

★ **Long John** 42 m HVS   1928
Pleasant climbing up the steep narrow wall dividing Ling and West Chimneys. Unfortunately, the difficult second pitch is out of character with the rest, being much harder, but it can be avoided. Start below a pinnacle, just left of Ling Chimney.
1   33 m (4b). Climb straight up to the bottom of the left-hand crack of Ling Chimney, then step left and climb the centre of the slab, until forced out left onto the edge. A short distance above, a ledge leads back right into the centre of the slab, which is climbed, trending left, to a platform above West Chimney. Either take a stance here, or climb the wall on the right to the top of the pinnacle. Step down from the pinnacle and belay a little higher.
2   9 m (5a). From the top of the pinnacle, a poorly protected and difficult move is made onto the wall above. Climb the wall more easily to a ledge.

★★ **Eagle's Nest Ordinary Route** (West Chimney) 107 m D   1892
A fine, old, traditional route that is now very polished. It also serves as a convenient descent from the other routes in this area, instead of finishing up the Ordinary Route and walking round. Start at the bottom of the obvious wide chimney.
1   30 m. Easy rocks lead to the bottom of the Chimney, which is climbed either by bridging or by the right wall.
2   12 m. Climb up and right through a crevasse to the top of Ling Chimney; then go up a smooth slab to a belay in the corner.
3   12 m. The easy chimney above is followed by a slab with polished holds.
4   18 m. A chimney on the left is followed by easy scrambling up broken rocks.
5   35 m. Following the scratches, scramble along the ridge.

Little John 26 m S   1947
A strenuous little route up the steep, left bounding wall of Eagle's Nest Ordinary Route. Start from the top of a pedestal 10 metres up the chimney on the left wall.
      Climb the slab on its left side to where it steepens then follow the grassy right-slanting crack to below the overhang. Pull through the overhang into the grassy crack above and up this to the top.

To the left of Eagle's Nest Ordinary Route the ground falls away steeply to the foot of Abbey Buttress, which is reached by carefully descending this steep and loose section of the path.

★★ Abbey Buttress   58 m   VD   1909

Good climbing with a devious and intimidating second pitch. Start from the foot of the buttress.

1   20 m. Climb straight up to a ledge, step right and follow a steep crack to a ledge.

2   20 m. Ascend the steep rock above to a wide ledge at 5 metres. Traverse left for 5 metres, then go straight up for 8 metres, where a traverse back right below an overhang can be made onto an arête that leads on good holds to a large ledge.

3   18 m. The crack on the right followed by the left corner of the buttress are climbed to a junction with Eagle's Nest Ordinary Route.

Abbey Buttress Variation   32 m   VD   1913

Start on the right of Abbey Buttress.

1   15 m. Make an upward traverse left to an obvious pinnacle on the skyline; then climb the steep slab on good holds to a stance at the right-hand end of the ledge traversed on Abbey Buttress.

2   17 m. Go straight up the wall above, on good holds to the overhang on Abbey Buttress which is then followed.

Eagle's Chain   110 m   VS   1945

A left to right girdle, starting at the foot of Abbey Buttress, crossing Eagle's Nest Buttress high up and finishing up Tricouni Rib. Pleasant climbing with some good exposed situations in its centre section.

1   20 m. Pitch 1 of Abbey Buttress.

2   10 m. Traverse right onto Abbey Buttress Variation, climb the wall to a ledge, then continue the traverse right, crossing Little John, into Eagle's Nest West Chimney.

3   10 m. Cross the wall on the right onto Long John and follow this, trending left, to a platform above West Chimney.

4   14 m (4a). Traverse horizontally right onto Eagle's Nest Ridge Direct, where a delicate and exposed step down is made into the Crow's Nest using sloping and polished holds (small wires to protect the second). Step down again, then traverse right to the grassy crack of Eagle's Crack. Climb the crack for about 2 metres, then traverse right to another grassy crack. Not an easy pitch to second.

5   28 m (4b). Step down and traverse delicately right across the steep wall to gain Crocodile Crack, above the crux. Climb the crack

for about 4 metres then make a slightly descending traverse right, crossing The Cayman, to a belay on Alligator Crawl.

6   18 m (4a). Make an upward diagonal traverse right to a junction with pitch 3 of Tricouni Rib, at the step across the gully, then continue up Tricouni Rib.

7   10 m (4a). Pitch 4 of Tricouni Rib.

The following two climbs are situated on the left bounding wall of Abbey Buttress and are approached from Eagle's Nest Gully.

The Merry Monk   30 m   MVS   1968
A pleasant little route up the thin crack line about 5 metres right of the obvious pod-shaped crack. Scramble up to the foot of the crack.
    (4b). Ascend the thin crack, which is awkward to start, and enter a shallow groove, breaking out left near the top.

The Pod   30 m   VS   1968
The obvious, deep, pod-shaped crack. Not as hard as it looks, but often wet.
    (4c). Scramble up easy rocks to the pod-shaped crack, which is climbed, exiting left at the top. Broken rocks lead to the ridge.

Sabre Ridge   30 m   VD   1920
This ridge divides Eagle's Nest Gully high above the chockstone. The approach is loose and unpleasant with the rewards minimal.
    Climb the arête for 7 metres; then go up the sharp left edge to a ledge. The short section of arête above is followed by scrambling to the top.

Cutlass Ridge   30 m   VD   1922
This climb is on the broken east wall of Arrowhead Ridge and starts high up the gully to the right of a grassy chimney. The climb is both vegetated and broken and deserves to be left in peace.
    Climb the steep buttress to a crack at 8 metres, which is followed for a further 8 metres to a steep slab. Ascend the slab, the climbing becoming progressively easier, to Arrowhead Ridge at the strid.

Murin Buchstansangur   25 m   E2   1988
The climbing is both shorter and easier to read than the name. Start from the top of a big block, left of Cutlass Ridge and about 15 metres higher than the foot of the slab taken by Time and Place.

(*opposite*)   Tophet Bastion, Tophet Wall
(*next page*)   Eagle's Nest Ridge Direct, Napes

(5b). Pull into a little corner below an overlap, just right of a wide crack. Climb thin, parallel cracks up to a diagonal break, then the pillar above, following its left-hand edge to the top.

Down to the left of Murin Buchstansangur is an obvious blank looking steep slab, with an overlap at half-height, which extends the full height of the east wall of the gully. The following two routes make the best of this area of unbroken rock.

Time and Place   35 m   E2   1982
Bold climbing that finds the easiest way round the problems. Start in the middle of the slab belaying at a short crack.
(5b). Climb the slab bearing left and make thin moves past a pedestal block on the left, but not using it! Traverse diagonally up right to within 2 metres of the right edge and climb direct over the bulge to a jamming crack. Traverse left into the middle of the slab and climb the thin crack to the top.

★★ The Tormentor   35 m   E4   1987
An eliminate line, taking on the problems avoided by Time and Place. A superb slab climb with a serious crux section up to the overlap. Start as for Time and Place.
(6a). Gain the lower left edge of the slab by climbing the short crack and stepping left along a grassy ledge. Pull onto the slab, and after 2 metres follow a faint weakness up and right to a runner, then pull back to good holds at the foot of a diagonal crack. (Junction with Time and Place.) Follow the crack until in the centre of the slab, then make some very scary moves straight up to the overlap (undercut hold and runner). Pull over and right on improving holds up to another diagonal break, then finish up the final thin crack of Time and Place.

Arrowhead Ridge – Easy Way   60 m   D   1892
A scrappy route missing the best part of the ridge. Start in Eagle's Nest Gully just left of The Tormentor slab.
1   22 m. Easy ledges, first left, then right and up, until a short traverse left ends at the gap between the Arrowhead and the upper section of the ridge.
2   8 m. From the gap, traverse right, then go up a crack to the top of the ridge.
3   30 m. Scramble along the ridge, passing the strid en route.

Long John, Napes   (*previous page*)
Arrowhead Ridge Direct, Napes   (*opposite*)

★★ **Arrowhead Ridge Direct**   80 m   VD   1896

An excellent and exposed climb, characterized by the distinctive Arrow-head at the top of the steep section. Start at the lowest point of the ridge.

1   15 m. Easy rocks followed by steeper climbing leads to a ledge.
2   25 m. The steep ridge ahead is climbed either direct or round the corner on the right to the top of a small pinnacle. Step off the pinnacle onto the slab, ascend to the base of the Arrowhead then make an exposed move on good holds to the top. From the base of the Arrowhead it is possible to traverse left to the gap between the Arrowhead and the upper ridge (easier).
3   10 m. Stride across the gap and pass along a horizontal section of the ridge.
4   30 m. Pitch 3 of Arrowhead Ridge – Easy Way.

Variation
South-East Variation   15 m   VD   1925

An alternative to pitch 2 of Arrowhead Ridge Direct. It can be reached from below, but the best way is to climb Arrowhead Ridge Direct to the top of the pinnacle on pitch 2, then descend the groove on the right for 8 metres, where a short ascending traverse is made to a good stance on the Easy Way.

2a. Climb the slab and a short way up the corner above, move out left onto the true arête, then go straight up to the top of the Arrowhead.

★ **Scimitar Ridge**   28 m   VD   1919

Immediately left of Arrowhead Ridge is the loose and nasty Arrowhead Gully. Scimitar Ridge lies high up this gully and is reached by scrambling, following the left-hand fork of that gully. An excellent little climb on good rock.

Climb straight up the ridge to a good ledge. The slab above leads to a large block on its left edge, then finish up the arête.

Left of Arrowhead Ridge the crag becomes very broken, the main feature being the Sphinx or Cat Rock (part of Sphinx Ridge) and all the climbs in this area are described in relation to it.

★ **Rainbow Ridge**   32 m   S   1922

Up and right of the Sphinx Rock and left of an overhanging nose is a clean slab of light coloured rock. The climb is reached by scrambling up Arrowhead Gully, then up steep grass on the left to the foot of the slab. Good open climbing on clean solid rock.

Climb the steep slab to a small ledge at 6 metres, then diagonally left to a detached block. Traverse right to the arête and follow it to the top. Alternatively, from the small ledge at 6 metres, traverse right to the arête and so to the top.

Gremlin's Crack   15 m   MVS   1946
Just right of Sphinx Ridge and level with the Sphinx Rock is a steep wall split by a dirty crack. Not recommended.

(4b). Climb the strenuous jamming crack.

The Sphinx or Cat Rock   5 m   VD   1889
One of the Lake District's first boulder problems and worth a try.

From the tail of the cat move right, then climb to the top of the rock.

Sphinx Ridge   15 m   D
The ridge immediately behind The Sphinx rock gives poor climbing with the difficulties being short. The route ascends easy rocks to a groove which leads to easy climbing above.

Westmorland Crags   (211 102)   Alt. 800 m   South Facing

These summit crags of Great Gable which lie immediately above the Napes Ridges are very broken but do offer an interesting scramble to the summit as an alternative to the grinding slog. The only route worthy of description is as follows:

Westmorland Ridge   36 m   VD   1932
Start at the foot of a small buttress on the right side of the crag.
1   13 m. Climb the wall above followed by scrambling to the foot of a pinnacle.
2   23 m. The ridge of the pinnacle leads up to a ledge, then over easy rocks to the top.

WASDALE

Yewbarrow

Bell Rib   (171 075)   Alt. 360 m   South Facing

This is the knott of rock above and right of Overbeck set high on the South West Ridge of Yewbarrow. The approach is steep and broken, the crag is no better. As the routes are of poor quality and seldom repeated; only then by a group of local enthusiasts, the descriptions are kept brief. Start from a grass terrace.

Route 1 (D, 1927). Starting near a large boulder climb the groove and easy rocks to the top. **Route 2** (VD, 1927). Start from the lowest point of the rock ridge just right of Route 1. Climb up to a ledge with a bollard on the right, then up a delicate slab on the left to finish up easy rocks. **Slab Climb** (HS, 1927). Starting just right of Route 2, climb diagonally up left then up the middle on small holds. **Mossy Face** (D, 1934). Start to the right of Slab Climb. Up easily to a ledge at 6 metres, then traverse right for 10 metres under a small overhang and climb the mossy face direct.

Great Door   (170 077)   Alt. 430 m   North Facing

The deep rock fault that separates Bell Rib from the rest of Yewbarrow. Only one route has been recorded on its dark, greasy walls and would be a complete waste of time and effort, that is assuming one could find it. **The North Door Climb** (S, 30 m, 1948). Start at a scratched corner on the true left of the gully running down to Overbeck. Traverse a hard corner to the left of a belay and finish straight up the wall.

Overbeck   (169 077)   Alt. 320 m   South West Facing

Overbeck is now the established name used for what is more accurately called Dropping Crag. The crag, which holds a fine sunny aspect overlooking Wastwater and The Screes, lies just left of a steep broken ridge which runs up to Bell Rib, the conical knott on the ridge of Yewbarrow. Until recently the routes were in the traditional mould being generally dark, polished chimneys and relatively easy slab routes but recently a number of harder routes have been added.

The rock is generally good and though mossy in parts, it provides a good place for a short day.

Park at Overbeck Bridge and follow the well worn track on the right-hand side of the wall up the south-west ridge of Overbeck crossing the wall high up at a stile, then traverse left across the fellside up to the base of the crag, just left of a scree shoot. (1 km and approximately 1/2 hr.)

The most obvious feature is the large corner of 'B' Chimney with the leaning detached pillar climbed by Femme Fatale on its left. High up and right of 'B' Chimney is the impending wall climbed by Queen of Change.

To suit the normal approach the routes are described from right to left with the best descent on the right, down the true left side of the gully.

Corner Climb   30 m   VD   1945
An easier version of Overbeck Buttress starting at a pillar at the ridge of the gully. Polished.
1   15 m. Go up then diagonally left to the grass ledge and flake belay on Overbeck Buttress.
2   15 m. Climb up and right, as Overbeck Buttress, but then step right, round the corner and follow the right side at the ridge, crossing Overbeck Buttress at the turn and up the wall to the top.

★ **Overbeck Buttress**   45 m   MS   1909
Good open climbing on clean rock but getting polished. Start below a rib at the lowest point of the crag.
1   20 m. Climb straight up the rib to a grass ledge and flake belay.
2   25 m. Move up and right, then ascend the steep wall on the left of the ridge until a delicate step right can be made; the 'turn' around the arête. Climb the wall direct to the top.

★ **Bowderdale Climb**   50 m   MS   1945
Another good route taking the obvious parallel cracks 5 metres left of Overbeck Buttress. Start below a mossy wall 5 metres left of Overbeck Buttress.
1   20 m. The mossy wall leads up to the grass ledge and flake belay on Overbeck Buttress pitch 1.
2   22 m. Climb straight up the parallel cracks above to a sentry box with a spike on the right. From the spike traverse left on shelving slabs then up on easier rocks to a belay below a corner. Junction with The Gargoyle.

3   8 m. Move up then out right round the bulging corner and climb the steep wall above on good small holds finishing out left at the top.

The Gargoyle   40 m   VS   1945
Interesting climbing up the corner crack and steep arête left of Bowderdale Climb. A strenuous but well protected crux pitch. Start at the left end of the large heather ledge, reached by various routes.
1   15 m (4b). Climb the mossy corner crack to a ledge below a steep corner.
2   10 m (4a). Traverse left along a narrow ledge and round the arête on a descending line to reach a terrace. Thread belay at floor level.
3   15 m (4c). Steep climbing up the wall to a spike on the right, then up left to the obvious leaning crack. Pull strenuously up the crack to good holds over the top. A good pitch.

Variation Finish   15 m   VS   1970
(4c). From the belay ledge on pitch 1 climb straight up the steep corner until below the capstone. Step out right onto the overhanging wall, then pull up and over to the top.

Central Route   47 m   S   1946
A very dirty and scrappy route that wanders up the centre of the crag. Start midway between the starts of Bowderdale Climb and Zig-Zag.
1   17 m. Follow the easy ledge up and right until an awkward move is made out left round a steep rib to gain a very mossy slab. Move up to belays level with the terrace below 'B' Chimney.
2   15 m. Traverse right then up to the ledge at the bottom of the slanting chimney. Either climb the dirty green chimney direct or escape out left onto the slab, then up the edge before moving back into the chimney to finish up the left wall onto a large grass ledge.
3   15 m. Walk along the grass ledge and climb the corner crack to the top.

North and Central   45 m   HS   1946
A series of variations on Central Route keeping just left of it but sharing its last pitch. Pitch 2 is bold. Start just left of Central Route at a recess.
1   20 m. Climb the awkward little chimney up to a ledge. Traverse left, then go up and right to the belay on Central Route pitch 1.
2   18 m. As Central Route to the ledge at the bottom of the slanting crack, then traverse left across the slab to the edge. Delicate moves now lead up and left into a scoop which is climbed pulling

over a bulge at the top and up to a grass ledge and junction with Central Route.

3   7m. The corner crack as pitch 3 of Central Route.

★ **Queen of Change**   50 m   E3   1984
A steep and direct line, spoiled only by the large escape ledges, with its crux pitch climbing a thin crack line up the impressive headwall. Start below a short steep clean wall in the centre of the crag, just right of a mossy wall.

1   15 m (5c). Make a series of difficult moves up the wall until a committing pull out left is made onto the easier mossy wall. Climb the wall to the grass ledge below 'B' Chimney.

2   15 m (5b). Step right and climb the slightly overhanging wall which gradually eases to a large grass ledge and belay below the thin crack line in the headwall.

3   20 m (6a). Difficult climbing up the thin crack leads to a large triangular hold, continue up to a horizontal break (rest), then trend right on small holds until a committing move is made into a flared crack running up diagonally right to the top. Belay well back. An exciting pitch.

There are three obvious chimneys in the middle of the crag, 'B' Chimney, Central Chimney and Ash Tree Chimney. These are reached by the prominent broad slab, which slopes up from the terrace for 7 metres to the narrow cat walk which foots all three chimneys.

'B' Chimney   25 m   D   1898
A traditional elbow and knee bruising exercise on very polished rock. Approach the base of the chimney via the cat walk or by the first pitch of Central Chimney.

1   25 m. Climb the chimney using traditional techniques to the top. The pitch may be split at 17 metres height.

Tim Benzedrino   40 m   E3   1978
The steep undercut wall just left of 'B' Chimney. The climbing is hard, bold and with one or two doubtful holds high up. Start as for Queen of Change.

1   14 m (5c). Pitch 1 of Queen of Change.

2   18 m (5c). Climb the short overhanging wall on the left and make a difficult finger pull up to a horizontal break in the wall above. (Side runners can be arranged in the horizontal break to protect these moves, placed from 'B' Chimney.) Gain a standing position on the break and continue up the crack line moving out left on

flat holds at the top, then back right to a large ledge. A bit run out.

3   8 m. Pitch 3 of Central Chimney.

★ **Femme Fatale**   42 m   E3   1988
An exciting route up the shallow groove in the obvious central undercut prow left of Tim Benzedrino. Start between the rib of Central Chimney and Queen of Change at a mossy flake crack.

1   14 m (4c). Climb the mossy flake crack, then step out right and up to a belay below and left of the undercut prow.

2   20 m (5c). Pull onto the rib above from the right and gain a good foothold. Delicate moves up the wall past a poor peg runner leads to good slots and protection, then ascend the groove to a precarious finish on a large ledge.

3   8 m. Pitch 3 of Central Chimney.

★ **Central Chimney**   36 m   S   1899
Difficult and polished climbing needing every technique in the book and more. Start directly below the chimney at a small arête.

1   10 m. Climb the arête to belay on the cat walk below the chimney.

2   18 m. Straight up the chimney passing a difficult overhanging narrow section to finish outside the top chockstone.

3   8 m. Using sloping polished holds step up onto the ridge, then move right and up to the top.

★ **Zig-Zag**   34 m   HVS   1944
Interesting climbing with an intimidating and bold top pitch, which unfortunately can be avoided by climbing the top pitch of Ash Tree Chimney. Start below a slanting groove right of the corner of the broad slab as Ash Tree Chimney Direct Start.

1   8 m (4a). Climb the slanting groove to belay on the cat walk.

2   12 m (4b). Starting just right of Ash Tree Chimney traverse the break and climb the arête to below a large triangular overhang, then traverse left under the overhang into Ash Tree Chimney.

3   14 m (5a). From the chimney break out onto the right wall just above the level of the overhang and move right into the centre of the wall. A difficult pull up the wall leads to good finishing holds at the break, then easily up the short wall to the top.

Ash Tree Chimney   24 m   VD   1899
Another traditional chimney route starting at the left-hand end of the cat walk just above the broad slab.

1   7 m. Climb the chimney and finish up the mossy left wall to a ledge with an ash and yew tree beside it. Belay on the right.
2   17 m. Step across into the chimney on the right and climb the narrow chimney-crack past a large flake to a cave beneath the chockstone. Either squirm up through a polished hole or more pleasantly move out right and traverse diagonally up the outside of the top blocks.

Variations
Direct Start   8 m   S   1946
1a Climb up the slanting groove right of the corner of the broad slab to the bottom of the chimney.

Variation Finish   15 m   D
2a Scramble up behind the yew to a shelf on the left, then up a steep corner on good holds followed by easy rocks to the top.

Variation   Ash Tree Groove   15 m   VS   1946
An alternative finish between the left-hand variation and the chimney. A route that receives few ascents and is very dirty. Not recommended.
2b (4b). Follow variation pitch 2a, but instead of moving left to the shelf, go straight up to a whitish wall. Climb the corner capped by an overhang until moving out right and up to a thin ledge. From the right-hand end of the ledge make a long reach up for a good incut and pull up followed by another but longer stretch for the next hold. Traverse right to the top of Ash Tree Chimney. Belay back and left to protect the second.

Troglodyte   28 m   VD   1970
An internal girdle of the central detached pillar providing a good wet day alternative. Potholing experience and a slim build a definite advantage on pitch 1. Start as for 'B' Chimney.
1   8 m. Follow 'B' Chimney for 5 metres then squirm along the passage left, negotiate a tight 90° bend and pop out into Central Chimney.
2   10 m. Follow the chimney up to a platform on the right.
3   10 m. Step into 'B' Chimney and follow the passage through to join the last pitch of Ash Tree Chimney which leads to the top.

Catamite Corner   30 m   E2   1988
A route of contrasting pitches, the first strenuous and well protected, the second bold. Start below the overhanging groove 4 metres left of the cat walk slab, just left of some large overhangs.

1   15 m (5c). Climb up onto a sloping ledge below the corner and ascend it strenuously exiting left at the top on good holds. Continue up to a grass ledge below a chimney and junction with The Curving Crack.
2   15 m (5c). On the right is a sharp arête. Climb its right-hand side with conviction to the top, then over easy rocks to finish.

The Curving Crack   30 m   HS   1946
The overhanging crack line curving to the right starting 10 metres left of Catamite Corner. Another neglected route now becoming very dirty.
1   15 m. Climb the crack to a bulge at 10 metres. Make a difficult move right to a ledge and scramble up grass to an oak.
2   8 m. Descend slightly and traverse round the corner on the right to the foot of a small chimney (North Chimney).
3   7 m. Climb the deceptively easy looking chimney to finish on the block overlooking Ash Tree Chimney Variation Finish.

Variation   8 m   HS
Avoids pitches 2 and 3 of the original route.
2a Climb the short crack behind the oak to finish.

Girdle Traverse   146 m   VS   1945
An interesting expedition starting at the right-hand end of the crag and finally descending Curving Crack. The climbing, although never really hard, does involve reversing some awkward sections of existing routes, often out of sight of ones partner and requires care with ropework, and protection.
1   20 m. Pitch 1 of Overbeck Buttress.
2   27 m. As pitch 2 of Corner Climb until level with the 'turn' of Overbeck Buttress. Traverse left, reversing the 'turn', and continue traversing to the crack of Bowderdale Climb above the sentry box. Follow Bowderdale Climb to the belay and junction with The Gargoyle. Care needed in protecting the second.
3   10 m (4a). Pitch 2 of The Gargoyle.
4   12 m. Reverse the slanting chimney on pitch 2 of Central Route to the ledge.
5   20 m (4b). Follow North and Central left to the scoop, then continue, via a delicate traverse, left into 'B' Chimney which is followed to the large ledge. A difficult pitch to second.
6   12 m (4a). Step left and descend Central Chimney to the traverse line on Zig-Zag, follow this into Ash Tree Chimney and descend the chimney to the belay on pitch 1.
7   15 m. Ash Tree Chimney Variation Finish.

8   7 m. Step left and reverse pitch 3 of The Curving Crack.
9   8 m. Reverse pitch 2 of The Curving Crack.
10 15 m. Reverse pitch 1 of The Curving Crack.

On the left side of the crag is the alternative descent via a polished chimney. The wall adjacent to this chimney provides a number of obvious short routes approximately 10 metres long and of varying grades that are suitable for top roping or soloing.

To the right of the gully and used by the right-hand descent route is a small outcrop containing two other short climbs that lay undisturbed.

Bowderdale Boulder, this lies on the right bank of Overbeck, a landmark in the valley below the crag. Numerous entertaining problems can be found on it.

Great Knott   (170 093)   Alt. 500 m   South West Facing

An attractive little crag with a superb outlook situated at the head of Overbeck overlooking Gosforth Crag Moss. The rock is clean and solid where it matters. The crag, which has been extensively developed, has produced only a few good routes but for completeness all the recorded routes are included.

From the car park at Overbeck Bridge follow the footpath on the right of Overbeck, crossing it at a foot bridge after 1½ km. The path then continues up the fell to join the Bowderdale track which is followed up the left-hand side of Overbeck. After 1½ km contour around Gosforth Crag Moss and up to the base of the crag (approximately 1hr.) The crag is easily identified by the central crack line and overhang climbed by Mr. Softee, flanked on each side by a square cut groove. The routes are described from left to right with the descent to the right.

Frozen Assets   23 m   VS   1989
At the extreme left end of the crag is a huge perched block high up. Start below the block.
      (4c). Climb the shallow groove then diagonally right under the block and up to the top.

Cold Climbs   23 m   VS   1989
The steep cleaned wall 7 metres right of Frozen Assets.
      (4c). Climb the wall to a break then the cracked rib on the left.

Neopolitan 23 m   VS   1988
The smooth water worn slab just right of Cold Climbs. Poor
protection and belays.
      (4b). Climb the centre of the slab then the arête on the left.

Chocolate Chip 25 m   MS   1988
      Climb the rib formed by the left side of the front of the buttress.

Naughty But Nice 17 m   MVS   1988
Start 3 metres left of the cleaned groove with a leaning flake at the
bottom.
      (4a). Up to a good ledge then climb the wall above on small holds
to the top.

Raspberry Ripple 20 m   D   1988
      The cleaned groove with a leaning flake at its base, exiting right
over hollow blocks to finish up the arête on the left.

Vanilla Fudge 25 m   VS   1988
Start just right of Raspberry Ripple.
      (4c). Climb the right wall of the groove, passing the overhang on
the left then up the leftward leaning scoop.

Mr. Softee 25 m   E2   1988
A good mixture of technical and strenuous climbing up the obvious
break in the centre of the buttress. Start directly below the left-facing
corner.
      (5c). Pull up into the bottom of the steep corner. Difficult moves
up the corner lead up to good holds and protection below the
overhang. Swing out right and pull strenuously up into the crack
above. Follow the crack to the top.

Wafer Thin 25 m   E2   1988
Good open climbing up the left wall of the groove climbed by
Tutti-Frutti. Start at the bottom of the groove.
      (5c). Pull up into the bottom of the groove then move out left to
a good ledge below the steep wall. Using small finger holds move
up the steep wall (small wire on the right) then move up and left
to good finishing holds.

Tutti-Frutti 25 m   VS   1988
Interesting climbing up the groove right of Wafer Thin.
      (4b). Pull up into the groove and follow it to the top.

The Cornet   25 m   HVS   1988
Start at the bottom of a V-groove behind an embedded flake right of
Tutti-Frutti.
  (5a). Climb the groove then cracks above over a slab to the top.

Cream Horn   25 m   HVS   1988
Sustained climbing with spaced protection up the arête right of The
Cornet.
  (5a). Step up right onto the arête and climb straight up to twin
cracks and protection. Follow the cracks and the arête to the top.

Angel Delight   25 m   VS   1988
Start just right of Cream Horn.
  (4b). From the top of a tooth shaped boulder climb the groove
followed by a crack line to finish up the arête.

Three Scoops Please   20 m   VS   1988
  (4b). Follow the line of scoops and corners to finish up the arête
just right of Angel Delight.

Middle Fell

Many short climbs have been made on the numerous small outcrops
that are scattered across the slopes of Middle Fell, some have been
recorded, others not. In an attempt to make some sense out of it all
a selection of the better outcrops and routes has been included for
those wishing to sample what is on offer. The surrounding rocks
should not be assumed to be virgin, as many other less worthwhile
climbs have been made.

Rough Crag   (153 082)   Alt. 350 m   North East Facing

This dark and seldom visited crag lies on the Netherbeck Face of
Middlefell. Although the rock is rough and solid it is often buried
under a carpet of moss which holds the moisture. The climbs
themselves tend to be serious and inescapable.

Park at the disused gravel pit or Netherbeck Bridge and follow the
well worn track up the left side of Netherbeck for 2 km, until a flat
area just beyond the waterfall is reached prior to Sandy Gill. Leave
the track and go up and back left over a boggy plateau followed by
rough ground to the bottom of the crag, which has a deep-cut gully

at its left-hand end, and a large square cut overhang on its right-hand side (approximately 1¼ hrs).

Masochists can go directly up the fell and after 1½ km be suitably rewarded.

The climbs are described from left to right with the descents to the right via a sheep track.

Left Gully Arête   73 m   S   1976
Climbs the left arête of Rough Crag Gully starting at the bottom of the gully.
1   22 m. Traverse up and left to gain a groove leading to a grassy platform. Pull up into the groove on the arête using a spike, then work up and left to a terrace.
2   35 m. Climb the broken arête above, passing a rowan to belay below a steep rib.
3   16 m. Up the grooved rib to the top.

Rough Crag Gully   60 m   HS   1976
The obvious deep cut gully at the left end of the crag. Vegetated, wet and nasty with an awkward crux.
1   32 m. Over a huge chockstone then easily up the gully to below the narrow vertical crux section. Strenuous moves eventually lead to good holds which allow a difficult pull up to a stance and belay on the right.
2   28 m. The right leaning gully above is climbed followed by easy slabs on the right, then back left to finish up a short gully.

Right Gully Arête   62 m   VS   1976
Good open climbing, in spite of the moss, up the right arête of Rough Crag Gully. Start just right of the gully below a steep mossy slab.
1   36 m (4b). Climb the slab until it forms a pinnacle. Step off this onto a cracked slab and go up to a bay below a groove. Traverse left onto the gully wall then make a high step up to below a slab that leads delicately up to an overlap. Pull right onto a rib then go up left across a slab to an arête. The scoop above leads to a terrace and tree belay.
2   26 m. Up a grooved ridge to the top.

Icicle   67 m   VS   1976
A good route up the obvious crack line 5 metres right of Right Gully Arête.
1   23 m (4b). Climb the crack past an awkward section, then move out left to gain a series of ledges that lead back up right to a terrace below a bulging wall.

2   17 m (4b). From the left-hand end of the terrace step up left onto
    a large hold then bridge awkwardly up the gangway out right to
    another terrace and tree belay.
3   27 m. Finish up the grooved slab behind the tree and easy rocks
    to the top.

Cheeky Charlie   65 m   VS   †   1978
10 metres up and right from Rough Crag Gully is an obvious,
relatively clean, slanting V-groove. After the initial groove the route
disappears under the moss. Start at the foot of the V-groove.
1   15 m (4c). Difficult moves up the groove are followed by a pull
    out left onto a platform. Step back right, across the groove and
    follow the break diagonally right past a niche to a spike belay.
2   12 m (4b). Climb the steep wall above the spike. Step left into a
    groove then go up and left to a ledge.
3   26 m (4b). Step down and right, then make an ascending traverse
    of the steep mossy wall on the right, crossing a bilberry ledge to
    gain a V-chimney. Climb the chimney.
4   12 m. Easy climbing to the top.

Immediately above the boggy plateau crossed on the approach to
Rough Crag is a buttress with an obvious waterslide. The following
route climbs the small buttress 4 metres right of this.

Starters   35 m   MVS   1975
Start below the steep little wall.
    (4a). Climb the wall working up from left to right to gain a crack
    leading to a heather ledge. The steep wall above is followed by
    an awkward mantelshelf out right to the top.

A route of Very Severe standard has been recorded up the broken
ground above the finish of Starters and is mentioned for completeness
only.

Approximately 100 metres above and right of the main buttress of
Rough Crag is a band of rock with the following recorded routes.

Descents possible to the right or left.

Left-Hand Buttress   32 m   VS   1982
Start at an ash tree below a wall on the left-hand side of the crag.
1   20 m (4b). After a difficult start the wall is climbed to a terrace.
2   12 m. Easy rocks lead to the top.

Forked Lightening   35 m   HVS   1982
The obvious steep crack line 4 metres right of the right-hand buttress.
Start at the sentry box.
1   20 m (5a). Climb the sentry box exiting right to gain the steep
     crack above and up this to a terrace.
2   15 m (4b). Climb the chimney crack 3 metres right to the top.

Iron Crag   (156 068)   Alt. 250 m   East Facing

An area of sound rock overlooking Netherbeck Bridge. Only the
recorded routes are described but other short easy climbs do exist on
the slabs up and right of the buttress. Park at the disused gravel pit
or Netherbeck Bridge and go straight up the fellside then follow a
stream up to the clean buttress (approximately 20 mins). The climbs
are described from left to right with descents on either side.

Iron Crag Ridge   60 m   D   1973
Start at the left corner of the buttress at a large spike.
     Follow the ridge taking variations to the right and left with belays
     as required.

Iron Crag Buttress   60 m   MVS   1973
A pleasant climb on good rock. Start 2 metres right of Iron Crag
Ridge.
1   30 m (4a). Climb the slab and thin crack to a ledge. Move right
     and up an awkward corner, then continue over slabs to a rock
     bay.
2   30 m (4a). The delicate rib on the right leads to a ledge followed
     by slabs and terraces to the top.

Right Band Buttress   60 m   S   1973
Another pleasant route. Start 7 metres right of Iron Crag Buttress
across a grassy bay at a crack.
1   30 m. Climb the crack, move right over slabs then straight up the
     centre of the buttress to a ledge. Climb the shallow chimney on
     the left.
2   30 m. Walk 5 metres left and climb the stepped slab, then a
     groove to a terrace.

Variation   30 m   1973
1a. Climb the mossy slab 5 metres right of the crack, traverse left,
     then go straight up the centre of the buttress to a ledge. Climb
     the shallow chimney on the left.

Goat Crag   (153 066)   Alt. 350 m   South East Facing

This broken crag, situated high up on the right-hand side of Goat Gill, is easily identified by a large white scar at its base. Although having been extensively developed by a local activist, the resultant routes are broken and unrewarding. Limited parking is possible just off the Wasdale Head road directly below the crag, with the approach being directly up the fellside on either side of Goat Gill.

The climbs are briefly described from left to right. The descent is to the left.

The first recorded route starts about 35 metres left and up from the white scar. **Deception** (MVS (4a), 1985). Climb the mossy scoop, then the arête and cracked wall. **Flakey Wall** (MVS (4b), 1985). Start 7 metres right of Deception. Climb the wall and corner. Move up left, passing a perched block on the right and straight up to finish. **Cracked Wall** (VS (4b), 1985). Start 7 metres right of Flakey Wall. Climb the wall and obvious leftward slanting crack to a ledge, then up the corner to the top. **Slab and Groove** (VS (4c), 1988). Start below a clean wall round the corner right of Cracked Wall. Climb the wall, move right into a groove and up to a ledge. A difficult pull through the overlap leads via a steep slab to the top. **Holly Tree Groove** (VS (4b), 1988). Start 10 metres right of Slab and Groove below a holly and large detached block. Step off the block and climb the groove above trending right. **Waterstreak Wall** (VS (4b,4c), 1968). The best route available. Start at an embedded flake below the white scar. Step off the flake and climb the slab, trending leftwards to an overlap with a doubtful block. Pull over then up and left into a groove and up to a ledge below a steep groove. Ascend the groove for 3 metres then swing out right to gain a small ledge. Straight up to finish. **Waterstreak Wall Direct Finish**. (HVS (5a), 1988). Climb the steep groove direct to the top. **The Flakes** (VS (4a,4b), 1988). Start 4 metres right of Waterstreak Wall. Climb a wall, over a perched flake and up to a large pedestal. Follow the crack line out left to a groove and up this to the top. **Rib and Slab** (VS 4b), 1988). Start 3 metres right of The Flakes below a holly tree. Climb the rib and slab, stepping right round a dubious spike to a ledge. Scrambling to finish.

Buckbarrow   (135 057)   Alt. 350 m   South East Facing

Buckbarrow is actually a series of small crags scattered across the fellside above the Gosforth to Wasdale road. It yields some excellent climbing on rock that is generally fast drying and provides a real alternative within the Wasdale Valley to the often wet higher crags on Scafell and Gable. Some of the crags being nominally south-west facing hold the sun late into the day and occupy a pleasant situation overlooking the west end of Wastwater.

On first acquaintance with Buckbarrow, the crags may seem a little broken, however, with some careful selection high quality routes on clean sound rock can be found.

Approaching from Gosforth, The Wasdale road reaches a high point after approximately 7 km at Harrow Head Farm. The crags can now be seen up on the left.

Due to the complexity of Buckbarrow, on first acquaintance it is worth driving along the valley until directly below the crag, where identification of the various buttresses and approaches can more easily be made using the crag diagrams. This advice is particularly relevant to the Lakeland Pioneers Area and Eastern Crags where the best approach is from above.

For approaches to Lower Crag, Long Crag, Amphitheatre Buttress, Lakeland Pioneers Buttress, and The Eastern Crags it is best to park on the right about $^1/_2$ km along from Harrow Head Farm on the side of the access road to 'Little Ground'. The path follows the right-hand side of Gill Beck starting from a point where it passes under the road.

For approaches to Witch Buttress, Gully Buttress, Moss Slabs and White Band Ghyll park about $^1/_2$ km further along the road, where the wall on the right drops back. From here a small path leads directly up to the Witch Buttress area.

Pike Crag and Buckbarrow Needle can be approached from either direction.

The crags are described from left to right as are the routes.

Lower Crag

The lowest piece of worthwhile climbable rock lies just 10 minutes from the road. Either approach direct or by contouring from the Gill Beck path. The only real point of interest is the sharp central pillar. Descend on the left.

BUCKBARROW CRAG

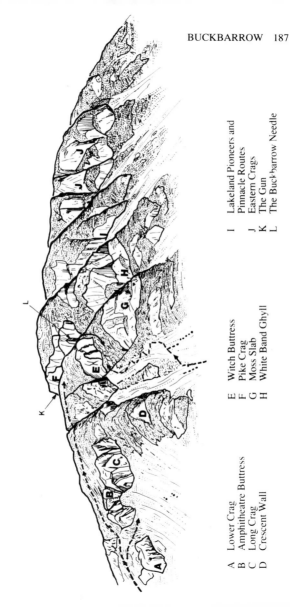

A Lower Crag
B Amphitheatre Buttress
C Long Crag
D Crescent Wall

E Witch Buttress
F Pike Crag
G Moss Slab
H White Band Ghyll

I Lakeland Pioneers and
   Pinnacle Routes
J Eastern Crags
K The Gun
L The Buckbarrow Needle

Bagatelle   36 m   MS   1970
A poor route starting up and left of Cassation at a dirty, easy-angled
buttress below an obvious diagonal fault line high up on the crag.
1   16 m. Climb the groove on the left followed by slabs.
2   20 m. Traverse down and right to the bottom of a groove. Climb
    the groove over a bulge into a niche, then exit right onto broken
    slabs which lead to the top.

Cassation   35 m   HS   1973
Start below the steep central pillar.
1   20 m. Climb steep rock to a bulge and gain a sloping ledge. Step
    awkwardly round a nose on the right, and then up to a ledge.
2   15 m. Follow the arête to the top.

Variation   20 m   VS
1a (4c). Climb steep rock to a bulge and gain a sloping ledge.
Continue up the groove above.

Amphitheatre Buttress

A steep, little crag at the top of the small amphitheatre up and left
of Long Crag. Not recommended. Descend on the left via steep grass,
then a broken rib that marks the left side of the buttress.

Amphitheatre Buttress   20 m   HVS   1973
Start just left of a small corner at the bottom of the descent rib.
    (5a). Pull over the bulge to gain the base of a steep slab, then
    make a difficult step up followed by a traverse right on small
    holds to an arête. Climb the arête to a ledge, traverse left then
    follow the steep arête to the top.

Girdle Traverse   30 m   VS   1973
Start at the right-hand edge of the wall next to a gully.
1   20 m (4c). Climb directly up the steep rock for 6 metres, then
    traverse left to gain the central groove which is followed up and
    left to a belay on the left edge.
2   10 m (4a). Climb the steep arête to the top.

Long Crag

A crag characterized by the steep blunt buttress in its lower central
section below a band of overhangs at half height. The climbing on
this central section is of good quality with strenuous, fingery moves

that require a positive approach. On either side and above, the angle eases to produce some routes of lesser grades and quality. A very accessible and fast drying crag, which is approached by following the Gill Beck path until a cairn marks the start of a sheep track, this contours above the Lower Crag, crossing a small stream before descending slightly across scree to the east of the crag (20 minutes).

To descend from the top of the crag traverse left over steep ground to above Amphitheatre Buttress, then follow the descent route for that crag. Descent from the Lower Buttress routes is by scrambling down the slab just left of the groove on pitch 1 of The Owl.

LONG CRAG

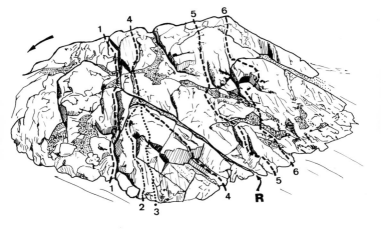

1	Injection	MVS	5	Hecate	VS
2	Un-Named Groove	HVS	6	Dang-a Ling	MVS
3	Red Garden Massacre	E3			
4	Lothlorian	HVS	R	Descent Ramp (Start of The Owl)	

Sideshow   30 m   S   1973
   A poor route that climbs a groove, starting about 20 metres up
   and left from the oak tree of Ejection, then up the broken rocks
   above.

Diamond Rib   52 m   MVS   1973
Broken but better than it looks. Start at an obvious diamond-shaped
block left of the oak tree of Ejection.
1   17 m (4b). Climb up the centre of the block, then up and left to
    the centre of the wall and up to a small ledge below a huge
    perched block. Pull out left and climb a V-groove to a ledge.
2   15 m. Climb the rib on the right to the overhang, traverse right
    to a break formed by hollow flakes and climb this to a ledge.
3   20 m (4a). Climb the pleasant slab above, step across a crevasse
    and climb a second slab to its top.

Ejection   45 m   VS   1973
A rather broken route but with an awkward start. Start at the oak up
and left from the toe of the buttress.
1   32 m (4b). From the oak awkward moves lead up to a rightward
    slanting crack, which is followed for a short distance until moves
    can be made up the wall above to a holly tree. Traverse left from
    the holly tree into a recessed corner, then go up the rib to grass
    ledges.
2   13 m. Climb the slabs above to the top.

Injection   40 m   MVS   1973
Just right of Ejection is a prominent corner and a little above this is
an obvious leaning groove. The groove provides an interesting
problem but the corner is very grassy and dirty in its lower section.
1   28 m. Climb the corner and wall on the right to an overhung
    ledge. Step back right and climb the steep corner, past a
    marauding holly tree, to finish up the left crack onto grass ledges.
    About 10 metres up the steep grass is the base of the leaning
    groove.
2   12 m (4a). Climb the groove.

Lower Buttress

About 15 metres right and down from the corner of Injection is a
very steep and compact buttress with a band of overhangs at half
height. The routes in this area take on a distinct character change.

★ **Un-named Groove**   25 m   HVS   1976

An excellent pitch that climbs the large shallow corner left of the overhangs. Start directly below the corner.

> (5a). Climb up into the base of the corner which is followed until forced out left at the top. Continue over easy ground breaking right to a tree belay.

Variation   25 m   VS   1976

> (4c). Where the corner steepens step out left onto the arête and climb up moving back right, into the groove at the top to finish.

Un-named Wall   25 m   HVS   1976

A good companion route to Un-named Groove.

> (5a). As for Un-named Groove to the base of the corner then step out right and climb up through the overlap finishing up a delicate slab to the tree belay.

The following three routes, after their initial steep fingery wall climbing, follow weakness's in the overhangs above giving them all an exposed and big route feeling.

★ **Red Garden Massacre**   32 m   E3   1986

A sustained problem with the protection difficult to place. Start below a steep crack line just left of Just Good Friends.

> (5c). Climb the awkward crack to where a move left leads to a large flat spike. The wall on the left is followed to an obvious slot, then climb above the slot to a ledge on a small arête. Continue up to breaks in the overhang that lead onto the slab above. Climb this to a tree belay.

★ **Just Good Friends**   32 m   E2   1986

A good sustained pitch.
Start in the middle of the wall at a diagonal crack containing two fossilized pegs.

> (5b). Swing up to the right along the crack to a good slot, then move back left along a gangway to the flat spike on Red Garden Massacre. Move right and up to a cone, then continue leftwards under an overlap until a break rightwards over the overhang can be made onto the top slab. Climb this to a tree belay.

★ **The Movie**   32 m   E2   1986

A fine pitch with an awkward start and an intimidating but well protected crux roof. Start just right of Just Good Friends.

(5c). Pull strenuously up the wall over small overlaps and continue leftwards up the steep slab to a break under the big roof. Climb the groove for a short distance, then make a difficult swing out right to gain a little undercut wall. (Jug at the top but a long reach). Continue rightwards onto easier ground above the big roof then up the slabs to a tree belay.

Lothlorian   70 m   HVS   1970
An interesting route with the difficulties being concentrated into the well protected overhanging crack on pitch 1. Start just right of the toe of the buttress below the obvious overhanging crack.
1   40 m (5a). Climb up to a sharp edged block below the overhanging crack. Pull strenuously over into the crack line above and follow it stepping out left at the top onto the rib. Climb the rib to a tree belay.
2   30 m (4a). The pleasant wall behind the tree is climbed on the left followed by slabs to the top.

Up and right of Lothlorian is the obvious easy angled groove climbed by The Owl, that runs up leftwards to the top of the Lower Buttress. Just left of this route is a convenient scramble descent for parties wishing to finish at the tree belay of Red Garden Massacre etc.

The Owl   53 m   VD   1973
Dirty and very broken in its upper section. Start at the bottom of the obvious leftwards slanting groove.
1   17 m. Climb the corner to a ledge.
2   18 m. Traverse right, across the wall on good holds, to a dirty rake. Easy ground leads up to a large flake belay at the base of a steep wall.
3   18 m. Climb up left over broken ground , then back right through a break onto easy slabs above the steep wall. Follow these to the top.

Variation   17 m   S   1979
A pleasant and worthwhile variation that makes a combination of this and pitch 2 of The Owl worth doing. Start 2 metres right of the original start below a groove.
1a. Climb the short wall to gain the groove then follow it leftwards to the belay ledge.

Variation Howl   18 m   E1   1988
A poor route.
3a. (5b). Climb the corner until above the level of the first overhang,
   then traverse right onto the steep wall using pinch grips. Go up
   the wall to an overlap, and pull over onto good holds in a groove.
   Move right and up to the top.

To the right of The Owl are some very dirty and uninviting slabs that
run up to below a steep headwall with a large square overhang at its
right-hand end. The headwall provides some interesting climbing but
unfortunately the approach pitches are poor.

Hecate   55 m   VS   1973
A good second pitch. Start just right of The Owl at the bottom of a
broken arête.
1   30 m (4a). Climb the arête, then go up the dirty slabs, trending
   left, to the large flake belay on pitch 2 of The Owl.
2   25 m (4b). Ascend the steep corner on the right, stepping right
   onto the rib at half height. Follow the shallow groove above,
   trending right then go straight up to finish.

Dang-a-Ling   60 m   MVS   1972
A good second pitch that climbs the clean wall just right of the large
square overhang, before being forced back left. Start about 6 metres
right of Hecate.
1   25 m (4a). Climb the slabs, past a doubtful flake, to a corner
   below the square cut overhang.
2   25 m (4b). Traverse right and up to the bottom of a crack in the
   clean wall. Up this, then traverse left on good holds above the
   overhang, and make a short descent to the left to reach a shallow
   groove. Go up the groove to a ledge below a small overhang.
3   10 m (4a). A line of good holds lead off right, beneath the
   overhang to a break. Finish up this.

Three routes have been recorded to the right of Dang-a-Ling but are
best left in peace. **Joint Effort** (VD, †, 1974), the rib left of a slabby
rake. This could not be unearthed during checking. **Kestrel** (HS,
1974) climbs a broken detached buttress on the right, but the approach
would deter most. **Bran Flake** (HS, 1988) climbs the obvious curving
crack in the small buttress on the right.

Girdle Traverse   82 m   VS   1974
Basically a poor route with one or two interesting moves starting up
Ejection then crossing the crag diagonally rightwards to finish up
Dang-a-Ling.

A Cut Above, Witch Buttress, Buckbarrow

1   30 m (4b). Climb up to the holly on Ejection and traverse right to the tree belay on Un-named Groove.
2   22 m (4b). Descend the groove line of The Owl for a short distance to the bottom of a steep diagonal black crack. Hand traverse the crack finishing with a difficult pull onto the slab above. Climb the crack above to the flake belay on The Owl.
3   20 m (4a). Traverse right and slightly down to a large block under a groove. Climb the groove then go up to the belay on pitch 2 of Dang-a-Ling. The quality of this pitch is improved by climbing pitch 2 of Hecate to belay under the small overhang as for Dang-a-Ling pitch 2.
4   10 m (4a). As pitch 3 of Dang-a-Ling.

Crescent Wall

100 metres right of and just below the level of Long Crag is a red wall, with an overlap at its right-hand end. The climbs here are dirty with some alarmingly loose flakes. **Crescent Wall** (HS, 1975) climbs the centre of the wall and over the roof via a crack. **Crescent Crack** (S, 1975) climbs the corner crack on the right starting behind the huge flake. **Crescent Ridge** (VD, 1975) takes the dirty V-groove right of the overlap.

Gully Buttress

This crag lies on the right-hand side of the open scree slope right of Crescent Wall at about the same level as and left of Witch Buttress. The crag, which has a steep left side and slabby face, is unattractive and receives few visits, even from the locals. The climbs are briefly described as follows with the best reference point being the shattered groove of Jamie about 15 metres up from the bottom left-hand toe of the crag.

Jim's Wall (VS (5a), 1986) climbs the steep wall and groove just left of Jamie to finish up the rib on the left. **Jamie** (VS (4c), 1973) up over broken blocks and climb the groove either finishing out left over steep loose ground or straight up the groove via the slightly easier **Direct Finish** (VS (4c), 1986). **Tramline** (VS (4c,4b) 1973) climbs the broken rock starting at a detached block left of the toe of the buttress followed by a crack on the left to finish up a wall and V-groove. **Slab and Groove** (MVS (4a,4a,), 1974) climb the slab and groove just right of Tramline to below an obvious groove which is followed, trending right, to the top. **Scorpion** (VS (4a,4b), 1973) start just left of an obvious crack in the front of the buttress. Climb the wall above a recess, then go up and left to a sentry box (poor protection). The steep rock on the right leads to the top. **Prickle** (MVS (-,4a), 1973) start 3 metres right of Scorpion. Climb the corner and wall above moving left into a groove. An awkward move leads up into an easier groove. Finish to the right.

Witch Buttress

The most obvious and cleanest piece of rock on the hillside being easily identified by its fine central detached pillar with a pleasant grassy ledge below. The left edge of this pillar is climbed by Wild West Show, one of the local test pieces. The climbing on Witch Buttress is amongst the best on the mountain with excellent quality routes in the harder grades on rock that is generally good, and quick drying. Just above Witch Buttress lies the long outcrop of Pike Crag which makes it possible to link together pitches on the lower and upper tiers resulting in some excellent long combinations. Approach by ascending directly up the hillside from the road (approximately 20 minutes).

The best descent is by following the rake down right (the upper section of White Band Ghyll) until reaching a small path that leads back left and down over a rock step to the base of the central pillar. The routes are described from left to right.

Gagarin   60 m   VD   1961
Start 18 metres left of the central detached pillar at the base of a rib on the right-hand side of a scree gully.
1   23 m. Climb the rib, bearing right to a ledge, then the short wall followed by a step up left onto a slab. The short corner above leads to a stance.
2   17 m. Move left to the edge, then climb up, breaking right, over mossy slabs to a clean rib. Belay's above a corner stance.
3   20 m. The easy ridge ahead leads to an obvious crack. Climb the crack followed by a ridge and slabs above.

A Cut Above   25 m   E1   1983
A pleasant pitch which climbs the left arête of Witch Buttress in its upper half. Start 4 metres right of the foot of the arête.
   (5b). Climb direct up the shallow corner to the groove of The Mysteron which is followed to where a diagonal crack leads out

left onto the arête. Follow this to a junction with Gagarin just left of the rib, up which it finishes.

★ The Mysteron   35 m   HVS

A good climb with the second pitch providing a safe introduction to the harder routes on the crag. Start below a large corner left of the central detached pillar.

1   10 m. Climb up and left to a large flake below the large overhanging corner of Imagine.

2   25 m (5b). Traverse left below a green wall to a groove. Climb this then make a committing move (crux) onto a small ledge high on the left. Continue straight up the crack until it is possible to step left into a crack that leads to the ridge and a junction with Gagarin. Finish up Gagarin.

★ Swipe   30 m   E2   1983

A technical and sustained pitch that climbs the leftward slanting ramp from the groove on Imagine.

(5c). As for Imagine pulling into the steep groove, then immediately move left onto the ramp and climb it until it almost finishes. Make a difficult pull into a short groove and follow it until the angle eases. Above is a cleaned wall, climb it direct to the top and a junction with Gagarin.

★★ Imagine   38 m   E1   1981

An excellent route giving steep and sustained climbing up the overhanging groove and continuation corner right of The Mysteron.

1   25 m (5b). Climb the large flake as for The Mysteron and pull into the steep groove on the right. Difficult moves up the groove lead to the roof (thread runner), pull over on undercuts and good jugs into the easier continuation corner which is followed, trending right, to below an undercut crack.

2   13 m (5a). Awkward moves give access to the crack that leads to the top.

Torch Song Trilogy   40 m   E5   †   1987

An eliminate line climbing the steep arête left of West Side Story direct. The climbing is very bold and dynamic and is poorly protected. Start at the bottom of the arête that forms the right-hand side of the corner climbed by Imagine.

1   25 m (6b). Climb the arête direct to a junction with West Side Story before the gangway, then continue straight up until rejoining it in its upper section which is then followed to the top, and the belay on Imagine.

2   15 m (5c). Climb the wall between the cracks of West Side Story and Imagine to the top.

★★ **West Side Story**   39 m   E4   1981
An excellent route giving sustained and exposed climbing with protection which is adequate but not obvious. The climb takes the groove line in the face right of Imagine. Start as for The Mysteron.
1   27 m (6a). Climb up left to a flake below the steep corner of Imagine. Pull up right across the wall onto a sloping ledge. Protection for the next few moves can be arranged high up on the gangway but is placed blind. Climb the rightwards sloping gangway to gain a shallow groove that leads up to a small overhang. Step left and follow a crack then an easier rib to a sloping ledge and the belay of Imagine.
2   12 m (4c). Step left and climb the crack and rib above to easy ground.

Agent Orange   35 m   HVS   1981
Climbs the left wall of Harmony via a rib and thin crack.
(5b). Climb the wide crack of Harmony until it is possible to pull onto the blunt rib on the left. Follow the rib and continuation crack to a ledge. Finish up the short crack on the right.

Harmony   35 m   HVS
The wide crack on the left side of the central pillar. Ignore the images created by the name as the climbing is very strenuous with a difficult and frustrating start.
1   23 m (5b). Climb the crack to a niche below a dirty groove. Continue up the groove and pull out right at the top, or climb the rib on the right.
2   12 m (4c). Pitch 2 of Witch.

To the right, between the cracks of Harmony and Witch is the detached central pillar containing a number of routes of high quality with crux pitches which are steep, hard and committing.

★★ **Wild West Show**   40 m   E5   1981
The left arête of the pillar. A sustained and exposed technical problem requiring a confident approach.
1   27 m (6b). Climb the arête for 5 metres (good protection round left of the arête but not obvious), make a long reach out right, then move up and back left onto the arête. Continue up the arête until forced out right again onto the wall at 12 metres. Step up,

then regain the arête, and continue more easily to the top of the pillar. A precarious pitch.

2   13 m (4c). The rib and groove above to the top.

★★ **Final Curtain**   40 m   E6   1989
Although effectively being a variation start to East Enders the end result is an extremely bold and serious undertaking requiring a positive approach on its poorly protected lower section. Due to its ground fall potential it is advisable to pad the large boulder at the bottom. Start at the large boulder between Wild West Show and East Enders.

1   27 m (6b). From the top of the boulder step up and left onto obvious footholds, then move up for 2 metres until a delicate traverse right can be made to an obvious undercling (nut runner). Make a long reach up left to a small hold on the bulging wall followed by some very difficult and committing moves up to a hold below a small overlap and a junction with East Enders. (It is possible to escape onto Wild West Show and good protection at this point if required.) Move left to an obvious undercut in the centre of the wall and reach up to a large but sloping hold. Continue more easily, trending right, to the top of the pinnacle.

2   13 m (4c). As pitch 2 of Witch.

★ **East Enders**   39 m   E4   1987
Steep and intimidating climbing up the right-hand side of the pillar, cunningly protected by small wires. Start as for Witch.

1   26 m (6a). Climb Witch for a couple of metres before moving left onto the rib which leads to a triangular overhang at 6 metres. Step left delicately, and climb the steep wall to the left-hand side of a small overlap. Move left to an obvious undercut in the centre of the wall and reach up to a large but sloping hold. Continue more easily, trending right, to the top of the pinnacle.

2   13 m (4c). As pitch 2 of Witch.

★ **Witch**   40 m   VS   1961
A justifiably popular route of traditional style taking the obvious chimney line on the right-hand side of the central pillar.

1   27 m (4c). Climb the chimney for 10 metres then move right with difficulty into a small niche. Good holds lead up the wall to regain the chimney/crack line above the overhang. Follow the crack to the top of the pillar.

2   13 m (4c). Step up and left into the open groove that leads to the top.

★★ Too Many Hands   40 m   E2   1981

An excellent steep pitch with spaced protection. 4 metres right of Witch and 15 metres from the ground is a large wedged block. A thin crack runs up the right-hand side of this block and through the overhang above. Start just left of the crack line, right of Witch.

(5b). Enter the fault/crack line from the left and follow it to the large wedged block. Climb the continuation crack above to a pinnacle then step off this into the hanging corner. A long reach gives access to the next short corner which is exited left onto a ledge at its top. Exposed moves now lead out right across the steep slab to the arête where easier climbing leads to the top.

★ Pace Maker   40 m   VS   1981

A surprisingly enjoyable pitch climbing the obvious corner 5 metres right of Too Many Hands. Start at the bottom of the corner.

(4c). Climb the corner to a bulge, step left into the next corner and follow this until forced out right to the rib that leads up to a ledge. Step diagonally left to a spike then up to a ledge below a steep corner. Climb the corner which is difficult to start, up to the top.

Just right of Pace Maker is a steep broken rib beyond which the crag falls back into an area of mossy slabs, starting a short distance up the fellside. The following route makes the best of the broken rib.

Captain Scarlet   45 m   HS

Start at the bottom of the rib.
1   30 m. Ascend the rib and wall above, trending right at 15 metres, then back left to a grass ledge.
2   15 m. From the right-hand end of the ledge, move up to another ledge, then traverse right and up a corner to the top.

Divertimento   33 m   VD   1973

The dirty slab just right of Captain Scarlet provides a convenient way to the top of Witch Buttress and no more.

Climb the slab to a ledge, then the corner above avoiding the bulge on the right.

The following two routes provide interesting pitches climbing the slabs and overlap right of Divertimento.

The Stitch   25 m   VS   1982

Start just right of Divertimento at a cleaned crack.

(4c). Climb the crack to the obvious break in the overlap. Climb this and the slab above to the top.

Satin   25 m   HVS   1983
Start at the same point as The Stitch.
(5a). Climb straight up to the overlap, pull over this and continue up the slab to the top.

★★ **Freebird**   67 m   E2   1983
A sustained girdle of the Witch Buttress providing three difficult pitches on good clean rock with thought provoking and exposed situations. Care required to protect the second. Start below an arête just left of A Cut Above.
1   20 m (5c). Climb the arête to a bulge, pull over this rightwards to step onto a small ledge (the crucial crux hold on Mysteron). Step up then go rightwards crossing Swipe to a belay in the corner of Imagine, just above the overhang.
2   12 m (5b). Step onto the rib on the right and descend 3 metres to below the overhang. Traverse right to a rib then descend this to a belay in the V-groove of Harmony. (The first section of this pitch reverses West Side Story.)
3   17 m (5c). Gain the rib on the right climbed by Wild West Show, then traverse right, to the centre of the pinnacle. Ascend slightly, then descend to the right rib and swing round this to below a small square roof. Continue horizontally right to belay on the large jammed blocks of Too Many Hands.
4   18 m (4c). Climb the right-hand of the two cracks above up to a bulge, then go diagonally right to a rocky shelf and a junction with Pacemaker. Step up left into a short corner, exit right and up to the top.

Moss Slab

A large and uninviting recessed slab about 60 metres below and right of the start of Witch. Approach as for Witch Buttress but take an ascending traverse right at a holly tree round to the bottom of the slab. The climbs in this area are generally of poor quality and are briefly described as follows. The arête on the left of the slab can be climbed at Difficult standard. **Left-Hand Route** (S, 1974), climb the left corner crack with a short section on the right slab at half height (the best route available). **Central Line** (VD, 1974), the centre of the slab. **J.C.B. G.T.** (MS, 1974), the name says it all. Climb the slab and corner on the right of Central Line. **Short and Brutish** (S, 1974), as for J.C.B. G.T. but trending right. **Dunn's Delight** (S, 1974), the rib, V-chimney and ramp right of Short and Brutish.

Pike Crag

The line of crags above Witch Buttress, starting on the right of a prominent pinnacle climbed by the Buckbarrow Needle. Although a little broken the crags have some excellent lines particularly in the area of the pinnacle. Approach as for Witch Buttress, then via its descent track on the right up to a rake that leads back left to the base of the pinnacle or by following the Gill Beck path up the shoulder until reaching the rock step that marks the left-hand end of the crag. The Gun will be seen directly ahead with an easy angled ascent/descent slab on its right (cairned).

A number of descents are available and are fairly obvious. Routes are described from right to left.

★ **Living in Sin**   15 m   E1   1984
A poorly protected and serious line up the thin crack in the bulging wall just right of the corner on Junkie and 10 metres right of the Needle.
>   (5a). Follow the crack to a scoop then a ledge. Step right and climb the arête to the top.

Junkie   22 m   E1   1981
A deceptively difficult little route starting below the steep green corner 5 metres right of Needless Eliminate.
>   (5b). Climb the corner to where the angle eases then step left into a groove. which leads to the top.

Mainline   22 m   E2   1981
A straightened out version of Junkie giving steep and fingery crack climbing. Start below the bulging crack between the obvious corner of Junkie and Needless Eliminate.
>   (5c). Climb the awkward crack direct until a long reach can be made onto easier ground above. Follow the groove of Junkie to the top.

★★ **Needless Eliminate**   22 m   E1   1979
A fine pitch climbing the groove and crack just right of The Buckbarrow Needle. Start in the corner just right of the crack of the right-hand start of The Buckbarrow Needle.

(5b). Hand traverse diagonally left to a large spike then pull onto a ledge on the right. Step back left and climb the well protected crack direct to the top.

Belter   23 m   E4   1983
Climbs the steep bulging arête up the front of the pinnacle using a thin crack on the right. Short and brutish. Start directly below the crack.
1   13 m (6b). Climb up to a bulge, (Friend slot high up or a good hand-hold, make your choice). A difficult pull through the bulge leads to easier ground and the top of the pinnacle.
2   10 m (4c). As pitch 2 of The Buckbarrow Needle.

★ **Needle Front**   23 m   E1   1979
Pleasant climbing on good rock up the left-hand side of the pinnacle. Start just right of The Buckbarrow Needle left-hand start.
1   13 m (5b). Climb up the wall just right of the crack, then follow a line of footholds onto the right arête, and up to the top of the pinnacle.
2   10 m (4c). As pitch 2 of The Buckbarrow Needle.

★ **The Buckbarrow Needle**   23 m   VS
An interesting climb of traditional character, the first pitch climbing the obvious crack on either the right of left-hand side of the pinnacle.
1   13 m (4b). Climb either of the cracks to the top of the pinnacle.
2   10 m (4c). Step off the pinnacle onto the wall above, and make a bold move up on small holds to easier ground above.

★ **Last of the Summer Wine**   22 m   E1   1982
Good climbing up the steep wall just left of The Buckbarrow Needle finishing with an intimidating crack up the overhanging wall. Start just left of The Buckbarrow Needle left-hand start at some small grassy ledges.
   (5b). Climb the groove and step right onto a flake, continue up the wall trending right until it is possible to swing across left into the base of the overhanging crack. (Good runner.) Straight up the crack to the top.

Atlantis   22 m   E2   1983
A sustained pitch. Start as for Last of the Summer Wine.
   (5b). Climb the thin crack and make a difficult move into a scoop, up this to the top.

Banana   20 m   VS
The obvious dirty fault line 3 metres left of The Buckbarrow Needle. More awkward than it looks.
(4c). Climb directly up the fault line and the deep groove above to the top.

Sunset Strip   40 m   VS   1975
Climbs the obvious crack running up the slab about 3 metres left of Banana. A good first pitch but then broken.
1   20 m (4b). Climb the crack to a good ledge, then step left onto a steep slab which is followed with increasing difficulty to a grassy bay.
2   20 m (4a). Up the corners above and over a doubtful block to a flake crack, Climb this to the top.

To the left of Sunset Strip this first section of crag gradually reduces in height to finish at a huge detached block where a grass rake leads back right to the top of The Buckbarrow Needle area. (The normal descent for routes in this section.) Numerous short routes exist in this area with various conflicting claims for first ascents and true lines. It is considered to be best left as a play area.

Above the grassy descent terrace the rocks are very broken and uninviting. Left of the huge detached block the crag improves again with some excellent routes of up to 40 metres in length. The most obvious line at its right-hand end is the wide diagonal crack of Santa Fe situated on the first section of continuous steep rock after the block.

Rooster   42 m   S   1975
Start below a steep little wall just right of Blind Faith.
1   12 m. Climb the wall on good holds to the terrace and belay under a rightwards slanting groove.
2   30 m. Enter the groove and follow it until a pull up left leads to a good ledge. Climb the crack and rib above to the top.

Blind Faith   37 m   HVS   1985
Steep climbing up the wall just right of the slanting crack of Santa Fe. Start below a right angled corner.
1   22 m (5a). Climb the corner to a grass ledge below an overhung scoop. Straight up over the overhang and the wall above to finish just right of the crack of Santa Fe.
2   15 m. Easy grooves to the top.

Santa Fe   40 m   VS   1982
Deceptive climbing up the wide diagonal crack. Start at the bottom
of a short groove below the crack.
      (4c). Climb the groove and wall above on large blocks. The crack
      is followed with difficulty to a ledge then up the groove on the
      left.

Mark Twain   30 m   VS   1975
Steep climbing with its fair share of moss and loose rock. Start as
for Santa Fe.
1   20 m (4b). Climb the slab into a niche below a bulge. Pass this
      on the left over loose blocks, then a steep mossy wall and a crack
      that leads to a grass ledge.
2   10 m. The V-groove above leads to the top.

About 7 metres left of Santa Fe is the groove line of Funnel with a
steep grooved wall on its right containing an obvious small square
overhang near the top. The following two routes climb this wall.

Hermes   35 m   HVS
Steep climbing up the grooved wall avoiding the overhang on the
right.
      (5a). Make awkward moves up the wall to gain the groove that
      runs up to the overhang. Climb the groove, then step out right at
      half height onto a narrow ramp and crack that leads up to a ledge.
      Finish up the groove.

★ **Flannel**   35 m   E1   1982
A good bold pitch tackling the problem avoided by Hermes.
      (5b). As for Hermes but continue straight up the groove to below
      the overhang. Difficult bridging up the groove leads to a small
      pocket below the overhang, this is followed by a bold pull up
      rightwards onto easier ground and up to the top.

Funnel   40 m   VD   1975
Interesting climbing with a difficult finish. Start below the cleaned
groove with a funnel shaped niche at half height.
1   30 m. Climb the groove to a grass ledge, then the chimney and
      slab to a spike belay in a grassy bay.
2   10 m. Straight over the bulge above to the top.

Jockey   40 m   HVS   †
Start as for Funnel.
(5a). Follow Funnel to the grass ledge then climb directly up the fault line to the top.

About 5 metres left of the groove on Funnel the crag splits into two tiers, with a distinct earthy right-facing corner and wide crack being formed. Just right of this corner a groove runs up into an obvious recess, with a continuation crack line above, this is climbed by The Jewel.

Alchemy   38 m   HVS   1985
Fingery climbing up the steep wall to the right of The Jewel. Start below a thin crack 3 metres right of The Jewel at an embedded block.
(5a). Make a difficult pull up the crack onto the wall and up to a niche on the right. Climb straight up from the niche to a grass ledge then the easy rib on the left to the top. (The pitch can be split at the grass ledge.)

The Jewel   38 m   VS   1971
An interesting problem that can be improved by gaining the recess via the crack start of Alchemy thus missing the normal earthy gully start.
(4c). Climb the nasty earth gully for 5 metres then traverse right into a groove that leads up steeply into a recess. Make a few moves up the crack out of the top of the recess, until forced out right and up to a ledge. The groove and rib on the right leads easily to the top.

The Crystal   25 m   E2   1982
Steep and fingery climbing up the clean wall left of The Jewel with a poorly protected crux. Scramble up past the foot of The Jewel to a grass ledge on the left.
(5c). Step up onto the wall, then make difficult moves on quartz holds up past a horizontal crack to gain a sloping hold. Move up to better holds and into a large scoop, cross this to the rib on the left then swing round the rib left and up to the top.

Joanne   40 m   HVS   1982
Starts at the lowest point of the lower tier, down and left of the start of The Jewel. The second pitch climbs the obvious crack line just left of The Crystal.
1   20 m (4a). Climb the wall bearing right to the grass terrace.

2   20 m (5a). Step across right into the steep crack (protection) and
    climb it to a slab. Climb the obvious groove above, step left at
    the top and finish up the wall.

The Runt   32 m   E2   1984
A steep little problem with the peg runner gained after the crux
moves, hence the usual long piece of in-situ tape. Well named. Start
as for Josephine.
1   14 m (4b). As pitch 1 of Josephine.
2   18 m (5c). Climb the blank, overhanging corner left of Joanne
    past the peg runner, then more easily to the top.

★ **The Catch**   32 m   E1   1983
A good climb with a sustained second pitch. Start as for Josephine.
1   14 m (4b). As pitch 1 of Josephine.
2   18 m (5b). Start below the overhanging wall 3 metres left of the
    corner of The Runt. Step up onto the wall then swing strenuously
    up and right to gain a small ledge on the easier angled wall above.
    Continue up delicately bearing left to a crack that leads to the
    top.

Josephine   32 m   VS   1975
Interesting climbing. Start 3 metres right of Borodino below a cleaned
groove.
1   14 m (4b). Climb the groove exiting right onto a grass terrace.
2   18 m (4b). Climb the corner left of The Catch to the top.

Borodino   32 m   HS   1971
Start on the left side of the lower tier, left of a holly tree.
1   15 m. Climb the left side of a small pinnacle, step left and then
    up to a grass terrace.
2   17 m. Move right to a corner and climb over the cracked blocks
    to a ledge. The overhanging groove above leads with difficulty to
    the top.

Shameless   20 m   MVS   1978
Start below a corner formed between the left end of the grass terrace
and the wall. Not recommended.
    (4a). Climb the corner and up an easy slab. At its top pull left
    into a groove and up to the top.

Left of the grass terrace crossed by Borodino is a prominent roof at
the top of a steep wall and corner which is climbed by Rob's Corner
and Rob's Roof. After this the crag gradually becomes very broken

until finally becoming a single rock step, and ending with The Gun the last of the recorded climbs.

★ **Cretin Hop**   23 m   E2   1982
The steep intimidating arête right of Rob's Corner. Good climbing on clean rock. Start at the bottom of the arête.
(5c). Climb the arête mainly on its slabby left-hand side until a move can be made into a niche round to the right of the arête. Pull out of the niche (crux) using the crack above, to good holds and the top.

Rob's Corner   23 m   VS   1975
Interesting climbing with one or two awkward moments. Start just left of Cretin Hop below a wall and obvious corner capped on its left-hand side by an overhang.
(4c). Make difficult moves up the wall, then climb the corner with increasing difficulty finishing up the right wall.

★ Variation   Rob's Roof   23 m   VS   1975
An improved finish with exposed moves over the roof.
(4c). As Rob's Corner but then traverse left under the roof to its centre. Pull over and up to the top.

The following two routes climb the broken ground left of Rob's Corner, starting with the rib **Goodness Nose** (VS (4c), 1978) which climbs a crack past a rock shelf then up a small buttress crossing a conspicuous nose on the right. **Cripes** (MVS (4a), 1978). Left of the top part of Goodness Nose is an obvious chimney corner. Climb the rib directly below, then the awkward chimney to the top.

About 40 metres left of Rob's Corner is a south-west facing pillar of rock which, given a certain level of artistic licence, is shaped like a revolver. The front of the pillar is climbed by The Gun and the obvious right-hand crack by Epidemic Crack.

Epidemic Crack   10 m   VS   1983
(5a). Climb up to an inverted-V roof. Pull through into the crack above and up to the top.

The Gun   10 m   HVS   1984
(4c). Climb the front face of the pillar, involving some long reaches and widely spaced protection.

To the left of The Gun are a series of short top-rope/bouldering problems which catch the last of the evening sun.

White Band Ghyll

From just below The Buckbarrow Needle, a grassy rake/gully runs diagonally down right (true left) to the base of the crags. The lower 30 metres is a deep gash capped by three chockstones giving the climb White Band Gully. On the crest of the right wall a line of white rock, The White Band, runs upwards and is followed by an indifferent route at difficult standard. This feature can best be seen from well below the crag. The right wall of the gully contains the main climbing and although being rather broken gives some pleasant pitches.

The ghyll can be reached from Moss Slab by traversing slightly down and right for 30 metres, then scrambling up the easy left ridge of White Band Gully into the ghyll proper.

The climbs are described starting at the bottom of the ghyll. Descent is by scrambling up, then moving off left and down to regain the top of the grassy rake.

The White Band   100 m   D
A poor route lacking direction that wanders up the line of the white rock band.

White Band Gully   32 m   S   1974
A traditional thrutch.
1   20 m. Climb the delicate slab on the left wall of the gully then pull into a cave below the chockstones.
2   12 m. Fight your way onto the first chockstone and climb the crack above to finish in the grassy gully.

The Gangway   38 m   VS   1974
Interesting climbing up the right edge of the gully. Start as for White Band Gully.
1   18 m (4b). Climb the awkward slabby ramp on the right edge of the gully until a move up right leads to a grass ledge.
2   20 m (4a). Move back left to the edge of the gully and climb up the wall until it is possible to step left across a niche. Continue traversing left to a sloping ledge below a slab, climb this on doubtful holds then step left into the grassy ghyll.

The next climb starts below a steep groove about 10 metres up the grassy ghyll and 4 metres left of a grassy bay with a large perched boulder.

Cromlech Groove   60 m   VS   1974

A scrappy route with a poorly protected first pitch.

1   24 m (4b). Climb the steep groove for 5 metres and make a committing move right, then up to a landing. Move up and left over a slab and grass ledge followed by a crack up to a stance.

2   12 m (4a). Step right and climb the groove to a ledge and up another short groove on the right.

3   24 m (4a). Traverse left for 9 metres and climb the steep narrow slab, moving right to a recess above a bulge on the left edge. Continue up to a terrace.

Up and left of Cromlech Groove is a recess where the cleaned crack of Serendipity leads out left. This crack is clearly visible from the road.

Centre Post   35 m   MVS   1974

Start below the recess. Some doubtful holds.

(4a). Move up right onto the rib and climb it until a move back left gains a groove that leads to a slab. Climb the slab either on its left or right-hand side to the top.

Serendipity   60 m   HS   1974

Pleasant but broken climbing.

1   20 m. Easily up the crack past a bulge, to a ledge. Step right and continue up the crack to another ledge.

2   30 m. The groove above leads to a terrace followed by scrambling up to below a cracked wall.

3   10 m. Up the wall to the top.

Tickle-me-Fancy   40 m   MVS   1974

Start just left of Serendipity below a steep grooved rib with an overhang on the right at its top. A good first pitch.

1   18 m (4a). Climb the groove to a small ledge, then move delicately right under the overhang to its right-hand side. Climb up then back left to a ledge. Belays high on the right.

2   22 m. Step left and climb the crack up the wall, then easier ground to the top.

Nameless Crack   36 m   VS
The dirty and uninviting prominent corner, capped by an overhang
and with a suspect chockstone at half height. Start below a corner,
just right of a pillar with a wide crack on its left-hand side, a few
metres left of Tickle-me-Fancy.
1   10 m (4a). Climb the corner crack to a grass ledge below the
     prominent corner.
2   26 m (4b). Continue up the corner, pull out left over a chockstone,
     then up the groove and wall above to the top.

Florence   40 m   HS   1974
Start 10 metres left of Nameless Crack below an obvious flake crack
that leads up to a grass terrace.
1   15 m. Climb the crack past a ledge followed by an awkward
     layback move up to a terrace.
2   25 m. The grooved ridge on the right is climbed past a reclining
     monolith to a grass terrace.

Zebedee   40 m   VD   1974
The square fronted buttress, bounded on the right by Florence. Start
below its lowest point.
1   15 m. Climb up to a bulge, pull over and up to a grass ledge.
2   25 m. As pitch 2 of Florence.

Left of Zebedee is a square cut chimney with a short buttress on its
left, containing a sentry box low down. This marks the start of the
next route.

Dougal   27 m   VS   1974
Two short difficult pitches complete with the ubiquitous grass ledge
and doubtful rock.
1   13 m (4c). Climb into the sentry box, pull up left onto a doubtful
     block then up the crack to the grass ledge.
2   14 m (4b). Up the wall above via a mantelshelf and climb the
     groove, then pull right into a second groove and up to the top.

Magic Roundabout   140 m   VS   †   1974
An ascending girdle of the right wall of White Band Ghyll. Some
good bits, some bad bits and a contrived start, but basically a
reasonable way of getting in some footage. Start as for The Gangway
at the bottom right-hand side of White Band Gully.
1   18 m (4b). As pitch 1 of The Gangway.
2   20 m (4a). As pitch 2 of The Gangway, then walk up the ghyll
     for 10 metres to the start of Cromlech Groove.

3   24 m (4b). As pitch 1 of Cromlech Groove.
4   30 m (4b). Traverse left, crossing a groove to the rib on Centre
    Post, then continue left into the crack on pitch 1 of Serendipity
    below the bulge. Traverse left, past a perched block to the groove
    on Tickle-me-Fancy which is followed until a crack leads off left
    to join Nameless Route halfway up the corner crack on pitch 1.
    Climb up to the grass ledge.
5   23 m. Go up and left to the crack on Florence which is followed
    up to a terrace.
6   25 m. As pitch 2 of Florence.

Lakeland Pioneers Buttress and Pinnacle Routes Area

East of White Band Ghyll is a wide scree gully that runs down
diagonally right eventually fanning out onto the fellside. Running up
the right-hand side of this gully are a series of small buttresses, that
in spite of their initial appearance, give some excellent short and
generally steep pitches. Due to their south-west aspect, the buttresses
catch the sun and dry quickly.

The main feature in the gully and a useful reference point is a 20
metres high detached, flat-faced pinnacle situated about halfway up
the gully on the right-hand side. Approach by the Gill Beck path up
the shoulder, as for Pike Crag, then scramble up the easy descent slab
right of The Gun and follow the track east over the rocky top.
Descend a rock step down to a grass hollow then bear off right and
descend the scree gully to the pinnacle. Alternatively walk from the
road straight up the fellside to the bottom of the gully (hard work
and boring – approximately 40 minutes).

Descents are generally to the left and care should be taken to avoid
dislodging loose rock above the crag. The routes are located with
reference to the pinnacle and described from left to right down the
gully.

Two routes have been recorded on a little buttress above Zeke at the
top of the gully and are briefly; **B.J.** (MVS, (4a), 1985), climbs the
centre of the wall following a groove and then slabs. **J.P.** (MVS, (4a),
1985), the cracked groove on the front edge. It should be noted that
the climbing in this area is very broken with numerous loose blocks.

Up to the left of Lakeland Pioneers Buttress is a small detached buttress with an obvious steep leftwards leaning crack on its left-hand side

Shorty 10 m HVS   1984
(5a). Pull over the small overlap at the bottom and climb the thin crack strenuously to the top.

Zeke 30 m MS   1984
Climbs the left arête of Lakeland Pioneers Buttress. Starting from the left climb the arête and continuation ridge to the top.

Harriet 30 m E1   1984
Start about 3 metres right of the left arête of the Lakeland Pioneers Buttress.
(5b). Climb up to the open groove, left of the prow, then up this awkwardly exiting right, and up the ridge more easily to the top.

Norma Jean 33 m E3   1984
Climbs the steep wall left of Lakeland Pioneers breaking out left at the top. The crux is protected by a peg runner which normally has a length of tape hanging from it. This helps in identifying the line. Start just left of Lakeland Pioneers.
1   15 m (5a). Climb the middle of the wall up to a ledge then continue up slightly left to a ledge and block belay.
2   18 m (6a). Step left and pull onto a ledge at 3 metres. The next few moves up to and past the peg runner, are hard but lead to good holds. Continue up left to the arête and more easily to the top.

★★ **Lakeland Pioneers** 35 m E1   1984
The best route on the gully walls climbing the crack, then the obvious right-facing corner above the break, left of the pinnacle. Start 2 metres left of the pinnacle below a corner crack.
(5b). Climb the corner crack starting at the right side of a V-shaped bay, and continue straight up, via an awkward mantelshelf to a ledge. Pull up into the steep right-facing corner that leads direct to the top. (This pitch can be split at the ledge.)

The Pinnacle Routes

Left Edge Route   18 m   HVS   1984
Exposed situations in its upper section.
    (5a). Climb the left-hand wall, then swing out onto the arête, and finish straight up to the top.

Pinnacle Face Direct   20 m   E3   1984
Climbs the gently overhanging front face of the pinnacle. A very fingery and sustained pitch with some suspect rock but adequately protected. Start just left of Pinnacle Face.
    (6a). Climb up leftwards for 3 metres, reach a large incut hold and move back rightwards to a peg runner. Difficult moves up leftwards lead past another peg runner and then more easily to the top.

Pinnacle Face   23 m   E1   1984
Poorly protected with a nasty landing. Start in the middle of the face.
    (5a). Step off the block onto the wall and make a scary pull up to gain a small ledge on the right. Move up right to a Thank God hidden side hold, then up to a big ledge. Continue up the easier groove on the left.

Right Edge Route   25 m   E1   1984
Good climbing up the right-hand (south) face of the pinnacle. Start at the bottom directly below a small overhang on the arête.
    (5b). Climb up to a peg runner under the overhang. Reach out right to small but good incut holds, then pull up onto the wall and straight up to an easier slab and the top.

Flakey Wall   30 m   HVS   1984
Right of the pinnacle is a chimney with an obvious and uninviting loose flakey wall on its right-hand side. Start 3 metres right of the chimney at a corner.
    (5a). Climb the corner on good holds, then up to an overhang at 12 metres. Swing across the wall on the right using large blocks and flakes with care. Step up and left into a groove and finish up this and a slab on the right to the top. Frightening.

Right of Flakey Wall is a steep grassy rake running up diagonally right which serves as a useful descent. About 12 metres up this rake is the steep dirty corner climbed by The Great Unwashed.

Old Strands   15 m   VS   1984
A serious pitch with some suspect rock. Start as for The Great
Unwashed.
    (4c). Climb the steep slab, move out left onto the arête and finish
    round the corner.

The Great Unwashed   17 m   HVS   1984
Strenuous climbing up the dark and dirty corner crack. Start directly
below the corner.
    (5a). Climb the corner to the top.

Below the grassy rake the rocks are very broken, but about 30 metres
down the gully from the pinnacle is an obvious crack with a niche
at half height (Crack Special) that runs up a relatively clean steep
slab. The following three routes start from this area. To descend move
up left for 10 metres then traverse left to the top of the grassy rake
that leads down left to the foot of Flakey Wall.

Attic Stairs   35 m   S   1985
Start just left of the crack of Crack Special below a groove.
    Up the groove and steep wall on excellent holds, avoiding a bulge
    on the left to finish up the rib of Crack Special.

Crack Special   35 m   VS   1985
A pleasant route with a good line. Start directly below the crack.
    (4b). Climb the crack past a sentry box, then the groove and rib
    to the top.

Back Stairs   35 m   HS   1985
Start 2 metres right of Crack Special below a hidden flake crack.
    Climb the crack and finish up the groove and rib of Crack Special.

At the bottom of the large scree shoot on its right-hand side (true
left) are two ruddy brown clean buttresses. The left-hand buttress,
which has a large embedded flake at its base, is climbed by the
following route.

Rusty Wall   25 m   E2   1984
Very steep climbing with a technical crux that is difficult to protect.
Start below the right side of the wall.
    (5c). Climb the steep crack up to a small overhang at 8 metres.
    Move left round the overhang then cross the smooth wall on the
    left to an obvious pinnacle. (Micro wire placements in the thin

horizontal crack). Step up onto the pinnacle and up to a ledge
that leads back right to finish via a crack on the right.

Eastern Crags

A complex area of broken crags situated high up on the steep broken
fellside. The best climbing is on the clean upper buttress which lies
directly above a terrace that separates the Upper and Lower Buttresses
and is easily identified from the road. The easiest access to the climbs
in this area is from above by abseil down onto the terrace.

From the top of the Lakeland Pioneers scree gully continue east along
a sheep track for about $1/2$ km crossing the top of Forked Gully and
Rowan Tree Gully until a line of small cairns leads down rightwards
over broken rocks to a peg and nut abseil point (approximately 40
minutes from the road).

The terrace can also be reached from below by climbing Centra.
Face-Lower Climb on the lower buttress but this is not recommended.

To reach the climbs in the vicinity of Long Climb, Forked Gully and
Toby traverse right from the base of White Band Ghyll over broken
rocks then across a wide scree gully followed by more broken rocks
to the bottom of the first big gully – Forked Gully. Unfortunately the
quality of the climbing does not really justify the tedious approach.
The buttress right of Forked Gully is easily accessible from here. The
left fork of Forked Gully can be used as a descent, whilst the right
edge of its right-hand fork is climbed by Quirk.

Long Climb 100 m D
  This route takes the left edge of the wide scree gully and roughly
  follows the line of the arête.

Forked Gully 30 m HS   1923
  The first large gully on the eastern crags with both its left-hand
  branch, which gives a scrambling descent, and difficult right-hand
  branch routes, proving to be thoroughly miserable places due to
  vegetation.

Smirk 38 VD   1975
Climbs the obvious groove 5 metres left and above the start of Quirk.
1   30 m. Climb the two short walls then the groove above to a stance
    and belay common to Quirk pitch 2.
2   8 m. The wall and groove on the left lead to the top.

EASTERN CRAGS

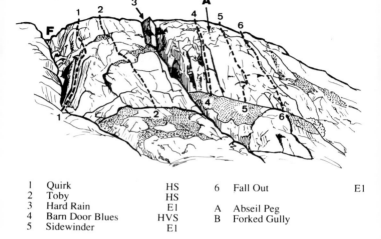

1	Quirk	HS	6	Fall Out	E1
2	Toby	HS			
3	Hard Rain	E1	A	Abseil Peg	
4	Barn Door Blues	HVS	B	Forked Gully	
5	Sidewinder	E1			

Quirk   72 m   HS   1974
This route climbs the right edge of the right fork of Forked Gully
and is very broken in its upper pitches.

1   30 m. Climb the arête for 3 metres, then the shallow groove
leading up left to grass ledges. Move delicately right to a second
grass ledge and block belays.

2   10 m. From the left-hand end of the ledge step up onto the wall
and climb a crack up right to a grass ledge and block belays.

3   22 m. From the left end of the ledge, pull up, then traverse left
for 10 metres. Climb up the easy rib to a terrace.

4   10 m. Cross the terrace and climb the left-hand groove, passing
a loose but useful finger of rock, then finish up a strenuous groove
on the left.

Fingers   40 m   HS   1974
Start 7 metres right of Quirk at a big V-groove.
1   20 m. Climb the slab on the left of the groove and belay as pitch
    1 of Quirk.
2   20 m. Traverse right for 5 metres then make an awkward move
    up right to a good hold. The rib on the right leads up to a terrace.

Between Forked Gully and Rowan Tree Gully is a broken buttress
with the following recorded routes of indifferent quality.

Left Face Climb   30 m   S   1973
Start just left of the grass ramp of Toby.
1   15 m. Climb up to the foot of a gangway.
2   15 m. Follow the cracks above, step left onto the arête, then back
    into widening cracks which lead to the top.

Toby   30 m   HS   1974
Start midway between Forked Gully and Rowan Tree Gully at the
bottom of a grass ramp.
    Climb up and trend left avoiding gorse, to a good spike. Step
    right, pull over a bulge and continue up to the top.

A route has been recorded in the vicinity of Toby but could not be
traced during excavations and is mentioned purely for the record.
Right Face Climb (1923).

Rowan Tree Gully   100 m   MS   1892
The next gully right of Toby gives scrambling in its lower section
with two 20 metres high chimneys at the top. The left one being
slightly harder. It is worth noting the description from 1945, "The
lower reaches of this under-gardened climb suffer from botanical
intrusions, and the holds may have to be dug for".

The next buttress right of Rowan Tree Gully is split by a terrace
into the Upper and Lower Buttresses.

Lower Buttress

The routes in this area are of poor quality being both dirty and broken
and at best provide an alternative access to the terrace and the Upper
Buttress. Approach from below.

Central Face – Lower Climb   25 m   S   1973
Start at the pinnacle leaning against the crag.
1   15 m. Climb the crack on the right-hand side of the pinnacle to
     its top.
2   10 m. The crack above leads to good holds and the terrace.

Several routes have been recorded starting from the grassy bay down
and right of the previous route but they are generally broken, dirty
and lack direction. In order to avoid any future rediscovery and
subsequent disappointment they are briefly described as follows.

Pinnacle Buttress (VS, 1974), from the left side of the grassy bay
climb the buttress and grooves trending left to cross the gully at half
height, then up broken rock to the top. **Rib and Groove** (VD, 1974),
start 3 metres right of Pinnacle Buttress and follow the rib running
up left to right. Traverse left over a flake, then up a groove to the
top. **Bright Interval** (MS, 1974), from the right-hand side of the
grassy bay climb the crack and slab to a ledge. Climb the wall and
crack above to finish up right of a clean wall to the top. **The Weakest**
(HS, 1974), climb the edge/rib right of Bright Interval then cross this
route to finish up the clean wall.

Upper Buttress

The only area really worth visiting on the Eastern Crags giving a
good selection or routes mainly in the Very Severe plus range on
steep generally clean and fast drying rock. Unlike the Witch Buttress
and Pikes Crag areas the crag still remains peaceful and remote.
Approach is by abseil as previously described.

The terrace at the bottom of the Upper Buttress runs diagonally up
left (west) into the upper section of Rowan Tree Gully which in turn
leads up to the diagonal slab and cracked headwall climbed by Hard
Rain.

Sideline   27 m   MVS   1986
A traditional thrash up the obvious chimney on the left of the head
wall. Start midway up the base of the diagonal slab.
     (4a). Climb the crack in the slab trending leftward to a perched
     block at the foot of the chimney. Climb the chimney to the top.

Hard Rain   37 m   E1   1986
A good pitch up the slab and cracked head wall right of Sideline.
Start as for Sideline.

(5b). Climb the crack in the slab trending leftwards to a perched block at the foot of the chimney, then trend right to a small hidden ledge below the bulging crack. Follow the disjointed crack strenuously, direct to the top.

Flanker   38 m   HS   1974

The easiest way up the crag, but not as easy as it looks. Start at the left end of the terrace below a groove that runs up from the bottom of a chimney. About 5 metres left of the large block at the bottom of Midsummer Madness.

Climb the scoop into the groove proper and continue past a huge block and square cut bulge until the angle eases. The right rib is followed trending right to the top.

Rib Tickler   38 m   VS   1987

Climbs the undercut rib between Flanker and the chimney of Danker. Start below a small slab just left of Flanker.

(4b). Climb the small slab until a pull can be made out right onto the rib. Follow the rib, and a steep cracked wall above to easy ground, then climb the obvious crack on the left to the top.

Danker   38 m   VS   1974

Climbs the steep dirty chimney/crack line 5 metres left of the Midsummer Madness block.

(4b). The chimney leads up to a ledge, step right onto a steep slab, then go up and back left into the chimney line. Finish up the grooved rib.

★ Barn Door Blues   38 m   HVS   1988

A sustained pitch with poor protection which follows the narrow V-groove just right of Danker.

(4c). Small but positive holds lead up the groove past a flake, then a head wall is climbed trending rightwards to the abseil point.

Just left of a line directly below the abseil point is a large detached block marking the start of the next three routes

★ Going Straight   38 m   HVS   1988

Steep fingery climbing up the wall directly above the detached block. Start from the top of the block below the centre of the wall.

(5a). A difficult pull is made up onto the wall (crux), then more easily up to a groove. Climb the groove to finish at the abseil point.

★ **Midsummer Madness**   38 m   HVS   1974
An interesting pitch with a short, well protected crux. Start from the
top of the block at its right-hand end.
> (5a). Using small holds step up right onto the steep slab. Climb
> up and left to good holds and protection, then make an awkward
> swing up into a groove on the left (crux). Follow the groove, then
> the rib on the right to finish up a steep crack to the abseil point.

★ **Shock Treatment**   38 m   E1   1989
A direct line up the obvious overhanging undercut V-groove just right
of Midsummer Madness. A long reach is useful on the crux. Start as
for Midsummer Madness.
> (5b). Follow Midsummer Madness up to the good protection at
> the top of the steep slab. Additional protection can be arranged
> on the right-hand side of the groove above (thread). The next few
> moves up and right into the groove are strenuous and committing.
> Continue up the groove to join the steep crack finish of
> Midsummer Madness.

Sidewinder   30 m   E1   1982
A good technical pitch up through the bulges right of Shock
Treatment. Start below a shallow corner 4 metres right of the
detached block.
> (5b). Climb the corner to its top and pull out right onto a small
> hanging slab. Go up the slab and step out right under a bulge
> then, using a hidden crack above, pull up and right to a good hold
> on the rib. Easy climbing up the rib, past a recess, leads to the
> top.

Central Face Climb   35 m   HS   1968
Start on the right beneath the obvious overhangs.
1   10 m. Easy rocks lead up to the base of the overhanging grooves,
    traverse right then up to a ledge at the foot of a groove.
2   25 m. Climb the groove and step left onto a slab at its top. Move
    up leftwards then back right to finish.

N.C.B.   40 m   VS   1988
Awkward climbing up the mossy groove just right of Central Face
Climb. Start as for Central Face Climb.
1   10 m. As pitch 1 of Central Face Climb.
2   30 m (4c). Climb the mossy groove up to the overhang and
    protection which is strenuous to place. Step right, pull up into the
    hanging groove just left of Fall Out, then follow the groove
    passing a good ledge to the top.

Cadbury   45 m   VS   1974
A disjointed and contrived route. Start down and right of Central Face Climb at two small rowans.
1   15 m (4a). Climb up left of a perched column then step onto it and up the slabs to the ledge on Central Face Climb.
2   30 m (4b). From the right-hand side of the ledge climb the light coloured groove (hard and avoidable until forced out right into a grassy groove. Follow the groove, then the steep crack up the rib on the left to finish over an overlap on good holds.

★★ **Fall Out**   45 m   E1   1986
The best route on the Upper Buttress giving steep climbing with widely spaced protection. Start 4 metres right of Cadbury on a glacis behind a large holly tree.
1   15 m (4c). Move up the wall into a heathery corner then step back left and climb the wall to the ledge on Central Face Climb.
2   30 m (5b). Climb straight up the corner between N.C.B. and Cadbury to an overlap where protection can be arranged in a slot. Pull over and up left to a small ledge, then straight up the crack above to another overlap. (Junction with Cadbury.) Pull straight over on good holds to the top.

Variation   15 m   E1   1989
More in keeping with the second pitch.
1a   (5b). Pull strenuously up the clean wall just left of the original start on small finger holds followed by easier climbing up to the Central Face Climb ledge.

Startling Starling   45 m   VS   1976
A poor route climbing the broken rocks right of Cadbury. Start just right of Cadbury beneath some large blocks.
1   10 m. Up over the large blocks to a grass terrace.
2   12 m (4a). Gain a sloping grassy ramp on the left then traverse right to reach a wide crack that leads up to block belays.
3   23 m (4b). Climb the groove above then over a bulge onto the wall to finish over a quartz bulge.

The right-hand bounding gully of the Upper and Lower Buttresses was climbed to give **Hidden Gully** (1923) but is now totally chocked with trees and vegetation.

Greendale Needle

About 30 metres right and below the level of the grass bay marking the start of Bright Interval is a pinnacle, conspicuous by its relative cleanliness, this is Greendale Needle. The climbing in this area is generally poor and unrewarding, the only route of any real interest being the Needle. Approach directly from below up the broken fellside to join an obvious grassy rake running up right. Follow the ramp to the base of the Needle (30 min).

Under the grassy bank directly below the pinnacle is a small buttress containing the obvious corner taken by Greendale Corner.

Tumbledown Chimney   40 m   VD   1974
The name says it all. Start 10 metres left of Greendale Needle below a rib.
1   15 m. Climb the rib to a good ledge.
2   25 m. Climb the chimney on the left, move right to a second chimney, then up this over some doubtful blocks to the top.

Greendale Needle   42   VS   1974
Start from the lowest point of the Needle.
1   25 m (4b). Follow the thin crack up over a square cut overhang to a sloping ledge. Climb the wall above to the top of the pinnacle.
2   17 m (4a). Descend the gap behind the Needle, then go up right to climb an awkward groove trending left.

Blue Peter   27 m   HVS   1989
Climbs the steep little buttress formed by the left edge of Greendale Corner. Poor protection.
     (5a). Climb straight up the centre of the buttress on widely spaced holds until a high step can be made onto easier ground. Belays at the top of Greendale Corner.

Greendale Corner   27 m   VS   1974
Start below the obvious corner.
     (4c). Climb straight up the corner to belay at the top.

Latterbarrow Crag   (127 028)   Alt. 200 m   South East Facing

This Wasdale outlier of superb sound granite commands a sunny position in woodland 1 kilometre south of Nether Wasdale. Its Lakeland fringe situation making climbing possible throughout the year. Though close to the road, the crag is tricky of access, and approaches other than the one recommended are liable to end in rhododendron thickets or larch jungle.

This is a private crag on private land and at the time of writing there is no agreement for access to climb. The following descriptions are included only for completeness of the guide. Please avoid causing aggrevation to the owners to enable the BMC to negotiate for access.

Leave cars on the verges near the entrance drive to Stangends on the Santon Bridge to Nether Wasdale road. Go over the stile opposite the drive and cross the field to its south-east corner where steps mount the wall. After crossing, walk 20 metres right then strike straight up the rough fell side through a thinning in the larch plantation to a ride which permits an approach to the fell summit. Time, about 20 minutes. The main crag lies down right, but the climbs are best attained by scrambling down a heathery rake diagonally left (east) to the belt of slabs marking the northern boundary of the outcrop. A cairn leans against the slabs some 10 metres left of their terminal spur.

Rubella   25 m   VD   †   1990
Start at the cairn.
> Climb the clean streak between the mossy fringes. Take the overhanging finish direct, then trend up right.

Rosanna   20 m   D   †   1990
Start 4 metres left of Rubella.
> The clean pink slab leads to a steep finish.

Primogeniture   15 m   M   †   1990
Start 2 metres left of a tree, 13 metres left of Rosanna.
> The attractive slab is climbable anywhere. A useful descent route.

Solivagant   20 m   VD   †   1990
Start 6 metres left of Primogeniture at a cairn.
> Climb the clean streak up the mossy slab to a bulge, then easier rock above.

Echappé 17 m MS †   1990
Start in the corner 3 metres left of Solivagant by a birch sapling and fallen flake.
> Follow the slabby corner for 9 metres then break out left up the wall via a steep fault line.

Nepotism 20 m E1 †   1990
Start 8 metres below and left of the birch and fallen flake of Echappé at a cairn.
1   11 m. Climb up the gangway system on the left wall, then traverse right to a large flake.
2   9 m (5b). Climb the flake, then, from its tip, the impending corner above to easy slabs.

Double Entendre 25 m MVS †   1990
Start 6 metres down and left from Nepotism at a cairn.
1   15 m (4a). An easy slab to a grass ledge, then directly up the overhang on the right to a glacis. Traverse right past the pink nose ahead to the big flake of the previous route.
2   10 m (4b). Follow the steep crack line sloping diagonally up the face on the left.

Veni Vidi Vici 25 m D †   1990
Start as for Double Entendre.
> A short slab, then the black crack ahead or the rock on either side lead to a ledge. Continue in the same line up the broken cracks, breaking out left near the top to a clean slabby finish.

Autumnal Ambience 25 m D †   1990
Start 5 metres down left from Veni Vidi Vici at a cairn.
> Easy twin cracks lead to a grass ledge, then steeper climbing up the rounded buttress ahead. Finish up the crack sloping diagonally left.

Solace in Senescence 27 m VD †   1990
Start 3 metres left of Autumnal Ambience. A pleasant climb.
> A series of short walls, then a fine strip of cracked slabs lead to an impending corner. Up this, then scramble up right to the top.

Late-Flowering Lust 25 m D †   1990
Start at the top of a short grassy rake 3 metres left of Solace in Senescence.
> The groove/crack line, finishing up either the prominent black crack or the face to its right.

Patriarch's Provenance   30 m   MS   †   1990
Start below and immediately left of Late-Flowering Lust at the toe
of a little subsidiary buttress.
   Climb the little buttress, then up a steep wall for 3 metres. Step
left to a crack system and climb direct to a corner and easier rock.

The Sequacious Doyen   25 m   VS   †   1990
Start at the back of a little grassy bay 6 metres left of Patriarch's
Provenance.
   (4c). The clean wall, following a blackish-green crack system.
Poor protection initially. Finish up a crack containing a suspect
jammed flake.

The Flatulent Pilaster   30 m   HS   †   1990
The steep cracked rib 7 metres down left from Sequacious Doyen.
An airy little climb.
   Follow the rib throughout, passing some dubious jammed blocks.

Messalina's Grotto   33 m   MVS   †   1990
The big square-cut hollow just left of the previous route's steep
cracked rib.
1   15 m (4b). A short wall to a lichenous slab, then the corner ahead
    (sometimes damp), by its right wall to the Grotto.
2   Bridge up the overhanging right corner of the Grotto and finish
    up short walls on the right.

Panegyric for a P.M.   30 m   MS.   †   1990
Start 3 metres left of Messalina's Grotto.
1   15 m. A short overhang leads to the lichenous slab, then follow
    an incipient ridge forming the left wall of Messalina's Grotto.
    Belay where the ridge joins the wall.
2   15 m. The lichenous wall above.

The Kafka Syndrome   30 m   MVS   †   1990
Start 2 metres left of Panegyric for a P.M.
   (4b). Overhanging steps lead to a ledge with a small bush, then
straight up the smooth lichenous wall.

Paternity Summons   30 m   VS   †   1990
Start 2 metres left of Kafka Syndrome below two steep
groove/corners.
   (4c). Vertical steps lead to a green corner, which is climbed on
its right to a small platform. The big, impending corner/groove
above is followed by an easier wall.

The Rubicund Rostrum 32 m HS †   1990
A good climb which uses the prominent black crack running up the
right side of the Rostrum, an obvious ruddy nose that dominates this
part of the crag. Start 4 metres left of Paternity Summons.
1   16 m. Up 5 metres to a little arête, followed to a cranny and
     stunted tree.
2   16 m. Gain the overhanging black crack via its right wall. The
     crack is easier than it looks and leads to the top of Rostrum.
     Finish up the exposed rib on the right.

The Lassitude of Hedonism 34 m VD †   1990
Takes the corner on the left side of the Rostrum, starting 4 metres
left of that route.
1   17 m. Easy steps bearing right, then a short corner to a platform
     and ancient nest on the left side of the Rostrum.
2   17 m. The steep corner above has good holds. From the top of
     the Rostrum, climb the wall on the right to an awkward finish.
     An easier option lies up left.

The Ravelled Sleave 35 m VD †   1990
Left of the Rostrum area is a wide vegetated defile, and left again is
the crags bounding spur climbed by this route. Start left of the lowest
point of the crag at a little orange-red wall.
     Pleasant climbing up the crest of the ridge, with easier variations
possible.

The Lycanthrope's Fang 24 m MS †   1990
From the crags lowest point, scramble up steeply diagonally left for
14 metres to an overhanging black wall.
1   7m. Up the wall, then diagonally left to a sharp little pinnacle.
2   17 m. From the pinnacle tip, mantelshelf onto the wall beyond.
     Climb this to a ledge, then bear right and finish up two awkward
     walls.

Eclecticism 78 m MVS †   1990
A left to right girdle, which permits several variations. This line
attempts to maintain a reasonable standard. Start just left of the lowest
point of the crags left-hand side below a little orange-red wall.
1   25 m. Up the broad spur for 13 metres (The Ravelled Sleave),
     then break out diagonally right to a stunted tree below an
     overhanging crack.
2   9 m. Traverse right to a shallow steep scoop which is climbed
     trending right to where an incipient ridge abuts a wall. Descend
     to the nook of Messalina's Grotto.

3   18 m (4b). Move round to the steep ridge on the right (The Flatulent Pilaster) and follow this route up over its crux to where the angle relents. A flat ledge leads delicately right past a suspect jammed flake in a crack to a stance below a prominent black crack.

4   11 m. Slabbier rock to the right, then trend slightly up right to the wide diagonal crack of Autumnal Ambience. Belay on a wide ledge.

5   5 m. Traverse easily right under the overhang, round the edge to the ledge and big flake of Double Entendre.

6   10 m (4b). The steep crack line slanting left up the face on the left. (Double Entendre).

The Screes

The large and imposing mass of rock, scree and steep broken fellside, overlooking the south-western end of Wastwater is generally disappointing but does provide some traditional wet and dark gully climbs. After a prolonged cold spell these gullies can give superb winter expeditions.

The buttresses themselves are basically unstable, though Low Adam Crag, can give a good day out. It is worth noting that as the area is a designated S.S.S.I, climbing should be restricted to the existing routes.

The Screes Gullies

The best approach is from the south-west end of Wastwater, where limited parking is available on the roadside at Wasdale Hall Lodge (143 043). Walk south-west along the road for ¹/₂ km to Woodhow and go through the metal kissing gate opposite. Follow the path across a field and down to a gate then along the river bank to cross over the River Irt via Lund Bridge. Turn left up the south bank of the river, crossing a concrete duct, to join the vehicle track leading to the Pump House. Continue along the lakeshore path for a short distance then strike off up the steep fellside to the gullies (approximately 35 mins).

The gullies are obvious with the deep cut cleft of 'C' Gully being easy to identify directly above the Pump House. About 100 metres left of 'C' Gully is 'B' or Great Gully, further left again is the wide scree funnel of 'A' Gully then 'F' or Seven Pitch Gully, this being the last gully of any interest.

The Gullies themselves are obvious and require no detailed descriptions, 'C' and 'B' being the hardest, although the climbing never gets too difficult, the climbs are up to 200 metres long are .

The gullies rarely dry out, as these are the traditional conditions for such routes they are graded for there conditions.

'C' Gully (VS, 1897), reasonably straightforward climbing in its lower section, passing a large capstone on the left to gain the large amphitheatre at half-height. Above this point the climbing becomes more awkward with escape routes being possible out right if required but they do lead out onto very steep broken fellside.

'B' or **Great Gully** (MVS, 1892), generally following the gully bed throughout except for a short excursion up its right-hand branch into a cave, before moving back left to regain the main gully. Up this via a large chockstone to the top.

Pens End Crag   (148 036)   Alt. 200 m   North West Facing

The crag lies 100 metres right and 50 metres up from the start of 'C' Gully, the obvious large grassy groove with trees at its base marking the start of The Bannister.

The rock is steep but loose and overgrown. The routes lack adequate belays and are badly protected. It is best avoided. The routes are described only for the sake of completeness. To descend follow a sheep track off right to a gully and descend this on its true left-hand side with care.

The Bannister (MVS (-, 4a, 4a), 1974). Climb up to an oak tree, step right and follow a break in the left wall of the groove moving out left at the top and up to a grass recess. Pull up the steep wall then move left to the arête that leads to the top. **Pump House Arête** (MVS (-, -, 4a), 1974). Climb the obvious disjointed arête right of The Bannister to a grass ledge. The wall above is climbed diagonally left to right, moving left onto the ridge and up to the top. **Peregrine** (VS (4a, 4b, -), 1974). The cracked wall 5 metres right and above Pump House Arête. The crack leads up to a large ledge, move right to below a groove, then starting from the left climb the groove over an overlap and move out left to the rib. Follow the rib moving out right and up to a ledge followed by scrambling to the top.

Low Adam Crag   (156 047)   Alt. 200 m   North West Facing

The only area of relatively clean stable rock on the screes, easily identified from the road junction on the opposite side of the lake. Contrary to previous reports in the old guide, the climbing is worthwhile when compared to other local developments, and is certainly worth a visit, albeit after a long dry spell. It gives an opportunity to climb on an isolated crag that catches the evening sun in a superb setting overlooking Wastwater.

The best approach is as for The Scree Gullies starting from the south west end of the lake but continuing along the lakeside track, through a boulder field then bearing diagonally right along a sheep track up to the base of the crag (1 hr from Wasdale Hall).

All the climbing is on the big steep buttress bounded on its right-hand side by a dirty gully (no descent) and the climbs are described from right to left to suit the approach. To descend follow a sheep track off right, crossing the top of the gully, and continue right for about 100 metres before going down over steep broken ground until level with the foot of the crag.

Thyroxin   60 m   VS   1962
Interesting open climbing with a good second pitch. Start just left and down from the base of the gully below a steep little subsidiary buttress. Shared belays with Adrenalin on pitches 1 and 3.
1   10 m (4c). Pull over the overhang above the block belay and climb the slab, moving left to a ledge.
2   15 m (4a). Traverse left across the slab then up its left edge to a ledge and large block belay. (Junction with Adrenalin.)
3   20 m (4b). Traverse left as for Adrenalin, negotiate the vindictive holly, then escape into the overhanging crack above, stepping right where the crack widens into a groove and climb it to belays in the steep cracked wall.
4   15 m (4b). Climb the crack above the belay followed by a short steep wall up the ridge. Easy scrambling leads to the top.

Adrenalin   60 m   VS   1958
The easiest route on the crag climbing the buttress just left of the large gully until forced out left. Start just left of Thyroxin below a deceptively easy looking crack.
1   10 m (4b). Climb the wall trending left then pull into the crack and up to the ledge.
2   20 m (4b). Climb straight up the rib to a small ledge at 5 metres. Traverse left, descending slightly, passing below a large poised

block and continue left across a corner to gain a leftwards sloping gangway. Make an exposed rising traverse left past an ill tempered holly to gain a ledge at the base of a groove.

3   15 m (4b). Climb the groove above the belay, step delicately out right onto a slab and up to belays in a steep cracked wall.

4   15 m (4b). Traverse right and slightly downward for 5 metres, then climb the crack line above, followed by easier rocks, first out right then back left to a ledge.

Easy scrambling leads to the top.

Aspro   47 m   E1   1974
Steep sustained climbing up the leftwards facing corner and continuation crack line starting about 10 metres left of Adrenalin. Unfortunately the first pitch is mossy and takes a long time to dry out.

1   15 m (5a). Climb straight up the corner and over the strenuous bulge to belays on the right.

2   17 m (5b). Pull into the steep crack above the belay and climb it with an awkward move into the groove above. (Very strenuous but well protected.) Continue up the groove to belays in the steep cracked wall as pitch 3 of Adrenalin.

3   15 m (4b). As pitch 4 of Adrenalin.

Up and left of Aspro is a huge fern covered ledge below a large green groove streaked white from bird activity. The following two routes start from this ledge which is reached by some steep scary scrambling.

Pituitrin   50 m   VS   1959
A dirty route especially if the large birds nest on pitch 2 has been occupied recently. Start below a thin crack at the right-hand side of the ledge.

1   14 m (4b). Climb the crack and make a difficult landing onto a large grass ledge.

2   18 m (4a). Step off the huge flake above onto the left wall and climb up to just below a ledge containing the birds nest. Traverse left round a rib and across slabs to a stance.

3   18 m (4b). The groove above leads to the top. Belay well back.

★ **Dexedrin**   45 m   VS   1964
Good climbing up the shallow bottomless groove left of Pituitrin. Start 5 metres left of Pituitrin at the extreme left end of the fern covered ledge.

1   20 m (4c). Climb the leftwards slanting gangway until it ends and make an awkward step left across a steep little wall to gain the shallow groove. Follow the groove stepping out left at the small black overhang onto a ledge. A good pitch.

2   25 m (4b). The rib above leads to a ledge and junction with Pituitrin. Finish as for pitch 3 of Pituitrin.

100 metres above and east of Low Adam Crag is a large pinnacle. This can be identified from the opposite side of the lake when it is picked out in the afternoon sun. The pinnacle itself is very steep and exposed, but it is also very dirty and disappointing. One route has been recorded on its long side, but it is not recommended. Approach as for Low Adam Crag but then continue diagonally up over steep broken ground and scree to the base of the pinnacle ($1^{1}/_{2}$ hrs from Wasdale Hall). Descend via the short side of the pinnacle by 10 metres of moderate scrambling.

Sheerline   45 m   HVS   †   1963
Climbs the steep crack and shallow groove up the centre of the large face. Start at the top of a grassy gangway.

(5a). Climb onto a grassy ledge then go down and left to the foot of the crack. using 1 nut for aid pull over the overhanging start and continue strenuously up the crack until the angle increases slightly. The steep wall right of the groove leads up past a doubtful flake then step back into the groove, and up this over an overhang to finish up an awkward corner. Easy scrambling to the top.

CLIMBING WALLS

Although artificial walls are not particularly numerous in Cumbria it has two of the top ten climbing wall in the Country, and a number of other walls are currently under construction or being planned and should be opened in the near future. Only the best or most readily accessible are described here:

Ambleside: Charlotte Masons College.　　　　BMC rating ★★
Good access, minimal regulations, low cost and excellent climbing. Unfortunately it tends to get very busy and has no changing facilities. Tickets available from Rock and Run and, The Golden Rule Hotel.
Access check; Tel: Charlotte Mason Collage (0966 33066)

Carlisle: The Sands Centre　　　　BMC rating ★★
Good access, minimal regulations, low cost and good climbing. There are excellent changing and shower facilities included in the price and alternative sports available. Tickets obtained at the Centre.
Access check; Tel: The Sands Centre (0228 27555)

Cockermouth Sports Centre
Good access, minimal regulations, low cost and good climbing. Good changing and shower facilities plus access to a multi-gym.
Access check; Tel: Cockermouth Sports Centre (0900 823596)

Whitehaven Sports Centre:　　　　BMC rating ●
Good access, minimal regulations, low cost, rather poor climbing. An afterthought on the rear of the centre, it is very small but high and lacks adequate facilities. Tickets available at the centre.
Access check; Tel: Whitehaven Sports Centre (0946 5666)

HASKETT BUTTRESS

1	The Dolorous Stroke	E1		7	The Dactylic Springald	E1
2	The Devious Slash	VS		8	The Ductile Slant	MS
3	The Detrital Slide	VS				
4	The Dexterous Shuffle	E2		H	Haskett Gully	
5	The Dipso Somnambulist	E2		W	Western Gully	
6	The Deleterious Sting	E1				

234

BLACK CRAG

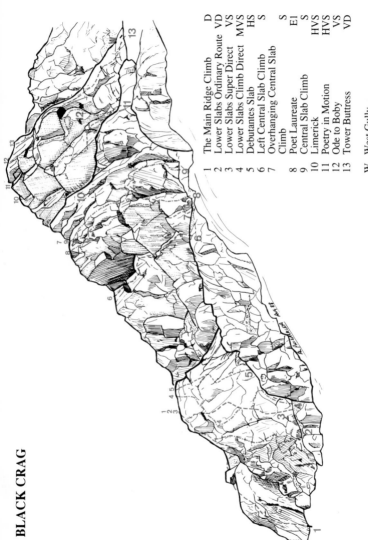

1	The Main Ridge Climb	D
2	Lower Slabs Ordinary Route	VD
3	Lower Slabs Super Direct	VS
4	Lower Slabs Climb Direct	MVS
5	Debutantes Slab	HS
6	Left Central Slab Climb	S
7	Overhanging Central Slab Climb	S
8	Poet Laureate	E1
9	Central Slab Climb	S
10	Limerick	HVS
11	Poetry in Motion	HVS
12	Ode to Boby	VS
13	Tower Buttress	VD
W	West Gully	

PILLAR – from JORDAN GAP

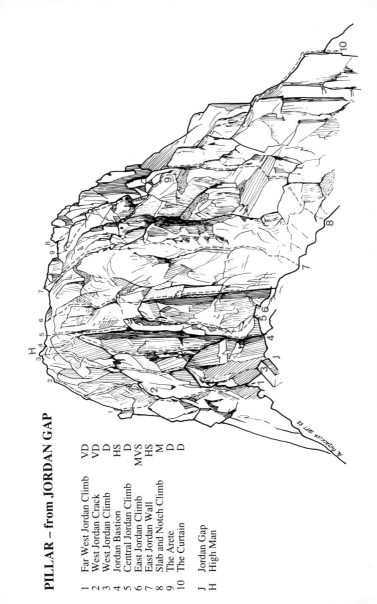

1	Far West Jordan Climb	VD
2	West Jordan Crack	VD
3	West Jordan Climb	D
4	Jordan Bastion	HS
5	Central Jordan Climb	D
6	East Jordan Climb	MVS
7	East Jordan Wall	HS
8	Slab and Notch Climb	M
9	The Arete	D
10	The Curtain	D

J Jordan Gap
H High Man

A. McMULLAN SEPT 88

SHAMROCK

1	Harlequin Chimneys	D	10	Vishnu		E2
2	Photon	MVS	11	Shamrock Tower		MVS
3	Eros	E2	12	Thanatos		HVS
4	Positron	MVS	13	The Magic Rainbow		E1
5	Electron	HVS	14	Necromancer		HVS
6	Tower Postern	HS				
7	Lepton	HVS	H	Great Heather Shelf		
8	Boson	HVS	W	Walker's Gully		MVS
9	Pauli Exclusion Principle	E2				

PILLAR – LOW MAN WEST FACE

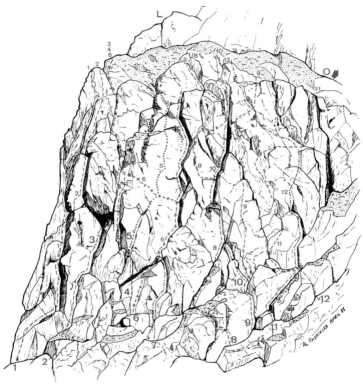

1	Charybdis	HVS
2	Goth	E1
3	Gaul	HVS
4	The Hun	VS
5	The Terrorist	E2
6	The Appian Way	HS
7	Attila	HVS
8	Nook and Wall Climb	S

9	Thor	MVS
10	The Devil's Entrance	MVS
11	Ledge and Groove Climb	S
12	West Wall Climb	VD
L	Low Man	
O	Old West Route (Descent)	

PILLAR – NORTH-EAST FACE

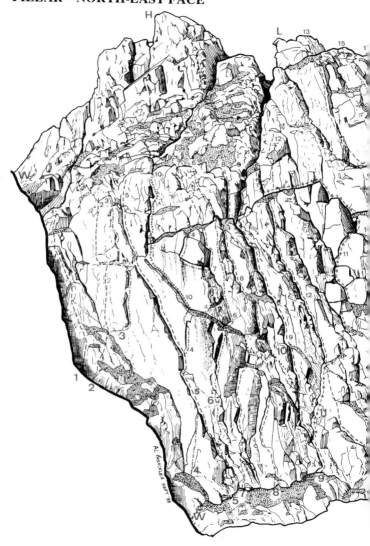

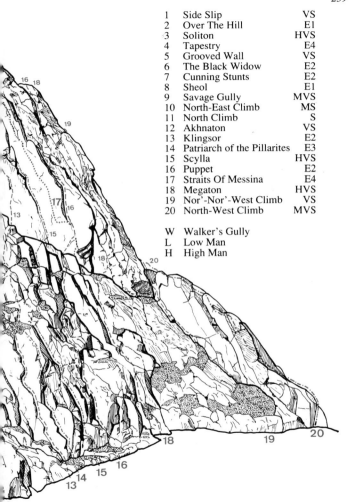

1	Side Slip	VS
2	Over The Hill	E1
3	Soliton	HVS
4	Tapestry	E4
5	Grooved Wall	VS
6	The Black Widow	E2
7	Cunning Stunts	E2
8	Sheol	E1
9	Savage Gully	MVS
10	North-East Climb	MS
11	North Climb	S
12	Akhnaton	VS
13	Klingsor	E2
14	Patriarch of the Pillarites	E3
15	Scylla	HVS
16	Puppet	E2
17	Straits Of Messina	E4
18	Megaton	HVS
19	Nor'-Nor'-West Climb	VS
20	North-West Climb	MVS
W	Walker's Gully	
L	Low Man	
H	High Man	

PILLAR – HIGH MAN WEST FACE

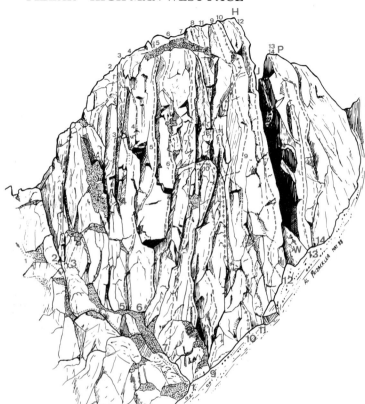

1.	The Old West Route (Descent)	
2	The Crumb	HS
3	The Pulpit Route	VD
4	Gondor	E2
5	Gomorrah	VS
6	Vandal	HVS
7	Sodom	VS
8	Cheekwooly	S
9	Rib and Slab Climb	HS
10	New West Climb	VD

11	South-West by West Climb	VS
12	South-West Climb	MVS
13	Sentinel	E1
14	Pisgah West Ridge	MS

H	High Man
J	Jordan Gap
P	Pisgah
W	West Jordan Gully

241

GABLE CRAG

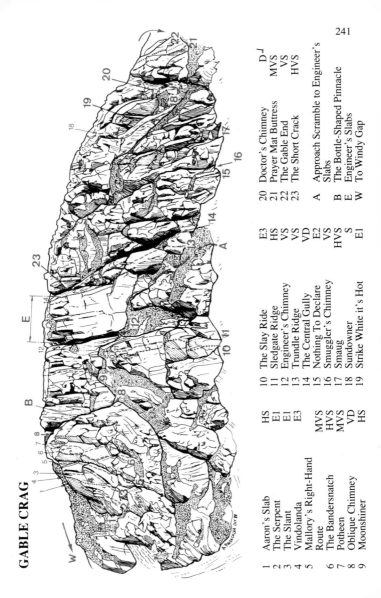

1	Aaron's Slab	HS
2	The Serpent	E1
3	The Slant	E1
4	Vindolanda	E3
5	Mallory's Right-Hand Route	MVS
6	The Bandersnatch	HVS
7	Potheen	MVS
8	Oblique Chimney	VD
9	Moonshiner	HS
10	The Slay Ride	E3
11	Sledgate Ridge	HS
12	Engineer's Chimney	VS
13	Trundle Ridge	VS
14	The Central Gully	VD
15	Nothing To Declare	E2
16	Smuggler's Chimney	VS
17	Smaug	HVS
18	Sundowner	S
19	Strike White it's Hot	E1
20	Doctor's Chimney	D⁻
21	Prayer Mat Buttress	MVS
22	The Gable End	VS
23	The Short Crack	HVS
A	Approach Scramble to Engineer's Slabs	
B	The Bottle-Shaped Pinnacle	
E	Engineer's Slabs	
W	To Windy Gap	

GABLE CRAG – ENGINEER'S SLABS

1	Engineer's Chimney	VS
2	Powder Finger	E3
3	Dream Twister	E3
4	The Troll	HVS
5	The Angle of Mercy	E1
6	Interceptor	VS
7	Snicker Snack	E3
8	Engineer's Slabs	VS
9	Mome Rath	E2

10	The Tombstone	E3
11	The Tomb	E2
12	Sarcophagus	E3
13	Engineer's Slabs – Unfinished Arete	VS
14	The Jabberwock	HVS
A	Approach Scramble	

KERN KNOTTS – RIGHT-HAND

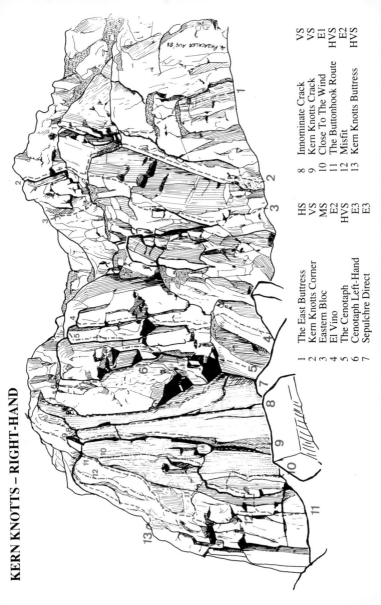

1	The East Buttress	HS
2	Kern Knotts Corner	VS
3	Eastern Bloc	MS
4	El Vino	E2
5	The Cenotaph	HVS
6	Cenotaph Left-Hand	E3
7	Sepulchre Direct	E3

8	Innominate Crack	VS
9	Kern Knotts Crack	VS
10	Close To The Wind	E1
11	The Buttonhook Route	HVS
12	Misfit	E2
13	Kern Knotts Buttress	HVS

A. PITZACKLER AUG '89

KERN KNOTTS – LEFT HAND

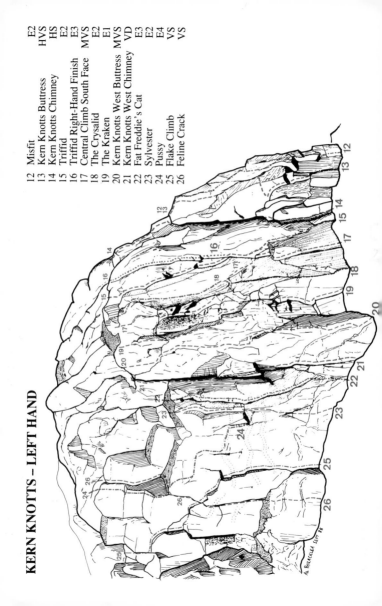

A. WHITECROSS. SEPT 88

THE NAPES – TOPHET WALL

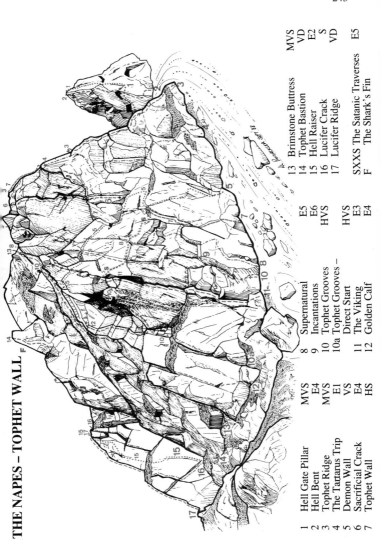

1	Hell Gate Pillar	MVS
2	Hell Bent	E4
3	Tophet Ridge	MVS
4	The Tartarus Trip	E1
5	Demon Wall	VS
6	Sacrificial Crack	E4
7	Tophet Wall	HS
8	Supernatural	E5
9	Incantations	E6
10	Tophet Grooves	HVS
10a	Tophet Grooves – Direct Start	
11	The Viking	HVS
12	Golden Calf	E3
		E4
13	Brimstone Buttress	MVS
14	Tophet Bastion	VD
15	Hell Raiser	E2
16	Lucifer Crack	S
17	Lucifer Ridge	VD
SXXS	The Satanic Traverses	E5
F	The Shark's Fin	

THE NAPES – NEEDLE RIDGE

1	Scrimshanker	VS
2	Buzzard Wall	D
3	Zeta Climb	VD
4	Belfry Buttress	HS
5	Belfry Crack	MVS
6	Chantry Buttress	MS
7	Salome	VD
8	The Lingmell Crack – The Needle	HS
9	The Wasdale Crack – The Needle	HS
10	The Arete – The Needle	HS
11	Needle Ridge	VD
N	Napes Needle	
G	The Gap	

THE NAPES – ARROWHEAD AND EAGLE'S NEST RIDGES

1	Eagle's Corner	MVS
2	Amos Moses	E1
3	Tricouni Rib	MVS
4	Crocodile Crack	HVS
5	The Cayman	E2
6	Eagle's Crack	VS
7	Eagle's Nest Ridge Direct	MVS
8	Ling Chimney	VD
9	Long John	HVS
10	Eagle's Nest Ordinary Route	D
11	Abbey Buttress	VD
12	Murun	
13	Buchstansangur	E2
	The Tormentor	E4
14	Time and Place	E2
15	Arrowhead Ridge – Easy Way	D
16	Arrowhead Ridge Direct	VD

XXX	Eagle's Chain	VS
NN	Napes Needle	
NG	Needle Gully	
DC	The Dress Circle	
EG	Eagle's Nest Gully	
AG	Arrowhead Gully	

To Tophet Wall and PR

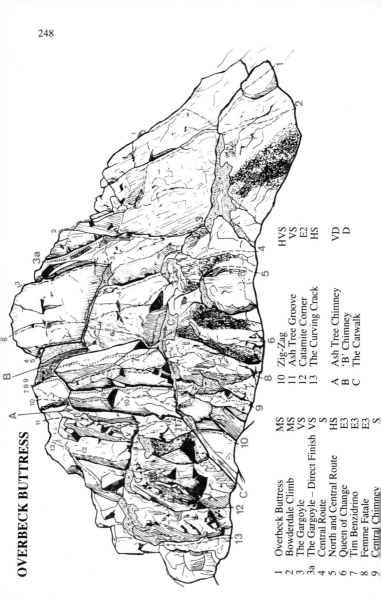

OVERBECK BUTTRESS

1	Overbeck Buttress	MS	
2	Bowderdale Climb	MS	
3	The Gargoyle	VS	
3a	The Gargoyle – Direct Finish	VS	
4	Central Route	S	
5	North and Central Route	HS	
6	Queen of Change	E3	
7	Tim Benzidrino	E3	
8	Femme Fatale	E3	
9	Central Chimney	S	
10	Zig-Zag	HVS	
11	Ash Tree Groove	VS	
12	Catamite Corner	E2	
13	The Curving Crack	HS	
A	Ash Tree Chimney	VD	
B	'B' Chimney	D	
C	The Catwalk		

BUCKBARROW – WITCH BUTTRESS AND PIKE CRAG

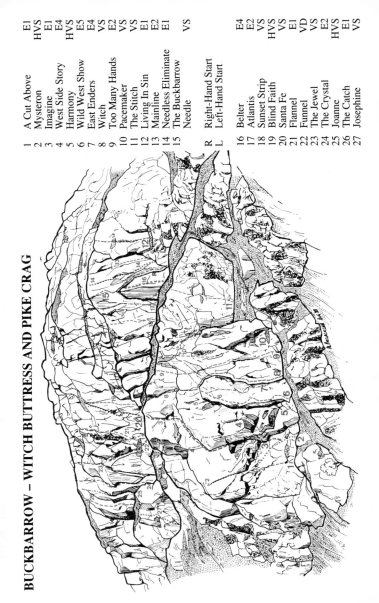

GRADED LIST OF CLIMBS

Due to their subjective origins, graded list are notorious for generating conflicting opinions on star ratings, adjectival grades and technical grades. This edition claims to be no better than any other guides and possibly worse with the first attempt at merging the Gable and Pillar areas with all of their character differences and the historical isolation of Pillar. The fact that very few climbers have a detailed knowledge across the grades in both areas will undoubtedly result in some anomalies but future editions can take care of these.

The graded list will very quickly come under the critical eye of those that use it as a yardstick on individual ability and progress, the league table and perceived status constantly under review during the never ending post mortems. On a good day no doubt, routes will appear overgraded but conversely the criticism of undergrading will be levelled by those struggling for an excuse.

The information contained within the graded list, with all of its flaws, is there for the planners, tickers, ego trippers and armchair dreamers alike but it is purely a guide: The rest is up to you.

E6
★★ Final Curtain (6b, 4c) — Buckbarrow
★★★ Incantations (5b, 6b, 6b) — The Napes

E5
Torch Song Trilogy (6b, 5c) — Buckbarrow
★★ Wild West Show (6b, 4c) — Buckbarrow
★★ Supernatural – Direct Finish (6b) — The Napes
★ The Satanic Traverses (6a) — The Napes
★★★ Supernatural (5c, 6a, 5b) — The Napes

E4
★ Golden Calf (6a, 4a, 6b) — The Napes
★ Sacrificial Crack (5a, 5b, 6a) — The Napes
Belter (6b, 4c) — Buckbarrow
★ East Enders (6a, 4c) — Buckbarrow
★ Straits of Messina (–, 6a, 6a) — Pillar Rock
★★★ Tapestry (5b, 6a, 5b) — Pillar Rock
★★ West Side Story (6a, 4c) — Buckbarrow
★★ The Tormentor (6a) — The Napes
★ Pussy (6a, 4b) — Kern Knotts
Hell Bent (5c) — The Napes
Moggy Traveller (6a) — Kern Knotts

E3

★★ The Viking (5b, 5c, 4b)	The Napes
★ Sepulchre Direct (6a)	Kern Knotts
Tim Benzedrino (5c, 5c, –)	Overbeck
★ Cenotaph Left–Hand (6a)	Kern Knotts
★★ Powder Finger (6a)	Gable Crag
★ Vindolanda (6a)	Gable Crag
Pinnacle Face Direct (6a)	Buckbarrow
Norma Jean (5a, 6a)	Buckbarrow
★ Triffid Right–Hand Finish (6a)	Kern Knotts
★ Femme Fatale (4b, 5c, –)	Overbeck
★ Fat Freddie's Cat (5c)	Kern Knotts
★ Queen of Change (5c, 5b, 6a)	Overbeck
★ Red Garden Massacre (5c)	Buckbarrow
★ The Tombstone (5b, 5c, 5b)	Gable Crag
★ Patriarch of the Pillarites (5c, 5c)	Pillar Rock
★★ Dream Twister (5c)	Gable Crag
★★★ Sarcophagus (4c, 5c, 5b)	Gable Crag
The Slay Ride (5c, 5c, 5b)	Gable Crag
★★★ Snicker Snack (5c, 5b)	Gable Crag

E2

★ Sylvester (5c)	Kern Knotts
★ Pauli Exclusion Principle (5c, 4b, 5a, –)	Pillar Rock
Scylla – Variation Direct Finish (5c)	Pillar Rock
● Left Wall (5b)	Bowness Knott
Rusty Wall (5c)	Buckbarrow
★ Triffid (5c)	Kern Knotts
Catamite Corner (5c, 5c,)	Overbeck
★ Swipe (5c)	Buckbarrow
★ Misfit (5c)	Kern Knotts
★★★ Cunning Stunts (5b, 5c, 5b)	Pillar Rock
★★ Free Bird (5c, 5b, 5c, 4c)	Buckbarrow
★ The Movie (5c)	Buckbarrow
★ Hell Raiser (5c, 5b)	The Napes
★★ The Crysalid (5a, 5c)	Kern Knotts
Mome Rath (5b, 5c)	Gable Crag
The Runt (4b, 5c)	Buckbarrow
Necromancer – Direct Start (5c)	Pillar Rock
★ Klingsor (5a, –, 5c, 5a, 5b)	Pillar Rock
★ Just Good Friends (5b)	Buckbarrow
The Black Widow (5a, 5c, 5a, 4c)	Pillar Rock
★★ The Cayman (5b, –,)	The Napes
Nothing to Declare (5a, 5b, 5a)	Gable Crag
Murin Buchstansangur (5b)	The Napes
★ Cretin Hop (5c)	Buckbarrow
Time and Place (5b)	The Napes
★★★ The Tomb (4c, 5b, 5a)	Gable Crag
★★ Gondor (4a, 5b, 5c)	Pillar Rock
Mainline (5c)	Buckbarrow

E2 (Contd.)

Atlantis (5b)	Buckbarrow
★★ Eros (5a, 5b, 5b, –)	Pillar Rock
★★ Too Many Hands (5b)	Buckbarrow
The Crystal (5c)	Buckbarrow
★ The Dexterous Shuffle (5c, 4b)	Haskett Buttress
Mr. Softee (5c)	Great Knott
The Terrorist (5c, –)	Pillar Rock
Wafer Thin (5c)	Great Knott
★ Puppet (4c, 5b, 4b, 5b)	Pillar Rock
Vishnu (5a, –, 5b, –)	Pillar Rock
El Vino (–, 5c)	Kern Knotts
★ The Dipso Somnambulist (5b, 4b)	Haskett Buttress
Fanghorn (5b, 5a)	Boat Howe Crags

E1

★ Over the Hill (5b, 5b)	Pillar Rock
★★ Imagine (5b, 5a)	Buckbarrow
★ The Deleterious Sting (5b, 4b)	Haskett Buttress
★★ The Angel of Mercy (5a, 5b)	Gable Crag
★ The Magic Rainbow (5b, 5a, –)	Pillar Rock
★ Sheol (5b, 5a, 4c, 4c)	Pillar Rock
★ Living in Sin (5a)	Buckbarrow
★ Hook Line and Sinker (5b)	Anglers' Crag
★ Numenor (5b, 5b)	Boat Howe Crags
The Tartarus Trip (4b, 5b)	The Napes
★ Shock Treatment (5b)	Buckbarrow
The Serpent (5b, 5a)	Gable Crag
★ The Dolorous Stroke (4a, 5b, 4a, 4c)	Haskett Buttress
★ Flannel (5b)	Buckbarrow
★ Close to the Wind (5b)	Kern Knotts
Sidewinder (5b)	Buckbarrow
★★ Goth (4c, 5b, 4a)	Pillar Rock
A Cut Above (5b)	Buckbarrow
★★ Spirit Level (4a, 5b, 5a, 5b, –, 4c)	Gable Crag
★★ Fall Out (4c, 5b)	Buckbarrow
Fall Out – Variation Start (5b)	Buckbarrow
★ Last of the Summer Wine (5b)	Buckbarrow
Wall Street (4b, 5a, 5b)	Bowness Knott
Right Edge Route (5b)	Buckbarrow
Harriet (5b)	Buckbarrow
The Dactylic Springald (5b, 4b)	Haskett Buttress
Strike While It's Hot (5b)	Gable Crag
The Kraken (5b, 5a)	Kern Knotts
Pinnacle Face (5a)	Buckbarrow
Junkie (5b)	Buckbarrow
Poet Laureate (4b, 5b)	Black Crag
Aspro (5a, 5b, 4b)	Low Adam Crag
★ Amos Moses (5a, 5b,)	The Napes
★ Needle Front (5b, 4c)	Buckbarrow

E1 (Contd.)
★ The Catch (4b, 5b)	Buckbarrow
Howl – Variation (5b)	Buckbarrow
Hard Rain (5b)	Buckbarrow
★★ Lakeland Pioneers (5b)	Buckbarrow
Sentinel (5b, –)	Pillar Rock
★ The Slant (5b, 5a)	Gable Crag
★★ Needless Eliminate (5b)	Buckbarrow
Roraima (–, 5b, 4b, 5a, 5a)	Pillar Rock

HVS
★ Smaug (5a, 5b, 4c)	Gable Crag
★ The Troll (5b, 5a)	Gable Crag
★ Limerick (5b)	Black Crag
Poetry in Motion – Variation Finish (5b)	Black Crag
★ Ximenes (5a, 5b, –)	Pillar Rock
★★ Poetry in Motion (4a, 5a, 4c)	Black Crag
Tophet Grooves (5b, 4a, 5a, 4c, 4b)	The Napes
The Short Crack (5b)	Gable Crag
Agent Orange (5b)	Buckbarrow
★ The Mysteron (5b)	Buckbarrow
Harmony (5b, 4c)	Buckbarrow
Odin (4c, 5b, 4b, 4b)	Pillar Rock
★★ The Buttonhook Route (5a, 5a)	Kern Knotts
★ Crocodile Crack (5a, –)	The Napes
Soliton (5a, 5a)	Pillar Rock
Blue Peter (5a)	Buckbarrow
West Cove Eliminate (5a, 4c)	West Cove
★ Un-named Groove (5a)	Buckbarrow
★ Necromancer (5a, 5a, –)	Pillar Rock
★★ The Jabberwock (4c, 5a, 4c)	Gable Crag
★★ Megaton (4c, 5a, 5a, 4c, 4c)	Pillar Rock
★ Kern Knotts Chain (4c, –, 4b, –, 5b, 5a, 4a)	Kern Knotts
Kern Knotts Buttress (4b, 5b)	Kern Knotts
Un-Named Wall (5a)	Buckbarrow
Demon Wall – Upper Traverse (5a)	The Napes
Satin (5a)	Buckbarrow
Gaul (4c, 5a, –)	Pillar Rock
Shorty (5a)	Buckbarrow
Flakey Wall (5a)	Buckbarrow
★ Going Straight (5a)	Buckbarrow
The Great Unwashed (5a)	Buckbarrow
★ The Prow of the Boat (5a, 5a)	Boat Howe Crags
Proton (5a, –, –, 5a, –,)	Pillar Rock
Tophet Grooves – Direct Start (5a)	The Napes
Alchemy (5a)	Buckbarrow
★★ Vandal (4c, 5a, 4a)	Pillar Rock
★ Barn Door Blues (4c)	Buckbarrow
Cream Horn (5a)	Great Knott
Bosun (4a, 4a, 5b, –)	Pillar Rock

HVS (Cont.)

Joanne (4a, 5a)	Buckbarrow
Hermes (5a)	Buckbarrow
Direct Obverse From The Gap (5a)	The Napes
★ Long John (4b, 5a)	The Napes
The Link (4b, –, 4c, 5a)	Pillar Rock
The Bandersnatch (5a, 4c)	Gable Crag
★ Charybdis (–, 4c, 4c, 5a, 5a, 4b, 5a)	Pillar Rock
The Eightfold Way (4a, 4b, 4a, –, 5a, 5a, 4c)	Pillar Rock
The Marriage (4a, 5a, 4c)	Bowness Knott
West Cove Eliminate (5a, 4c)	West Cove
Forked Lightening (5a, 4b)	Rough Crag
Blind Faith (5a, –)	Buckbarrow
Odin Variation (4b, 4b, 5a)	Pillar Rock
Jocky (5a)	Buckbarrow
Landlubber (4c, 4c, 4b)	Boat Howe Crags
Amphitheatre Buttress (5a)	Buckbarrow
★ Thanatos (4b, 5a, –,)	Pillar Rock
★ Midsummer Madness (5a)	Buckbarrow
Lepton (4c, 5a, 4c, 4c)	Pillar Rock
★★★ Electron (5a, 4b, 4c, 4b)	Pillar Rock
Left Edge Route (5a)	Buckbarrow
Catalepsy Corner (5a, 4a)	Anglers' Crag
★ Abacus (5a, –)	Green Gable
Attila (–, 4c, 5a)	Pillar Rock
Lothlorian (5a, 4a)	Buckbarrow
★ Scylla (–, –, 4c, 5a, 4c)	Pillar Rock
The Devils Exit (–, 5a, 4c)	Pillar Rock
Sheerline (5a)	Low Adam Crag
The Cenotaph (4c)	Kern Knotts
The Cornet (5a)	Great Knott
Starboard Fender – Direct Finish (4c)	Boat Howe Crags
The Gun (4c)	Buckbarrow
★ Gog (5a)	Anglers' Crag
Waterstreak Wall – Direct Finish (5a)	Goat Crag
★ Zig-Zag (4a, 4b, 5a)	Overbeck

VS

★★★ Grooved Wall (–, 5a, 4b, 4c)	Pillar Rock
The Girdle Traverse	Pillar Rock
★ Demon Wall (5a, 4b, 4c, –,)	The Napes
Shep (4c)	Anglers' Crag
The Gargoyle – Variation Finish (4c)	Overbeck
★ Smuggler's Chimney (4a, 4c)	Gable Crag
Epidemic Crack (5a)	Buckbarrow
Jim's Wall (5a)	Buckbarrow
The Jewel (4c)	Buckbarrow
Akhnaton (4c, –, 4c, 4b)	Pillar Rock
The Delectation Sinistrose (4a, 4b, 4b, 4b, 4a, 4c)	Haskett Buttress
Feline Crack (4c)	Kern Knotts

VS (Contd.)

★ The Hun (4c, 4b)	Pillar Rock
★★★ Engineer's Slabs (4c, 4c)	Gable Crag
★★ Ode to Boby (4a, 4c, 4b, 4c)	Black Crag
Vanilla Fudge (4c)	Great Knott
Engineer's Slabs – Unfinished Arête (4b, 4c, 4c)	Gable Crag
Peregrine (4a, 4b, –)	Pens End Crag
★ Interceptor (4c, 4c, 4c)	Gable Crag
The South-West by West Climb (–, 4c–, 4a)	Pillar Rock
★ Kern Knotts Crack (4b)	Kern Knotts
Neopolitan (4b)	Great Knott
Prophylactics (4c, 4b)	Cove Crag
Triton	Pillar Rock
★ Dexedrin (4c, 4b)	Low Adam Crag
★ Tophet Girdle (–, 4a, –, 4c, 4a,4a)	The Napes
★ Strider (–, 4b, –, 4c, 4a, 4a, –,)	Pillar Rock
Old Strands (4c)	Buckbarrow
Eagle's Chain (–, –, –, 4a, 4b, 4a, 4a)	The Napes
The Gargoyle (4b, 4a, 4c)	Overbeck
Greendale Corner (4c)	Buckbarrow
Scrimshanker (4c)	The Napes
Steeple Crack (4c)	Haskett Buttress
Thyroxin (4c, 4a, 4b, 4b)	Low Adam Crag
Cheeky Charlie (4c, 4b, 4b, –)	Rough Crag
Goodness Nose (4c)	Buckbarrow
Sante Fe (4c)	Buckbarrow
★ Angel's Step (4c)	Anglers' Crag
Eagle's Crack (4c, 4c, –)	The Napes
Cheekwooly – Variation (4c)	Pillar Rock
★ The Buckbarrow Needle (4b, 4c)	Buckbarrow
Shamrock Tower – Variation (4c)	Pillar Rock
Banana (4c)	Buckbarrow
★ Pace Maker (4c)	Buckbarrow
The Detrital Slide (4a, 4c, 4a)	Haskett Buttress
Cromlech Groove (4b, 4a, 4a)	Buckbarrow
N.C.B. (–, 4c)	Buckbarrow
★ Green Gash (4c)	Bowness Knotts
Cassation – Variation (4c)	Buckbarrow
Un-named Groove – Variation (4c)	Buckbarrow
★ Nor'-Nor'-West Climb (–, –, –, 4b, 4c, 4c, –, –,)	Pillar Rock
Flake Climb (4c)	Kern Knotts
The Stitch (4c)	Buckbarrow
★ Rob's Roof – Variation (4c)	Buckbarrow
Rob's Corner (4c)	Buckbarrow
★ Witch (4c, 4c,)	Buckbarrow
Magic Roundabout (4b, 4a, 4b, 4b, –, –,)	Buckbarrow
Dougal (4c, 4b)	Buckbarrow
Delta (4b)	Green Gable
Kern Knotts Corner (–, 4c)	Kern Knotts
Boot Strap (4b, 4a, 4b, 4a, 4b)	Pillar Rock

VS (Contd.)

Girdle Traverse (Amphitheatre Buttress) (4c, 4a)	Buckbarrow
The Pod (4c)	The Napes
Side Slip (4b, 4c, 4a)	Pillar Rock
Jamie (4c)	Buckbarrow
Jamie – Direct Finish (4c)	Buckbarrow
★ Lower Slabs Super Direct (4c)	Black Crag
Nor'-Nor'-West Climb – Variation Finish (4c)	Pillar Rock
Frozen Assets (4c)	Great Knott
The Devious Slash (4b, 4b, 4a)	Haskett Buttress
Pituitrin (4b, 4a, 4b)	Low Adam Crag
Scorpion (4a, 4b)	Buckbarrow
Slab and Groove (4c)	Goat Crag
Tramline (4c, 4b)	Buckbarrow
Adrenalin (4b, 4b, 4b, 4b)	Low Adam Crag
★★ Innominate Crack (4b)	Kern Knotts
Engineer's Chimney (–, 4a)	Gable Crag
Three Scoops Please (4b)	Great Knott
Sodom (–, 4a, 4b, 4b)	Pillar Rock
Cold Climbs (4c)	Great Knott
Girdle Traverse (–, –, 4a, –, 4b, 4a, –, –, –, –)	Overbeck
Mark Twain (4b, –,)	Buckbarrow
Girdle Traverse (Long Crag) (4b, 4b, 4a, 4a)	Buckbarrow
The Faux Pas (–, 4b, 4a)	Scoat Fell Crag
The Gangway (4b, 4a)	Buckbarrow
Octopus (4a, 4b, –,)	Scoat Fell Crag
Aaron (4a, 4a)	Green Gable
The Gable End (4b)	Gable Crag
Hecate (4a, 4b)	Buckbarrow
Sunset Strip (4b, 4a,)	Buckbarrow
Icicle (4b, 4b, –)	Rough Crag
★★ Fie (–, 4b)	Green Gable
Girdle Traverse – Fie Finish (4b)	Green Gable
Corkscrew Slabs (–, 4b)	Gable Crag
Gomorrah – Variation Finish (4b, –,)	Pillar Rock
'C' Gully	The Screes
Central Climb South Face – Variation Start 1a (5a)	Kern Knotts
★ Gomorrah (–, 4b, 4b, 4b)	Pillar Rock
Trundle Ridge (–, 4b, 4b, 4b)	Gable Crag
Josephine (4b, 4b)	Buckbarrow
Tutti-Frutti (4b)	Great Knott
Moving Fingers Groove (4a, 4a, 4b)	Steeple West Buttress
Central Climb South Face – Variation Start 1b (4b)	Kern Knotts
Holly Tree Groove (4b)	Goat Crag
Ash Tree Groove – Variation (4b)	Overbeck
Crack Special (4b)	Buckbarrow
Rib and Slab (4b)	Goat Crag
Nameless Crack (4a, 4b)	Buckbarrow
Angel Delight (4b)	Great Knott
Desperate Dan (4b)	Anglers' Crag

VS (Contd.)

Waterstreak Wall (4b, 4b)	Goat Crag
The Needle Perimeter	The Napes
Danker (4b)	Buckbarrow
Right Gully Arête (4b, –,)	Rough Crag
Left-Hand Buttress (4b, –)	Rough Crag
Greendale Needle (4b, 4a)	Buckbarrow
Cadbury (4a, 4b)	Buckbarrow
Startling Starlings (–, 4a, 4b,)	Buckbarrow
The Flakes (4a, 4b)	Goat Crag
Rib Tickler (4b)	Buckbarrow
Cracked Wall (4b)	Goat Crag
Ejection (4b, –,)	Buckbarrow
Pinnacle Buttress	Buckbarrow

MVS

★ Photon (4b, 4c, –, 4a, 4b, –)	Pillar Rock
★★ Walker's Gully (–, 4a, 4b, –, 4c)	Pillar Rock
Gremlin's Crack (4b)	The Napes
Three Blind Mice (4a, 4b, 4b)	Black Sail Buttress
Brimstone Buttress (4b, –, –,)	The Napes
★★★ North-West Climb (–, 4a, 4b, 4a, 4b)	Pillar Rock
● Hadrians Wall (–, –, –, 4b, 4b, –)	Pillar Rock
The Merry Monk (4b)	The Napes
Tricouni Rib (–, 4b, 4a, 4a)	The Napes
★ Central Climb South Face (4b, 4b)	Kern Knotts
★★★ South-West Climb (4b, 4b, 4b)	Pillar Rock
The Devils Entrance (4a, 4a, 4b, –)	Pillar Rock
★ Thor (4a, 4b)	Pillar Rock
Err (4a, 4b)	Pillar Rock
★ Kern Knotts West Buttress (4b, –,)	Kern Knotts
Tophet Ridge (–, 4b, –)	The Napes
Shamrock Tower (–, 4a, 4b, 4a, 4a, –)	Pillar Rock
Potheen (–, 4b)	Gable Crag
Dang–a–Ling (4a, 4b, 4a)	Buckbarrow
Flakey Wall (4b)	Goat Crag
Labyrinth (4a, –, 4b)	Bowness Knott
Directrix (4b)	Elliptical Crag
The Cat Run (4a, 4b)	Black Sail Buttress
★★ Eagle's Nest Ridge Direct (4a)	The Napes
Hell Gate Pillar (4a)	The Napes
Diamond Rib (4b, ,– ,4a)	Buckbarrow
Pumphouse Arête (–, –, 4a)	Pens End Crag
★ Prayer Mat Buttress (4b)	Gable Crag
● Belfry Crack (4b)	The Napes
Positron (4a, 4b, –, –, 4a, –,)	Pillar Rock
Savage Gully (–, 4b, 4a, 4b)	Pillar Rock
Lower Slabs Climb Direct (–, 4b)	Black Crag
Eagle's Corner (–, –, 4a, –)	The Napes
Tickle-me-Fancy (4a, –)	Buckbarrow

MVS (Contd.)

Injection (–, 4a)	Buckbarrow
Prickle (–, 4a)	Buckbarrow
Deception (4a)	Goat Crag
Great Gully	The Screes
Slab and Groove (4a, 4a)	Buckbarrow
Centre Post (4a)	Buckbarrow
B.J. (4a)	Buckbarrow
A Face Remembered (4a)	Angler's Crag
The Dream Merchants (4b, 4a)	Scoat Fell Crag
East Jordan Climb (4a)	Pillar Rock
Cripes (4a)	Buckbarrow
J.P. (4a)	Buckbarrow
Sideline (4a)	Buckbarrow
Mallory's Right-Hand Route (4a, –)	Gable Crag
Shameless (4a)	Buckbarrow
Starters (4a)	Rough Crag
Iron Crag Buttress (4a, 4a)	Iron Crag
★ Breakwater Slabs, Grooved Arête (4a, –)	Boat Howe Crags
The Banister (–, 4a, 4a)	Pens End Crag
Naughty but Nice (4a)	Great Knott

HS

Crescent Wall	Buckbarrow
The Curving Crack	Overbeck
The Curving Crack – Variation 2a	Overbeck
Cassation	Buckbarrow
★ The Wasdale Crack	The Napes
★ The Obverse Route	The Napes
★ The Arête	The Napes
Forked Gully	Buckbarrow
★ The Lingmell Crack	The Napes
★ The Crowley Route	The Napes
★ Kipper's Chimney	Pillar Rock
★★★ Tophet Wall	The Napes
★ North Climb – The Hand Traverse	Pillar Rock
No Ewe Turns	Cove Crag
East Jordan Wall	Pillar Rock
Rough Crag Gully	Rough Crag
● Tower Postern	Pillar Rock
The Crumb	Pillar Rock
★ Sledgate Ridge	Gable Crag
Black Crack Route	Bowness Knott
Hailstorm	Bowness Knott
The East Buttress	Kern Knotts
Captain Scarlet	Buckbarrow
Starboard Arête Direct	Boat Howe Crags
★★ Kern Knotts Chimney	Kern Knotts
Jordan Bastion	Pillar Rock
Moss Slab	Boat Howe Crags

HS (Contd.)

Branflake	Buckbarrow
Horizon Climb	Boat Howe Crags
North and Central	Overbeck
Moonshiner	Gable Crag
★★★ Rib and Slab Climb	Pillar Rock
★★ The Appian Way	Pillar Rock
Borodino	Buckbarrow
Slab Climb	Bell Rib
Quirk	Buckbarrow
Fingers	Buckbarrow
Florence	Buckbarrow
Aaron's Slab	Gable Crag
Belfry Buttress	The Napes
Central Corner	Black Crag
Alligator Crawl	The Napes
Central Face Climb	Buckbarrow
Flanker	Buckbarrow
The Weakest	Buckbarrow
Kestral	Buckbarrow
Toby	Buckbarrow
Forgotten Wall	Anglers' Crag
★ Crystal Groove	Anglers' Crag
Back Stairs	Buckbarrow
Twin Ribs Climb	Pillar Rock
Serendipity	Buckbarrow
Debutantes Slab	Black Crag

S

★★★ North Climb	Pillar Rock
The Higher Needle Girdle	The Napes
Stern Girdle Traverse	Boat Howe Crags
Skyhook	Bowness Knott
Temptation	Anglers' Crag
★ Overhanging Central Slab Climb	Black Crag
Left-Hand Route	Buckbarrow
Left Gully Arête	Rough Crag
★ Lucifer Crack	The Napes
★ Nook and Wall Climb	Pillar Rock
Ledge and Groove Climb	Pillar Rock
Crescent Crack	Buckbarrow
Green Peace	Green Gable
Larboard Arête	Boat Howe Crags
● Tyrozet	Bowness Knott
Little John	The Napes
● Sirloin Climb	Pillar Rock
Short and Brutish	Buckbarrow
East of Eden	Green Gable
Calculus	Green Gable
Pedestal Wall	Pillar Rock

S (Contd.)

Centipede	
● Bowness Girdle	Raven Crag
★ Rainbow Ridge	Bowness Knott
Left Central Slab Climb	The Napes
The Slab Climb	Black Crag
Right Face Route	Lower Kern Knotts
Beta – Variation	Elliptical Crag
West Jordan Gully	Green Gable
Travesty Cracks	Pillar Rock
★ Central Chimney	Scoatfell Crag
The Buttress	Overbeck
Route 1	Lower Kern Knotts West
White Band Gully	Mosedale Buttresses
Route 2	Buckbarrow
American Dream	Mosedale Buttresses
Wide Gully	Gable Crag
Pisgah from Jordon Gap	West Cove
Central Slab Climb	Pillar Rock
Sundowner	Black Crag
Right-Hand Buttress	Gable Crag
The North Door Climb	Iron Crag
Easter Traverse	Great Door
Heinz Route	Mosedale Buttresses
Great Doup Pinnacle	Gable Crag
Breakwater Slabs and Lighthouse	Great Doup
Central Route	Boat Howe Crags
● Shamrock Gully	Overbeck
East Buttress	Pillar Rock
Ash Tree Chimney – Direct Start	Haskett Buttress
Sideshow	Overbeck
The Owl – Variation	Buckbarrow
Dunn's Delight	Buckbarrow
Left Face Climb	Buckbarrow
Cow Pie	Buckbarrow
Nor'-Nor'-West Climb – Variation Start	Anglers' Crag
Central Face Lower Climb	Pillar Rock
Attic Stairs	Buckbarrow
Western Buttress	Buckbarrow
Rooster	Great Doup
Windy Ridge	Buckbarrow
● Snowstorm	Gable Crag
North-West Climb – Kirkstile Variation	Bowness Knott
Cheekwooly	Pillar Rock
	Pillar Rock

MS

Back of the Napes	The Napes
Pisgah West Ridge	Pillar Rock
★ Bowderdale Climb	Overbeck
The Ductile Slant	Haskett Buttress

MS (Contd.)

Magog	Crag Fell Pinnacles
Chantry Buttress	The Napes
Starboard Arête Direct	Boat Howe Crags
Eastern Bloc	Kern Knotts
★ Overbeck Buttress	Overbeck
★ Epsilon	Green Gable
Bagatelle	Buckbarrow
Eta	Green Gable
Starboard Direct	Boat Howe Crags
Chocolate Chip	Great Knott
Bright Interval	Buckbarrow
Contravallation Ridge	Steeple
Zeke	Buckbarrow
Rowan Tree Gully	Buckbarrow
J.C.B. G.T.	Buckbarrow
Kirk Fell Ghyll	Kirk Fell
Eastern Crack	Crag Fell Pinnacles
Shadow Wall	Anglers' Crag
Phantom Groove	Anglers' Crag
★ North-East Climb	Pillar Rock

VD

The Pulpit Route	Pillar Rock
★★ Abbey Buttress	The Napes
Abbey Buttress – Variation	The Napes
★ West Wall Climb	Pillar Rock
★ Tophet Bastion	The Napes
★ Tower Buttress	Black Crag
Troglodyte	Overbeck
The Main Ridge Climb	Black Crag
Long Chimney	West Cove
Ling Chimney	The Napes
Smirk	Buckbarrow
★★ Needle Ridge	The Napes
Timshel	Green Gable
Tumbledown Chimney	Buckbarrow
Salome	The Napes
Steeple Buttress	Steeple
Funnel	Buckbarrow
Central Line	Buckbarrow
Zebedee	Buckbarrow
Omega	Green Gable
Starboard Fender Ordinary Route	Boat Howe Crags
Starboard Chimney	Boat Howe Crags
Sabre Ridge	The Napes
Cutlass Ridge	The Napes
★ Scimitar Ridge	The Napes
Ash Tree Chimney	Overbeck
★★ Arrowhead Ridge Direct	The Napes

VD (Contd.)

Arrowhead Ridge – S.E. Variation	The Napes
Gagarin	Buckbarrow
★★★ New West Climb	Pillar Rock
Kern Knotts West Chimney	Kern Knotts
Scarab	Raven Crag
Corner Climb	Overbeck
Shamrock Buttress	Pillar Rock
The Owl	Buckbarrow
Rib and Groove	Buckbarrow
Caleb	Green Gable
Evening Chimney	Black Crag
Hind Cove Buttress	Hind Cove
Alpha	Green Gable
Pyfo	Kern Knotts
Coastguard Climb	Boat Howe Crags
Route 2	Bell Rib
Jaga	The Napes
Hatchway and Rigging	Boat Howe Crags
Zeta Climb	The Napes
Route 2	Hind Cove
Crack Chimney and Slab	Black Crag
Divertimento	Buckbarrow
● The Shamrock Chimney's	Pillar Rock
The Sphinx or Cat Rock	The Napes
Route 1	Hind Cove
Oblique Chimney	Gable Crag
Beta	Green Gable
Lower Slabs Ordinary Route	Black Crag
West Jordan Crack	Pillar Rock
Sea Wall Arête – Variation 3a	Boat Howe Crags
Lucifer Ridge	The Napes
Ridge and Gully Climb	Hind Cove
Westmorland Ridge	The Napes
Mallory's Left-Hand Route	Gable Crag
Joint Effort	Buckbarrow
Crescent Ridge	Buckbarrow
The Central Gully – Direct Finish	Gable Crag
Barney Buttress	Gable Crag
● Solo Slabs	Black Crag
Far West Jordan Climb	Pillar Rock

D

Harlequin Chimneys	Pillar Rock
Sphinx Ridge	The Napes
Great Doup Buttress	Great Doup
Left-Face Route	Elliptical Crag
Mossy Face	Bell Rib
The Main Ridge Climb	Black Crag
★★ Eagle's Nest Ordinary Route (West Chimney)	The Napes

D (Contd.)

Iron Crag Ridge	Iron Crag
West Gully	Black Crag
Ash Tree Chimney – Variation 2a	Overbeck
Arjuna	Green Gable
Route 1	Bell Rib
Arrowhead Ridge Easy Way	The Napes
West Jordan Climb	Pillar Rock
★ Gamma	Green Gable
Theta	Green Gable
Girdle Traverse – Theta Finish	Green Gable
Long Climb	Buckbarrow
The White Band	Buckbarrow
The Great Chimney	Pillar Rock
Doctor's Chimney	Gable Crag
North Face	Green Gable
Epsilon Chimney	Green Gable
Route 6	Mosedale Buttresses
Sea Wall Arête – East Buttress	Boat Howe Crags
Buzzard Wall	The Napes
The Crack	Lower Kern Knotts
North-East Chimney	Pillar Rock
Raspberry Ripple	Great Knott
'B' Chimney	Overbeck
North-East Arête	Pillar Rock
● Dan's Mine	Anglers' Crag
Route 5	Mosedale Buttresses
Central Jordan Climb	Pillar Rock
Dan's Groove	Anglers' Crag
Slab and Chimney Route	Lower Kern Knotts West
The Curtain and Arête	Pillar Rock

M

★ **The** Slab and Notch Climb	Pillar Rock
Pendlebury Traverse	Pillar Rock
The West Route	Lower Kern Knotts

FIRST ASCENTS

1826 July 9	**The Old West Route, The Old Wall Route** J Atkinson *(see Historical).*	
1863 Aug 14	**Slab and Notch Climb** J W E Conybeare, A J Butler, E Leeke, J C Leeke, T R C Campbell, J D Poyer, J W Pratt *N.B. It is not certain whether the first ascent via the Slab went through the Notch or round by the Ledge – the-so-called Easy Way.*	
1872 Sept	**Pendlebury Traverse** F Gardiner, W M Pendlebury, R Pendlebury, (Probably others)	
1882 Aug-Sept	**West Jordan Climb** W P Haskett-Smith	
1882 Aug-Sept	**Central Jordan Climb** W P Haskett-Smith	
1884 Aug-Sept	**East Jordan Climb** W P Haskett-Smith *On 27 July 1919, the East Jordan Climb was made independent of the Central Jordan Climb by giving it a new start and a slightly different finish. H M Kelly, C G Crawford, C F Holland, N E Odell.*	
1884 Sept	**Needle Ridge** W P Haskett-Smith *2 January 1911. From the lowest point. A G Woodhead, S F Jeffcoat, J Laycock.*	
1886 June 27 or 30	**The Needle** W P Haskett-Smith *11 July 1910. By the left end of the Mantelshelf. L B Smith, W B Brunskill, J Mallinson, T C Pattinson. This may have been done previously by G B Gibbs. On this date T C Pattinson passed through the crack from west to east. 23 April 1892. The Lingmell Crack. O G Jones, Mrs Commeline, J N Collie (the last named led to the shoulder). 28 August 1893. The Crowley Route. E A Crowley. 17 September 1894. The Arête. W H Fowler. On 21 January 1904, the crack on the right of Western Crack was climbed by W C Slingsby. 26 August 1912. The Obverse Route. S W Herford, W B Brunskill. 29 April 1928. Direct Obverse from the Gap. H G Knight, H M Kelly, W G Standring.*	
1887 March 5	**The Great Chimney, The Arête** and **The Curtain** W P Haskett-Smith (*See Historical*). *It is uncertain when these climbs were first done, but the date of the third ascent of The Curtain is given as 18 April 1899.*	
1889 March	**The Sphinx** or **Cat Rock** W P Haskett-Smith	
1890 Dec 29	**Shamrock Gully** (By Right-Hand route of Great Pitch) G Hastings, Chas Hopkinson, J W Robinson *A previous ascent had been made by the help of a snowdrift. On 29 December 1896 the Left-Hand route of the Great Pitch was first climbed by O G Jones, W J Williams, G D Abraham, A P Abraham.*	

1891 July 27	**North Climb** (Savage Gully exit)	W P Haskett-Smith, G Hastings, W C Slingsby

N.B. This was by the Westerly Variation, but the Stomach Traverse Route, to the Split Blocks only, had been climbed by Haskett-Smith and his brother Edmund previously when exploring the North Face.
On 13 February 1892 the Hand Traverse was first done by G A Solly, G Hastings, H A Gwynne, E Greenwood, W C Slingsby. (This was also by the Westerly Variation).
The Nose Direct was first climbed about 1893 by J Collier, S B Winser, and probably others.
26 August 1921. Intermediate Variation by H M Kelly, R E W Pritchard, J H Doughty, H Coates.

1892 April 15	**Eagle's Nest Ridge Direct**	G A Solly, W C Slingsby, G P Baker, W A Brigg

A route years ahead of its time. Requiring combined tactics in an incredible situation with no protection.
11 September 1910. Pope's Variation. H R Pope, E T W Addyman.

1892 April 15	**Rowan Tree Gully**	N Collie, W W King, W Brunskill, G B Gibbs
1892 April 17	**Eagle's Nest Ordinary Route** (West Chimney)	G A Solly, M Schintz
1892 April 17	**Arrowhead Ridge**	W C Slingsby, H Waller, R W Brant, G P Baker, W A Brigg

(To the recess behind the Arrow.)
31 March 1893. Finishing along the ridge. G A Solly, M Schintz, R W Brant, H C Bowen.

1892 April 21	**East Pisgah Chimney** (Right)	O G Jones

(Right.)
The Left-Hand Chimney was climbed on 26 May 1923 by H M Kelly. Probably been done before.

1892 Dec 27	**Great Gully**, The Screes	G Hastings, J W Robinson, J N Collie
1892 Dec 31	**Oblique Chimney**	J Collier, B Goodfellow, E Talbot, H J Woolley, S B Winser
1893 Dec 26	**Kern Knotts Chimney**	O G Jones, W H Fowler, J W Robinson

28 April 1894. Variation on left of slab. F O Wethered, C Schuster, H Kempson.

1894 Sept 23	**The Shamrock Chimney**	R S Robinson, J W Robinson, L R Wilberforce, W H Price
1886 March 14	**Arrowhead Ridge Direct**	A G Topham, H Walker, W C Slingsby

Direct over the top of the Arrowhead.
8 October 1925. South-East Variation. F Graham.

1896 April 7	**The Central Gully, Direct Finish**, Gable Crag	F Leach, V Blake, T S Booth

28 September 1903. Chimney between Direct and Easy exit. H V Reade, G Arbuthnot.

1896 April 26	**Doctor's Chimney**	Dr. Simpson, C W Patchell

1897 Jan 1	**Hind Cove Gully** *First ascent was evidently made on this date, and the only name mentioned in connection therewith is that of R C Gilson, though there were probably others.*
1897 April 27	**Kern Knotts West Chimney** O G Jones, C W Patchell
1897 April 28	**Kern Knotts Crack** O G Jones, H C Bowen *July 1898. Lower part of Crack direct. W R Reade, W P McCullock.*
1897 April 29	**'C' Gully**, The Screes O G Jones, H C Bowen
1898 March 31	**Pisgah from Jordan Gap** J S Sloane, T Brushfield, S Mason
1898 July 21	**West Jordan Gully** W P McCullock, W R Reade *9 September 1912. Alternative Start by H B Gibson, G S Sansom.* *3 September 1921. Alternative Finishes by H M Kelly, Morley Wood, H Coates.*
1898 Dec	**'B' Chimney**, Overbeck O G Jones, G D Abraham
1899 Jan 7	**Walker's Gully** O G Jones, G D Abraham, A E Field *Alternative Start route.* *A famous epic, as the gully was in very bad condition.* *5 September 1898. First Section direct by J F, R W, H Broadrick.* *June 1909. Additional Finish by F W Botterill and others.*
1899 Jan 8	**Ash Tree Chimney** O G Jones, A E Field, J W F Forbes, G D Abraham *2 October 1946. Variation Start and Ash Tree Groove. A P Rossiter.*
1899 July 30	**Engineer's Chimney** G T Glover, W N Ling *20 June 1924. Variation. H S Gross, M H Hewson.*
1899 Sept 11	**Central Chimney**, Overbeck C W Barton, W G Barton *6 September 1944. Direct start. A B Gilchrist, R Armitage.*
1899 Oct 15	**Ling Chimney** W N Ling, G T Glover
1900 Oct 1	**Great Doup Buttress** G D Abraham, A P Abraham, E E Stock, W E Webb, F Kennedy T T Townley
1901 May 26	**New West Climb** G D Abraham, A P Abraham, C W Barton, J H Wigner
1901 Aug 27	**Savage Gully** C W Barton, G D Barton, L F Meryon *On 3 June 1901 P A Thompson climbed this gully alone, but he had the moral support of a rope from above for the last two pitches.* *At Easter, 1892 or 93, G A Solly, whilst doing the North Climb, led the last pitch of this gully.* *18 June 1968. Variation start W Young, J C Eibeck, W S Lounds.*
1906 June 8	**North-West Climb** (by Taylor's Chimney) F W Botterill, L J Oppenheimer, A Botterill, J H Taylor *23 August 1906. By Lamb's Chimney, R Lamb, W L Collinson, R Horton, E W Steeple.* *1913 (?), Alternative Finish. D G Murry, E B Beauman.* *1 August 1937. Kirkstile Variation by F Graham, R S T Chorley.*

1908 April 22	**Long Chimney**, West Cove B Hoessly J D Hazard, E E Roberts, F Boyd
1908 April 22	**Haskett Gully** W P Hasket-Smith, L J Oppenheimer, H Scott-Tucker *(L J Oppenheimer led the cave pitch.)*
1908 Sept	**Mallory's Left-Hand Route, Mallory's Right-Hand Route** G H L Mallory, G L Keynes *July 1968. Variation Start to Right-hand Route* *P L Fearnehough, G Oliver.*
1909 April 7	**Abbey Buttress** F Botterill, J de V Hazard
1909 April 9	**Smuggler's Chimney** J S Sloane, M Gimson, A Gimson, J G Henderson
1909 May 6	**West Jordan Crack** H B Gibson, W B Brunskill
1909 May 6	**Far West Jordan Climb** H B Gibson, W B Brunskill
1909 May 24	**Shamrock Buttress** (Route 2) H B Gibson, F W Botterill, J H Davidson *Originally the variation but proves the best climbing.* *Route 1 Variation, 1902 Easter. G D Abraham, A P Abraham,* *W G Clay, H G Beeching.*
1909 June 4	**Pisgah West Ridge** F W Botterill, H B Gibson *(both the ordinary route and variation).*
1909 June	**North-East Arête** F Botterill, H Williamson, E S
1909 July 15	**Overbeck Buttress** E T W Addyman and others
1910 Easter	**Black Crack** H B Lyon, L J Oppenheimer, J M Davidson *The Black Corner was climbed by W Heaton Cooper on 10* *September 1933.*
1910 Easter	**Easter Crack** E A Baker, H Westmorland
1910 Aug 15	**Left Face Route** H B Lyon, G S Sansom
1910 Aug 15	**Right Face Route**, (Direct) W B Brunskill *15 May 1910. First done by traversing out of Black Crack 40* *feet up. – H B Lyon, W B Brunskill, L B Smith.*
1910 Aug 15	**Small Chimney** H B Lyon and others
1910 Aug 15	**Small Crack** H B Lyon and others
1911 Sept 29	**South-West Climb** (New West Climb Finish) H R Pope, W B Brunskill *24 July 1919. Direct Finish to Jordan Gap. C F Holland,* *R F Stobart, Dorothy E Pilley.* *27 July 1919. Direct Finish to High Man. H M Kelly,* *C F Holland, C G Crawford, N E Odell.*
1912 April 12	**Kern Knotts West Buttress** G S Sansom, S W Herford
1912 April 21	**North-East Climb** ^G D Abraham, A P Abraham *In the above ascent the last three pitches of the climb as given* *in this guide were apparently avoided. These were evidently* *done for the first time on 30 May 1912 by a party composed of* *C F Stocks, Miss Capper, C S Worthington, J Gaspard.*
1913 Easter	**Wide Gully** D G Murray, E B Beauman *18 April 1908. Chimney Variation. J D Hazard, E E Roberts.* *11 September 1912. Branch Gully. E E Roberts.*
1913 Sept 7	**Abbey Buttress Variations** G H L Mallory

Upper part only called Mallory's Variation.
Remainder on 17 June 1924 by H S Gross, M H Hewson.
These variations combine to make independent route.

1913	**Slab Climb** S W Herford, J Laycock
1919 June 13	**Tophet Bastion** H M Kelly, E H Pryor, A R Thomson, Mrs Kelly, C G Crawford
1919 July 29	**Rib and Slab Climb** C F Holland, H M Kelly, C G Crawford
1919 July 29	**West Wall Climb** H M Kelly, C F Holland, C G Crawford
	Originally named West Face of Low Man.
1919 July	**Scimitar Ridge** C F Holland
1919 Aug 3	**East Jordan Wall** C G Crawford, C F Holland
1919 Aug 3	**Jordan Bastion** C G Crawford, C F Holland
1919 Aug 5	**Kern Knotts Buttress** H M Kelly, R E W Pritchard
1919 Aug 7	**Central Climb, South Face** H M Kelly, R E W Pritchard, A P Wilson
	September 1933. Variation Start. J H Jameson.
	31 March 1956. Variation. J A Austin, R B Evans.
1919 Aug 7	**Flake Climb** H M Kelly, R E W Pritchard, A P Wilson, G H Jackson
1919 Aug 9	**Sodom** H M Kelly, C F Holland
	In early editions of the guide this was known as Route 1.
	On 12 September 1911, O Tindale and others did the last two pitches of this route as a finish to New West Climb.
1919 Aug 9	**Gomorrah** H M Kelly, C F Holland
	In the early editions of the guide this was known as Route 2.
	15 May 1932. Ridge Variation. M Linnell, A S Piggott.
	19 June 1967. Direct Start. W Young, R Schipper.
	22 July 1967. Variation Finish. J C Eilbeck, P W Lucas.
	The names of Routes 1 and 2 have been changed, to Sodom and Gomorrah respectively. These were, in fact, the original names as is best explained by a quote from a letter received from H M Kelly: "It was Holland, under the stress of a slight contretemps on Route 2, which might have ended in disaster, who suggested Sodom and Gomorrah as titles, on the way home on that memorable day. But the suggestion was for a time kept to ourselves and the more prosaic titles entered in the Hotel Log Book, I think the same day".
1920 May 30	**The Slab Climb** H M Kelly, G S Bower
1920 Aug 30	**Sabre Ridge** H M Kelly, R E W Pritchard
1920 Sept 11	**Nook and Wall Climb** H M Kelly, C F Holland, R E W Pritchard
1921 April 9	**Innominate Crack** G S Bower, B Beetham, J B Wilton
1921 Oct	**Routes 1, 2, 3, 4, 5** and **6** Mosedale Buttresses F Graham
1921 Nov 10	**The Buttress** F Graham
1921 Nov 11	**Chantry Buttress** F Graham
1922 June 5	**Buzzard Wall** F Graham, M Wood
1922 July 27	**Cutlass Ridge** F Graham
1922 July 27	**Rainbow Ridge** F Graham
	June 1934. Variation. F G Balcombe, C J A Cooper.

1923 May 24	**Hind Cove Buttress**	H M Kelly, B Eden-Smith
1923 May 24	**Routes 1 and 2**, Hind Cove	H M Kelly, B Eden-Smith
1923	**The Appian Way**	H M Kelly, R E W Pritchard

Rumour has it that the route was named as a pun on 'pee on the way'.

1923 July 13	**Forked Gully**	H M Kelly, R E W Pritchard

(Right fork: ascent and descent).

1923 July 13	**Right Face Climb**	H M Kelly, R E W Pritchard
1923 July 13	**Hidden Gully**	R E W Pritchard, H M Kelly

(descent only).

1923 July 14	**Tophet Wall**	H M Kelly, R E W Pritchard

15 August 1925. Direct Start. M de Selincourt.

1924 April 20	**The West Route**	H M Kelly, R E W Pritchard
1924 April 20	**Easter Traverse**	F Graham, H S Gross

(H S Gross led last pitch.)

1924 June 16	**The East Buttress**	H S Gross
1924 June 19	**Eagle's Corner**	C D Frankland, B Beetham

June 1925. Variations. H S Gross, M H Hewson.
12 October 1946. Variation. M Schatz, G G Macphee.

1924 Sept 25	**Zeta Climb**	F Graham
1925 April 19	**Sea Wall Arête – East Buttress**	G Basterfield, T Graham Brown
1925 April 19	**Starboard Chimney**	G Basterfield, T Graham Brown
1925 May 30	**Hatchway and Rigging**	L C Letts, T Graham Brown
1925 May 31	**Breakwater Slabs** and **Lighthouse**	G Basterfield, G Lee, T Graham Brown
1925 June 7	**Larboard Arête**	G Basterfield, K B Milne
1925 June 21	**Rib and Gully Climb**	H M Kelly, B Eden-Smith
1925 Aug 19	**Tricouni Rib**	C D Frankland, M M Barker
1925 Sept 8	**Belfry Crack**	F Graham, G M Wellburn
1925 Oct 9	**Aaron**	F Graham
1925 Oct 9	**North Face**	F Graham
1925 Oct 16	**Lucifer Crack**	F Graham
1926 April 3	**Coastguard Climb**	J De V Hazard, T Graham Brown
1926 April 3	**Starboard Arête by Clinker**	J de V Hazard, T Graham Brown

The Clinker has now disappeared.

1926 April 4	**Stern Girdle Traverse**	J de V Hazard, T Graham Brown
1926 April 4	**Horizon Climb**	J de V Hazard, T Graham Brown
1926 May 24	**Prayer Mat Buttress**	G Wood-Johnson, E Wood-Johnson, T R Burnett, K Ward, W G Hennessy, A Wood-Johnson
1927 April 6	**Route 1**, Bell Rib	G Wood-Johnson, E H Marriot
1927 May 6	**Slab Climb**, Bell Rib	E C Williams, E Wood-Johnson
1927 May 6	**Route 2**, Bell Rib	E Wood-Johnson, E C Williams
1927 Aug 6	**Great Doup Pinnacle**	G Wood-Johnson, E Wood-Johnson, M M Barker
1927 Oct 23	**Alpha**	G C Macphee, H S Gross, C M Barnard
1927 Oct 23	**Eta**	G G Macphee, H S Gross, C M Barnard
1927 Oct 29	**Gamma**	G G Macphee, C M Barnard
1927 Oct 29	**Theta**	C M Barnard, G G Macphee
1927 Oct 29	**Beta**	C M Barnard, G G Macphee

12 May 1928. Direct ascent of top pitch. G G Macphee and Kate Ward.

1927 Nov 27   **Epsilon**   G G Macphee, G S Bower, H S Gross

1928 April 11   **Long John**   H G Knight, H M Kelly
June 1932. Top Pitch. C J A Cooper, E Wood-Johnson, E D G Lewers.

1928 April 27   **Kern Knotts Chain**   H G Knight, W G Standing, H M Kelly
(left to Right.)

1928 April 28   **Grooved Wall**   H M Kelly, H G Knight, W G Standing
(W G Standing led the last pitch.)

1928 April 29   **Kern Knotts Chain**   H M Kelly, W G Standing, H G Knight
(Right to Left.)

1928 May 12   **Delta**   G G Macphee, K Ward

1928 May 12   **Epsilon Chimney**   G G Macphee, K Ward
Probably climbed by numerous members of the club meet. May 1910.

1928 May 28   **Breakwater Slabs, Grooved Arête**   H S Gross, G Basterfield, B Tyson

1928 May 28   **Harlequin Chimneys**   H G Knight, W G Standing, W Eden-Smith

1929 June 26   **Main Ridge Climb**   E Wood-Johnson, A Wood-Johnson, E W Milne, W G Hennessy

1929 June 26   **Tower Buttress**   E Wood-Johnson, C J Astley Cooper, A Wood-Johnson, W G Hennessy

1929 June 26   **Left-Hand Route, Right-Hand Route, West Buttress**   A Wood-Johnson, E Wood-Johnson, C J Astley Cooper, W G Hennessy

1929 June 26   **Lower Slabs Ordinary Route**   E Wood-Johnson, E W Milne

1929 June 27   **Lower Slabs Climb Direct**   E Wood-Johnson, C J Astley Cooper, A Wood-Johnson, W G Hennessy
28 June 1929. 'Third pitch and Direct Finish.' E Wood-Johnson, W G Hennessy.

1929 June 28   **Left Central Slab Climb**   E Wood-Johnson, W G Hennessy, A Wood-Johnson

1929 June 28   **Overhanging Central Slab Climb**   E Wood-Johnson, W G Hennessy, A Wood-Johnson
Variation. 25 June 1929. Central Slab Climb. E Wood-Johnson, A Wood-Johnson, E W Milne, W G Hennessy.

1929 June 28   **West Gully**, Black Crag   A Wood-Johnson, W G Hennessy

1929 June 28   **Crack, Chimney and Slab**   A Wood-Johnson, W G Hennessy

1931   **Girdle Traverse**   M Linnell, A B Hargreaves, A W Bridge
The party started up South-West Climb and finished up Grooved Wall Climb.
24 April 1957. C J Crowther and T W Gallon had the idea of a Girdle in the opposite direction but miss out many of the best pitches.

1932 June 25   **Nor'-Nor'-West Climb**   A T Hargreaves, G G Macphee
3 August 1936. Variation Start by W G Standing, W C Light.
18 March 1954. Direct finish by W F Dowlen, R Greenwood.

1932 June	**Tophet Ridge** S Watson, R Holmes, B Porter, C Cowen
1932 June	**Westmorland Ridge** S Watson, R Holmes, B Porter, C Cowen
1932 June	**Kern Knotts Corner** (by easy exit) S Watson, R Holmes, B Porter, C Cowen *1934. Direct finish. S Watson, A Watkins, P Brown.*
1933 April 14	**Hadrian's Wall** A T Hargreaves, W Clegg, W Eden-Smith, R E Heap, W G Milligan
1933 Sept	**Fie** C J A Cooper
1933 Oct 22	**Ledge and Groove Climb** A T Hargreaves, G Barker, R E Heap
1934 April 1	**The Pulpit Route** A S Piggott, G R Speaker, H M Kelly
1934 June 7	**The Buttonhook Route** F G Balcombe, C J A Cooper
1934 June 8	**Engineer's Slabs** F G Balcombe, J A Shepherd, C J A Cooper *A magnificent lead which was not repeated for over 11 years.*
1934 June	**Lucifer Ridge** F G Balcome, J A Shepherd
1934 June	**Engineer's Slab – Unfinished Arête** F G Balcombe, J A Shepherd
1934 June	**Hell Gate Pillar** F G Balcome, C J A Cooper, M M Barker
1934 Sept 12	**Mossy Face** B Ritchie, H M Kelly
1935 April 28	**Starboard Fender** T H Savage, R H Fidler, R M Lupton, D Usher
1937 Aug 1	**Pedestal Wall** R S T Chorley, F Graham *10 October 1938. Alternative Start by F Graham, M W Guinness.*
1937	**Centipede** D J Cameron, W Heaton Cooper
1937	**Scarab** D J Cameron, W Heaton Cooper
1937	**Solo Slabs** J B Chadwick
1938 Whit	**South-West by West Climb** A Birtwistle, W K Pearson
1938 June 20	**Phantom Groove** J Williams
1938 Aug 28	**Brimstone Buttress** A T Hargreaves, S H Gross, R E Hargreaves, J J Heap, A M Nelson
1939 May 28	**Sirloin Climb** A T Hargreaves, S H Gross, R E Hargreaves, A M Nelson, C J A Cooper
1939 June 17	**Moss Slab** A Gregory, F Grundy
1939	**Barney Buttress** B Beetham
1940 May 12	**Shamrock Tower** S H Cross, A T Hargreaves, A B Hargreaves, R E Hargreaves, A M Cross *1986 Variation (pitches 2 & 3).*
1940 May 18	**Evening Chimney** J B Chadwick, H R Carter
1940 June 2	**The Prow of the Boat** S H Cross, A T Hargreaves, R E Hargreaves, A M Cross
1940 June 16	**Eagle's Crack** R J Birkett, R Holmes, G Rawlings
1940 June 21	**Starboard Arête Direct** D M K Home
1940 Oct 13	**Tophet Grooves** R J Birkett, V Veevers *June 1968. Direct Start. P L Fearnehough, J E Howard.*
1941 June 16	**The Needle Perimeter** R L Plackett, A Burnstead
1941 June	**Tower Postern** S H Cross, A T Hargreaves
1942 June 25	**Back of the Napes** T A H Medlycott, Miss Medlycott
1942 Aug 9	**East Buttress** W Peascod, A Barton, F L Jenkins
1943 July 23	**Western Buttress**, Great Doup F L Jenkins
1944 April 10	**Kirk Fell Ghyll** L Kellett, J E Blackshaw, C E F Dee

1944 July 2	**Zig-Zag** J Wilkinson, D W Jackson	

Last pitch top-roped, led by D C Birch in 1947.
Pitch 2 and 3 originally known as Jackson and Wilkinson Zig-Zag.

1944 Sept 7   **Windy Ridge**   A R Dolphin, C Smith, J Skinner
1945 April 10   **Demon Wall**   A R Dolphin, A B Gilchrist
12 October 1974. Variation. The Upper Traverse. J Lamb, C Downer.

1945 April 11   **Tophet Girdle**   A R Dolphin, B Black
1945 July 19   **Twin Ribs Climb**   J Wilkinson, D W Jackson
1945 Aug 27   **Bowderdale Climb**   A P Rossiter, B Bloch
1945 Sept 4-24 **Girdle Traverse** (short course) N to S, Overbeck A P Rossiter (solo)
S to N, including pitches 9 and 10, by P Rossiter (Solo) 13 January 1946.

1945 Sept 6   **Eagle's Chain**   J Wilkinson, J Umpleby
1945 Sept 24   **The Gargoyle**   A P Rossiter (Solo)
1st pitch climbed on 7 September 1945 by A P Rossiter (Solo).

1945 Sept   **Corner Climb**   A P Rossiter, B Bloch
1946 Jan 5   **Central Route**   A P Rossiter, B Bloch
March 2 1970. Variation Finish. R Triesidder, R Howarth.

1946 April 15   **Octopus**   J Wilkinson, C A Bunton, H Ironfield
1946 July 11   **Curving Crack** and **North Chimney**   A P Rossiter, B Bloch
(Crack alone, A P Rossiter, 2 September 1945.)

1946 July 14   **Gremlin's Crack**   D Haworth
1946 Sept 28   **North and Central**   A P Rossiter
1946 Oct 2   **Ash Tree Groove** (by Direct Start and Zig-Zag)   A P Rossiter
1947 April 18   **Heinz Route**   B Beetham
1947 Sept 27   **Little John**   J G Ball, J W Cook
1948 April 14   **The North Door Climb**   A P Rossiter, N S Brooke
1948 July 21   **Magog, Eastern Crack**   J Williams, D Williams
1950 Feb 19   **Black Crack Route**   W Peascod W J Allen
1950 April 10   **Hailstorm**   W Peascod, G Rushworth (alt)
1951 Sept 16   **Jaga**   G B Fisher, F Bantock, P Taylor
1954 Oct 10   **Salome**   G Fisher, D Oliver
1955 April 20   **The Cenotaph**   P Ross, R Scott, D Wildridge
1957 April   **Steeple Buttress**   D A Elliott
1957   **Snowstorm**   F Crosby, A Watson
1958 June 15   **Corkscrew Slabs**   A H Greenbank, J Wilkinson, A E Wormell
1958 June 15   **Sledgate Ridge**   A H Greenbank, J Wilkinson, A E Wormell
1958 July 5   **Moonshiner**   J Wilkinson, J Umpleby
1958 July 5   **Sundowner**   J Wilkinson, R S Knight, J Umpleby
1958 Nov 23   **Adrenalin**   R Shaw, I Clough (alt)
1959 March 14   **Pituitrin**   A H Greenbank, A D Simpson
1959 May 17   **Girdle Traverse**, Green Gable   J D Oliver, K C Ogilvie
1959 June 3   **Labyrinth**   A G Thorbrun, R Macleod
1959 July 6   **Green Gash**   A G Thorburn
1959 June 13   **Vandal**   G Oliver, J M Cheesmond, L Willis
1959 June 13   **Goth**   M de St Jorre, N Hannaby

Two hard routes done in one day. It was 18 years since the last new route had been done on the Rock.

1959 Aug 11	**Aaron's Slab**	J Wilkinson, A E Wormell, P B Wormell
1960 April 18	**Odin**	B Ingle, P Crew

Alternate leads, pitches 1-3.
30 April 1967. Pitch 4 added by A G Cram, K Robson.
23 October 1965. Variation Finish – P Ross, C Bonington (alternate leads). The party did pitches 1-3 of Odin and the route was named Shamrock Eliminate.

1960 April 23	**Crocodile Crack**	G Oliver, G Arkless, P Ross, N Brown
1960 May 22	**Alligator Crawl**	G Oliver, G Arkless
1961 March 2	**Witch**	P Walsh, M Burke

A hint at the quality that was available but ignored.

1961 April 15	**Gagarin**	D N Greenop, E Ivison, P Magoriam
1961 May 14	**Angel's Step**	D Byrne, J Young, W Young
1962 Sept 24	**Thyroxin**	D Elliot, W Young
1962 Oct	**Pyfo**	D N Greenop, E Ivison (alt)
1963 June 9	**Scylla**	A G Cram, W Young

Direct Finish. Climbed using aid by A G Cram 1966.
May 1974. Direct Finish climbed free. J Lamb, P Botterill.

1963 July 9	**Sheerline**	R D Brown, J A Hartley
1964 July	**Dexedrin**	W Young, I Singleton, J Williams
1964 Sept 12	**West Cove Eliminate**	A G Cram, T Martin

A piton was used as the overhang was wet.

1964 Sept 30	**Charybdis**	A G Cram, W Young
1964	**Skyhook**	A G Cram, W Young (alt.)
1965 April 2	**Sheol**	A G Cram, T Martin
1965 Aug	**Scrimshanker**	L Brown, J S Bradshaw
1966 April 30	**Puppet**	A G Cram, B Whybrow

Pitches 1-4.
July 1963. Pitch 5. D Yates and party as a finish to Scylla.
19 June 1967. Complete. A G Cram, L Rodgers.

1966 Sept 20	**The Hun**	L Brown, S Bradshaw

The layback crack was avoided.

1966 Sept 29	**Electron**	A G Cram, J C Eilbeck
1966 Sept 29	**Proton**	R Schipper, W Young

Alternate leads. 2 slings were used for aid on pitch 1.
Climbed free by T Martin on the second ascent, 1966.

1966 Sept 30	**The Tomb**	A G Cram, W Young

1 point of aid used on pitch 2 at the overlap. Now climbed free.
Variation climbed by P Nunn on 2nd ascent.

1967 April 15	**Attila**	R Schipper, W Young

Variation. E Spofforth, J Ratcliff 22 June 1975.

1967 April 16	**The Sentinel**	R Schipper, T Martin

3 slings were used for aid.
Climbed free by A G Cram, W Young on the second ascent, 1967.

1967 April 29	**Gondor**	A G Cram, K Robson

1 peg for aid.
Climbed free. G Tinnings, 1978, on a slightly different line.

1967 April 29	**Akhnaton** W Young, R Schipper (alt)
1967 June 1	**Interceptor** P L Fearnehough, N J Soper
1967 June 10	**Directrix** J C Eilbeck, P W Lucas
1967 June 13	**Thor** R Schipper, C Bonington
1967 June 27	**The Troll** A G Cram, L Rodgers

1 point of aid used on pitch 1 at the block overhang. Now climbed free.

1967 July 22	**Bootstrap** J C Eilbeck, P W Lucas
1967 July 22	**Positron** J C Eilbeck P W Lucas
1967 Sept 16	**Photon** W A Barnes, A Jackman, J C Eilbeck, D A Elliott (var)

18 May 1968. Direct Finish. W S Lounds, J C Eilbeck.

1967 Sept 23	**Kipper's Chimney** W A Barnes, A Jackman, D A Elliott
1968 April 12	**Ximenes** A G Cram, W Young
1968 April 12	**Necromancer** A G Cram, W Young (var)

29 June 1986. Variation Start. R Kenyon, A G Cram.

1968 April 21	**Waterstreak Wall** J Harris, N J Soper (alt)
1968 May 18	**Eros** W S Lounds, J C Eilbeck
1968 May 18	**Thanatos** W S Lounds, J C Eilbeck (alt)
1968 May 19	**Lepton** W S Lounds, J C Eilbeck (alt)
1968 May 29	**Tyrozet** D N Greenop, A McGregor, D Bonney
1968 June 1	**Bosun** W S Lounds, J C Eilbeck (alt)
1968 June 21	**Eightfold Way** W S Lounds, J C Eilbeck

Alternate leads. Pitch 2, W Young, T Martin, June 1968.

1968 June	**Central Face**, Buckbarrow P L Fearnehough, P Phipps
1968 July 6	**Vishnu** W S Lounds, J C Eilbeck (alt)
1968 July 13	**The Black Widow** T Martin, J Wilson, G Cowan

Four pitons for aid. First free ascent W Lounds, A Charlton, 8 August 1969.

1968 July 29	**The Link** W Young, J C Eilbeck (alt)
1968 July	**Belfry Buttress** J E Howard, P L Fearnehough
1968 July	**The Pod** P L Fearnehough, G Oliver
1968 Aug	**The Slant** M Burbage, L J Griffin, P L Fearnehough, G Oliver

In 1955 P Nunn led the top pitch only.

1968 Sept	**The Merry Monk** P L Fearnehough, G Oliver
1969 April 5	**Contravallation Ridge** D N Greenop
1969 April	**The Greater Traverse** W Young, R Schipper (alt)

The first complete crossing in $5^1/_2$ hours of the Eightfold Way, The Link and The Girdle Traverse of Pillar.

1969 May 3	**Moving Finger Grooves** D N Greenop, G Jennings (var)
1969 May 24	**Three Blind Mice** N A J Rogers, C H Taylor, I Roper (alt)
1969 May 27	**The Cat Run** C H Taylor, J Taylor, A Kelly
1969 May 28	**The Marriage** D N Greenop, G Jennings
1969 June 1	**Numenor** I Roper, N A J Rodgers

3 points of aid used on 1st ascent.
Climbed without aid: W Lounds, K Bliss. 30 August 1973.

1969 June 12	**The Dolorous Stroke** G Jennings, D N Greenop, R Briggs
1969 June 14	**Landlubber** I Roper, N A J Rogers
1969 June 14	**Fanghorn** I Roper, N A J Rogers

3 points of aid used on 1st ascent.

Pitch 1 climbed with 1 point of aid: W Lounds, K Bliss. 30 August 1973.

1969 June 15   **The Viking**   A McHardy, P Braithwaite
On the first ascent pitch 2 was climbed with virtually no protection. A very bold lead.
A gem stolen from under the noses of the locals establishing a new great on Gable.

1969 July 15   **The Ductile Slant**   D N Greenop

1969 Aug 29   **The Detrital Slide**   D N Greenop, G Jennings (var)

1969 Sept 6   **The Devious Slash**   D N Greenop, A McGregor (var)

1970   **Bagatelle**
Pitch 2 W E Pattison.
Pitch 1 H Jenkins, A W Dunn, 25 November 1973.

1970 March 8   **Troglodyte**   A Malheim, D Sanderson

1970 May 29   **The Delectation Sinistrose**   D N Greenop, G Jennings (alt)

1970 June 4   **The Jabberwock**   R Valentine, J Wilkinson
Pitch 3 originally the Direct Finish to Engineer's Slab – Unfinished Arête, first climbed by P Ross, D P Lockey, 15 June 1958.

1970 June 4   **Trundle Ridge**   R Valentine, J Wilkinson

1970 June 13   **Potheen**   D Miller, J Wilkinson

1970 June 13   **The Bandersnatch**   D Miller, J Wilkinson

1970 June 15   **Lothlorian**   L A Goldsmith, D A Banks (alt)

1970 June 20   **The Serpent**   C Read, W L Robinson (alt)

1970 Aug 29   **Err**   W L Robinson, K S Perry (alt)

1970 Aug   *A number of routes were claimed on Latterbarrow Crag during this month by A Shepard, J Costick, A Jones and A Barber (all members of the Karabiner MC), and a small supplement was produced. The exact lines are not known at present and will have to be checked against current claims in due course.*

1971 Feb 1   **Borodino**   J Lindsay, J W Bremner

1971 March   **The Jewel**   J Gosling, E Thurrell

1971 May 2   **Travesty Cracks**   D N Greenop, A D Baldwin (alt)

1971 May 2   **The Dream Merchants**   D N Greenop, A D Baldwin (alt)

1971 May 2   **The Faux Pas**   D N Greenop, A D Baldwin (alt)

1971 Sept 11   **Ode to Boby**   D N Greenop, H Thomas (var)
Believed climbed by C Bonington in early 1960's.
26 May 1987. Direct Finish. J Loxham.

1971 Sept 11   **Spirit Level**   A G Cram, W Young (var)
1 point of aid used on pitch 1. Now climbed free.

1972 May 20   **Megaton**   W Young, W A Barnes

1972 Aug 15   **The Devil's Entrance**   R Bennett, Miss R Lavender

1972 Aug 26   **Soliton**   W S Lounds, J C Eibeck, K A Willis

1972 Oct 14   **The Magic Rainbow**   D W Hodgson, J Workman
Pitch 1. W Young, I Singleton, 1966.

1972   **Ding-a-Ling**   J Wilson

1973 April   **The Owl**   R Bennett, A Shaw, A Mitchell
1979. Variation 1a. W E Patterson, J W Bremner.
1988 May. Variation Howl. J Carradice, P S Mackrill

1973 May 6	**Injection** R Bennett, R Lavender	
1973 May 18	**Hecate** R Bennett, R Lavender	
1973 May	**Divertimento** H Jenkins, A Dunn (alt)	
1973 June	**Cassation** H Jenkins, A W Dunn	
1973 July 25	**Sideshow** W E Patterson, J W Bremner	
1973 July 25	**Diamond Rib** J W Bremner, W E Pattison (alt)	
1973 July	**Amphitheatre Buttress** J W Bremner, W E Patterson	
1973 July	**Girdle Traverse**, Amphitheatre Buttress W E Pattison, J W Bremner	

Original 2nd pitch left out due to unstable rock.

1973 July	**Central Face – Lower Climb** H Jenkins, A W Dunn
1973 Sept 9	**Jamie** W E Patterson, A W Dunn

September 1986. Direct Finish. J Palmer, W E Pattison

1973 Oct 21	**Ejection** J W Bremner, W E Pattison
1973 Oct 28	**Tramline** J W Bremner, W E Pattison, R Bennett (alt)
1973 Oct 28	**Scorpion** W E Pattison, R Bennett, J W Bremner (alt)
1973 Oct 28	**Prickle** R Bennett, J W Bremner, W E Patison (alt)
1973 Nov 25	**Left-Face Climb** A W Dunn, H Jenkins
1973 Nov	**Iron Crag Ridge** W E pattison, A W Dunn, J Bremner
1973 Nov	**Iron Crag Buttress** W E Pattison, A W Dunn, J Bremner
1973 Nov	**Right Band Buttress** W E Pattison, A W Dunn, J Bremner

Variation 1a. W E Pattison, A W Dunn, J Bremner.

1974	**Girdle Traverse**, Long Crag D A Banks, R Goldsmith, A Brown
1974 Jan 20	**Left-Hand Route** J W Bremner, W E Pattison (alt)
1974 Jan 20	**Dunn's Delight** J W Bremner, A W Dunn, W E Pattison (alt)
1974 April 6	**El Vino** A Stephenson, S Miller
1974 April 6	**The Kraken** S Miller, J Stephenson
1974 April 20	**Centre Line** J W Bremner (Solo)
1974 April 21	**J.C.B. G.T.** H Jenkins, A W Dunn (alt)
1974 April 21	**Cromlech Groove** W E Pattison, J W Bremner (alt)
1974 April 21	**Tickle-me-Fancy** H Jenkins, A W Dunn
1974 May 1	**The Gangway** W E Pattison, J W Bremner (alt)
1974 May 1	**Serendipity** W E Pattison, A W Dunn, J W Bremner (alt)
1974 May 4	**Klingsor** C Read, W L Robinson
1974 May 5	**White Band Gully** J W Bremner, W E Pattison (alt)
1974 May 5	**Majic Roundabout** W E Pattison, J W Bremner
1974 May 5	**Short and Brutish** W E Pattison, J W Bremner (alt)
1974 May 15	**Triton** A Stephenson, R G Willison
1974 May 19	**Florence** A W Dunn, W E Pattison (alt)
1974 May 19	**Zebedee** W E Pattison, A W Dunn
1974 May 19	**Dougal** W E Pattison, A W Dunn
1974 May 27	**Pinnacle Buttress** J W Bremner, J D G Bremner
1974 May	**Centre Post** W E Pattison, J W Bremner (alt)
1974 May	**Vindolanda** P Long, J Adams

One point of aid used on first ascent.
Climbed free by P Botterill, J Adams on 10 July 1977.

1974 June 2	**Cadbury** W E Pattison, J W Bremner
1974 June 2	**Flanker** W E Pattison, J W Bremner
1974 June 9	**Bright Interval** H Jenkins, J W Bremner, A W Dunn

1974 June 11	**Tumbledown Chimney**	A W Dunn, W E Pattison (alt)
1974 June 11	**Greendale Needle**	W E Pattison, A W Dunn (alt)
1974 June 12	**The Weakest**	J W Brewmmer, H Jenkins
1974 June 15	**Strider**	J D Wilson, P Semphill, B Smith
1974 June 16	**Quirk**	W E Pattison, S Daglish, J Daglish

Pitches 1 and 2 by W E Pattison, S Daglish , J Daglish.
Pitches 3 and 4 W E Pattison, W J Bremner, 17 June 1974.

1974 June 17	**Fingers**	W E Pattison, J W Bremner, A W Dunn
1974 June 19	**Toby**	J W Bremner, W E Pattison, A W Dunn
1974 June 19	**Joint Effort**	P Moffat, P Hogg, H K Gregory
1974 June 23	**Danker**	W E Pattison, J W Bremner
1974 June 25	**Gaul**	J D Wilson, T Martin
1974 June 27	**Midsummer Madness**	W E Pattison, J W Bremner (alt)

Originally climbed in 2 pitches with 1 point of aid on the crux

1974 June 30	**The Crumb**	R Bennett, Miss R Lavender
1974 June	**Pumphouse Arête**	W E Pattison, A W Dunn
1974 June	**Peregrine**	W E Pattison, A W Dunn
1974 June	**The Bannister**	W E Pattison, A W Dunn (alt)
1974 July 13	**Aspro**	N Barnes, S Clarke, A Jackman, I Angell
1974 July 14	**Cheekwooly**	R Bennett, Miss R Lavender

The first section only, known as Cheek, was given an
independent finish called Wooly on May 14 1988, A Phizacklea,
R Wightman.

1974 Sept 9	**Slab and Groove**	A W Dunn, W E Pattison
1974 Oct 13	**Kestrel**	R Bennett, R Lavender
1974	**Rib and Groove**	W E Pattison (Solo)
1974	**Greendale Corner**	W E Pattison, A W Dunn
1975 Feb 25	**Smirk**	W E Pattison, A W Dunn
1975 May	**Crescent Wall**	W E Pattison, A W Dunn
1975 May	**Crescent Crack**	W E Pattison, A W Dunn
1975 May	**Crescent Ridge**	W E Pattison, A W Dunn
1975 July 22	**Steeple Crack**	R G Hutchinson, J W Earl (alt)
1975 Aug	**Josephine**	W E Pattison, A W Dunn
1975 Aug 17	**Rooster**	W E Pattison, A W Dunn
1975 Aug 17	**Mark Twain**	W E Pattison, A W Dunn
1975 Aug 20	**Funnel**	W E Pattison, A W Dunn
1975 Sept	**Sunset Strip**	W E Pattison, A W Dunn
1975 Dec	**Starters**	W E Pattison, A W Dunn
1975	**Rob's Corner**	R Tressider A.N.O.

Variation 1975, Rob's Roof. R Tressider A.N.O.

1976 Feb	**Icicle**	W E Pattison, A W Dunn

A cold start to the development of Rough Crag.

1976 March	**Rough Crag Gully**	W E Pattison, A W Dunn
1976 April	**Left Gully Arête**	W E Pattison, A W Dunn
1976 May 9	**Right Gully Arête**	W E Pattison, A W Dunn
1976	**Un-named Wall**	C Wornham, J Williams, C Greenhow
1976	**Startling Starlings**	W E Pattison, A W Dunn
1976 Aug 28	**Side Slip**	W Young, A G Cram (alt)
1976 Oct 24	**The Crysalid**	S Clegg, J Lamb (alt)

1977 July	**Supernatural** P Whillance, D Armstrong (var)
	Climbed in stages.
	The first E5 in the Gable Area, and a sign of things to come.
	Direct Finish added 22 July 1984, P Whillance, D Armstrong.
1977 July 10	**Sarcophagus** P Whillance, D Armstrong (alt)
1977 Aug 9	**The Cayman** P Whillance, D Armstrong
1978 April 23	**Triffid** P Botterill, J Lamb
1978 May	**Cripes** W E Pattison, J W Bremner
1978 May 21	**Golden Calf** P Botterill, J Lamb (var)
1978 May 30	**Goodness Nose** J W Bremner, A J Bremner
1978 June 3	**Shameless** J W Bremner
1978 June 4	**Cheeky Charlie** W E Pattison, B Curley, J Bremner
1978 June 18	**Sacrificial Crack** J Lamb, P Botterill, J Taylor
	The chalenge laid down by P L Fearnehough in October 1976 is successfully taken on. Not repeated for 9 years.
1978 June	**Un-named Groove** W E Pattison (solo)
1978	**Tim Benzedrino** N Halliday, T Sawbridge
	First ascent claimed at extremely severe, but found to be very hard on checking, with many known failures.
1979 June 3	**The Angel of Mercy** J Lamb, P Botterill
1979 June 23	**Needle Front** J W Earl, P Stewart
1979 June 23	**Needless Eliminate** P Stewart, J W Earl
1979	**Feline Crack** J Lamb, M Hetherington, J Fotheringham
1980 March 16	**Dan's Groove** K Ball
1980 March 16	**Cow Pie** K Ball
1980 March 16	**Desperate Dan** K Ball, D Martin
1980 April 20	**Tapestry**
	Pitch 2 and 3 A Stephenson, C Sice (alt) W Young, R G Wilson.
	Pitch 1 A Stephenson, W Young, April 1982.
	Said to be fit to hang on any wall.
	After a decade of E4 and above grades elsewhere, Pillar had its first modern route of the so called new wave cleaned and inspected prior to first ascent.
	A fine effort by a strong local team.
1981 April 8	**Cunning Stunts** A Stephenson, W Young
	Aptly named.
1981 April 13	**Wall Street** W Young, A Stephenson
	8 April 1981. Variation pitch 2a. A Stephenson.
1981 April 15	**Imagine** A Stephenson, J Wilson
	Buckbarrow was re-discovered and the race was on.
1981 April 25	**Wild West Show** D Armstrong, P Whillance (var)
	A raiding party scores with its first plum. (A bit hard for the locals?).
1981 May 2	**Agent Orange** C Sice, A Stephenson, J Wilson
1981 May 2	**Too Many Hands** A Stephenson, C Sice, J Wilson, W Young, A Edwards
	A local gang bang!!

1981 May 2	**Pace Maker**	J Wilson, A Stephenson, C Sice

Too Many Hands and Pace Maker were a logical straightening out of the original recorded routes of Tandeka (VS) and Dibra (VS).

1981 May 4	**West Side Story**	P Whillance, M Hamilton, D Armstrong (alt)
1981 May 17	**Junkie**	P Botterrill, J Lamb
1981 June 28	**Triffid Right-Hand Finish**	J Lamb, P Boterill (var)
1981 June 28	**Cenotaph Left-Hand**	P Botterill, J Lamb

Four extremes in one day from a strong Carlisle team brings Kern Knotts up to date.

1981 June 28	**Sylvester**	T Furness, P Rigby (var)
1981 June 28	**Sepulchre Direct**	J Lamb, P Botterill

A solution to the problem created by the loss of the original 1st pitch of Sepulchre in a rockfall.

Sepulchre was climbed on 22 June 1930 by J A Musgrove, N Richards, E S Wilson, M Beaty, J Brady, A J Buck.

A direct finish which the present route uses was climbed as a variation in 1975 by J Lamb.

1981 Aug 9	**Misfit**	A Stephenson, W Young

Aid point used for cleaning on 1st ascent. Now Free.

1981 Aug 9	**Roraima**	J Grindley, B Thompson
1981 Oct 3	**Mainline**	A Stephenson, H McDonald
1982 March 13	**Catalepsy Corner**	K Ball, D Martin
1982 March 13	**Aneurysm**	K Ball, D Martin
1982 April	**Santa Fe**	J Wilson, B Smith
1982 April	**The Stitch**	J Wilson, R Smith
1982 April 29	**Time and Place**	M Leoroyd, H Griffith
1982 May	**Last of the Summer Wine**	J Wilson, B Smith

Perfect casting!

1982 June	**Left-Hand Buttress**	W E Pattison, J Bremner
1982 June	**Forked Lightening**	W E Pattison, J Bremner
1982 Sept	**Flannel**	G Smith, J Carradice
1982 Sept	**The Crystal**	G. Smith, J Carradice
1982 Sept	**Cretin Hop**	G Smith, J Carradice
1982 Oct 9	**Sidewinder**	A Stephenson, J Wilson
1982	**Joanne**	B Smith J Wilson
1983 March 28	**Satin**	P Strong, D Hinton
1983 April 1	**Atlantis**	P Strong, D Hinton
1983 April 7	**Swipe**	D Hinton (unseconded)
1983 April 8	**The Catch**	J Wilson, D Hinton (alt)

Named after one way of stopping a leader fall.

1983 May 16	**A Cut Above**	A Stephenson, W Young
1983 May 19	**Freebird**	A Stephenson, W Young (alt)
1983	**Epidemic Crack**	G Smith, J Carradice, J Adams
1983	**Belter**	D Hall, P Strong
1984 April 29	**Living in Sin**	P Strong, C Daly

1984 May 26	**The Runt** T Walkington, B Rogers
	The pre-placed protection peg arrives on Buckbarrow.
	Long sling also used on first ascent, allowing protection to be
	gained before the crux.
1984 May 26	**Lakeland Pioneers** B Rogers, T Walkington
	The start of another sharp short development project.
1984 May 27	**Left Edge Route** B Rogers, T Walkinton
1984 May 27	**The Gun** T Walkinton, B Rogers
	Climbed before but not recorded.
1984 May 28	**Pinnacle Face Direct** T Walkington, B Rogers
	Pre-top roped.
1984 May 28	**Pinnacle Face** T Walkington, B Rogers, A Kenny
1984 May 28	**Right Edge Route** T Walkington, B Rogers, A Kenny
1984 June 2	**Flakey Wall** B Rogers, T Walkington
1984 June 3	**Old Strands** B Rogers, T Walkington
1984 June 3	**Rusty Wall** T Walkington (unseconded)
1984 June 9	**Norma Jean** T Walkington, B Rogers
	Pre-top roped.
1984 June 10	**Harriet** B Rogers, T Walkington
1984 June 10	**Zeke** B Rogers, J Foster
1984 June 10	**Shorty** T Walkington, B Rogers
1984 June 10	**The Great Unwashed** B Rogers, T Walkington
1984 June 10	**Straits of Messina** P Whillance, D Armstrong (alt)
1984 June 30	**Queen of Change** I Turnbull, D Hall
	Overbeck at last receives some long needed attention.
1984 Aug 15	**Incantations** P Whillance, D Armstrong (var)
	Pitch 3 on 22 August 1984. P Whillance, D Armstrong.
1985 March 26	**Alchemy** A Wilson, J Wilson
1985 March 27	**Blind Faith** J Wilson, A Wilson
1985 Oct	**BJ** W E Pattison, J Pattison
1985 Oct	**JP** W E Pattison, J Pattison
1985 Oct	**Crack Special** W E Pattison, J Pattison
1985 Oct	**Back Stairs** W E Pattison, J Pattison
1985 Oct	**Attic Stairs** W E Pattison, J Pattison, J Nellis
1985	**A Face Remembered** S Maskrey, G Greenhow
1985	**Flakey Wall** W E Pattison (solo)
1985	**Cracked Wall** W E Pattison (solo)
1985	**Deception** W E Pattison (solo)
1986 April 9	**Just Good Friends** J D Wilson, P Strong
	An old route signals the start to a short burst of activity on
	Long Crag.
1986 April 16	**Red Garden Massacre** D Hinton, J D Wilson
1986 May 3	**Sideline** J Daly, M Gibson
1986 May 3	**Hard Rain** K Phizacklea, D Geere, J Daly
1986 May 3	**Fall Out** K Phizacklea, D Geere, J Daly
	Variation 1a. Added D Kirby (solo) on 17 September 1989.
1986 May 16	**The Movie** P Strong, J D Wilson, A Wilson
1986 July 15	**Snicker Snack** C Downer, A Hall
1986 Sept	**Jim's Wall** J Balmer, W E Pattison

1987 April 25	**Hell Bent** A Phizacklea, D Kirby
1987 April 25	**The Tartarus Trip** A Phizacklea, D Kirby
1987 April 28	**Lower Slabs Super Direct** J Loxham
	Solo with a back rope.
1987 April 28	**Poet Laureate** J Loxham
	Cleaned and soloed with a back rope.
1987 May 16	**Powder Finger** C Downer, A Redfearn
1987 May 26	**Poetry in Motion** J Loxham
	Cleaned and soloed with a back rope.
	7 May 1988. Variation Finish. R Wightman, A Phizacklea.
1987 June 20	**Amos Moses** P Long, T Parker
	Supercedes a route called Crinkler's Cracks climbed on 19 May 1973 by R Valentine, J Wilkinson.
1987 July 5	**Torch Song Trilogy** M Berzins, C Sowden
1987 July 13	**Dream Twister** C Downer, A Hall
1987 July 14	**Over The Hill** J Loxham, P Botterill (alt)
	First cleaned and top-roped in May 1986 by Jim Loxham and named to reflect the age of the first ascentionists.
1987 Aug 2	**Rib Tickler** W E Pattison, P Buckland
1987 Aug 8	**The Tormentor** A Phizacklea, A H Greenbank
1987 Sept 27	**Hell Raiser** A Phizacklea, A H Greenbank, J C Lockey
1987	**East Enders** D Armstrong, J Williams
1988 April 17	**Chocolate Chip** W E Pattison, P Buckland
	The start of a short intense period of development on Great Knott.
1988 April 17	**Tutti-Frutti** W E Pattison, P Buckland
1988 April 23	**Prophylactics** A Phizacklea (solo)
1988 April 23	**No Ewe Turns** A Phizacklea (solo)
1988 April 24	**Calculus** S Brailey, S Hubball
	The upper section was originally Alpha Variation by A Wood-Johnson, Mabel M Barker, 21 April 1935.
1988 April 24	**Omega** S Hubball, S Brailey
1988 April 24	**Abacus** S Hubball, S Brailey
1988 April 24	**Caleb** S Hubball, S Brailey
	Four new routes in one day, the first for 55 years.
1988 May 1	**Mr. Softee** D Kirby, P Melville
	The result of checking on rumoured activity.
1988 May 7	**Timshel** S Hubball, S Brailey
1988 May 7	**The Dexterous Shuffle** A Phizacklea, R Wightman
1988 May 7	**The Deleterious Sting** A Phizacklea, R Wightman
1988 May 7	**The Dactylic Springald** R Wightman, A Phizacklea
1988 May 7	**The Dipso Somnambulist** R Wightman, A Phizacklea
	(Nice routes, a shame about the names).
1988 May 8	**Naughty but Nice** J Jackson, W E Pattison
1988 May 8	**Raspberry Ripple** W E Pattison, P Buckland
1988 May 8	**The Cornet** W E Pattison, P Buckland
1988 May 8	**Three Scoops Please** J Jackson, P Melville
1988 May 9	**Cream Horn** D Kirby, J Jackson
1988 May 9	**Angel Delight** J Jackson, P Melville

1988 May 14	**Wafer Thin** D Kirby, P Melville
1988 May 14	**Pauli Exclusion Principle** R Wightman, A Phizacklea

An on sight lead, rare these days!

1988 May 14	**The Terrorist** A Phizacklea, R Wightman

Even rarer on Pillar these days. Two new routes climbed in one day.

1988 May 15	**Neopolitan** P Buckland, W Mollineaux
1988 May 15	**Vanilla Fudge** W E Pattison, P Melville
1988 May 15	**Smaug** A Phizacklea, R Wightman (alt)
1988 May 15	**The Gable End** R Wightman, A Phizacklea
1988 May 16	**Arjuna** S Hubball (solo)
1988 May 21	**Murin Buchstansangur** A Phizacklea, R Wightman
1988 May 22	**American Dream** S Brailey, S Hubball, S Day
1988 May 30	**East of Eden** S Hubball, S Brailey
1988 May 30	**Greenpeace** S Brailey, S Hubball
1988 June 5	**Close to the Wind** R Kenyon (unseconded)

*Incorporating Awe, the variation on The Buttonhook Route, 29
August 1965, G W B Tough, J E Harding*

1988 June 6	**Patriarch of the Pillarites** S Miller, J Loxham

*The result of an earlier visit by S Miller (May 1981). The
combination of Klingsor variation start, and a new hard pitch
gave another hard addition to the rock.*

1988 June 12	**Nothing to Declare** A Phizacklea, D Kirby
1988 June 12	**Strike While It's Hot** A Phizacklea, D Kirby

The result of industrial action during a long hot summer.

1988 June 15	**The Tombstone** A Phizacklea, S Carruthers

Pitch 2 top roped on first ascent, then led.

1988 June 15	**The Short Crack** A Phizacklea, S Carruthers
1988 June 27	**The Slay Ride** A Phizacklea, C Gregg
1988 June 20	**Limerick** J Loxham (solo)

*Cleaned and top-roped before being climbed with a back rope.
The last section of the route (the overhanging crack) had been
climbed before by A Phizacklea, R Wightman 7 May 1988.*

1988 June	**N.C.B.** J Balmer, J Wilson
1988 July 27	**Slab and Groove** W E Pattison, P Buckland
1988 July 31	**The Flakes** W E Pattison P Buckland
1988 July 31	**Waterstreak Wall Direct Finish** D Kirby, P Melville, W E Pattison
1988 Aug 7	**Holly Tree Groove** P Buckland, W E Pattison
1988 Aug 7	**Rib and Slab** W E Pattison, P Buckland
1988 Aug 7	**Barn Door Blues** P Collis (solo)
1988 Aug 7	**Going Straight** P Collis (solo)
1988 Oct 30	**Femme Fatale** A Phizacklea, D Kirby B McKinley
1988 Oct 30	**Catamite Corner** A Phizacklea, B McKinley

*Two new routes in one day helping in bringing Overbeck up to
date.*

1989 April 19	**Final Curtain** I Turnbull, J Balmer
1989 May	**Frozen Assets** W E Pattison, P Buckland
1989 May	**Cold Climbs** W E Pattison, P Buckland
1989 May 29	**The Satanic Traverses** A Phizacklea, R Wightman, D Lampard

1989 June 17	**Mome Rath** A Phizacklea, D Kirby
1989 June 25	**Blue Peter** W E Pattison, P Buckland
1989 Sept 17	**Shock Treatment** D Kirby (solo)
	Cleaned and inspected on abseil.
1989	**Eastern Bloc** A Phizacklea
1989	**Pussy** A Phizacklea
1990 May 28	**Moggy Traveller** A Phizacklea, A Rowell
1990 May 28	**Fat Freddies Cat** A Phizacklea, A Rowell, D Kells
1990 July 14	**Debutantes Slab** J Loxham, A Loxham
1990 Nov 8	**Rubella** D N Greenop
1990 Nov 8	**Rosanna** D N Greenop
1990 Nov 8	**Primogeniture** D N Greenop
1990 Nov 8	**Solivagant** D N Greenop
1990 Nov 8	**The Ravelled Sleave** D N Greenop
1990 Nov 8	**The Lycanthrope's Fang** D N Greenop
1990 Nov 9	**Veni Vidi Vici** D N Greenop
1990 Nov 9	**Autumnal Ambience** D N Greenop
1990 Nov 20	**Solace in Senescence** D N Greenop
1990 Nov 20	**Echappé** D N Greenop
1990 Nov 21	**Late-Flowering Lust** D N Greenop
1990 Nov 21	**Patriarch's Provenance** D N Greenop
1990 Nov 21	**The Sequacious Doyen** D N Greenop
1990 Nov 21	**The Flatulent Pilaster** D N Greenop
1990 Nov 22	**Messalina's Grotto** D N Greenop
1990 Nov 22	**Panegyric for a P.M.** D N Greenop
1990 Nov 22	**The Kafka Syndrome** D N Greenop
1990 Nov 22	**The Lassitude of Hedonism** D N Greenop
1990 Nov 26	**Double Entendre** D N Greenop
1990 Dec 1	**Nepotism** D N Greenop, G Greenop, B J Porter (var)
1990 Dec 1	**Paternity Summons** C Greenop, D N Greenop, B J Porter (var)
1990 Dec 1	**The Rubicund Rostrum** D N Greenop, C Greenop (var), B J Porter
1990 Dec 1	**Eclecticism** G N Greenop, B J Porter, C Greenop

Note

Details of the first ascents of the following routes are not known, any information or claims would be appreciated. Please send them to the Editor.

The Bowness Girdle, Left Wall; Bowness Knott. Robinson's Pinnacle, Short Side; Crag Fell Pinnacles. Dan's Mine, Forgotten Wall, Shaddow Wall, Temptation, Andreas Revenge, Like It or Lump It, Midge Arête, Shep, Gog, Hook Line and Sinker, Crystal Groove; Angler's Crag. Central Corner; Black Crag. Shamrock Tower Variation, The Devils Exit; Pillar. Starboard Fender Variation; Boat Howe Crags. The Kraken Variation; Kern Knotts. The Slab and Chimney Route; Lower Kern Knotts West. Sphinx Ridge; The Napes. Un-named Groove Variation, Bran Flake, The Mysteron, Harmony, Captain Scarlet, The Buckbarrow Needle, Banana, Hermes, Jockey, Nameless Crack, Long Climb; Buckbarrow.

Addendum Note
It has been reported that a number of routes were climbed on Latterbarrow Crag around August 1970 by A Shepard, J Costick, A Jones and A Barber, members of the Karabiner Club, and a supplement produced. It is thought that many of these correspond with those claimed by D Greenop during November and December 1990. This discrepancy will be checked and rectified in future editions.

MOUNTAIN ACCIDENTS

Procedure for Climbers in the Lake District

There has recently been considerable change in the procedures for mountain rescue in the Lake District. This change has been brought about by many factors, including the increase in the number and availability of rescue teams, the developments and improvements in equipment and techniques, and the increased availability (thanks to the R.A.F.) of helicopters for mountain rescue purposes.

Consequently, only minor casualties should come within the scope of treatment and evacuation by the climber's companions. The rule for all other cases is to make the casualty safe, to initiate the treatment, and to send expeditiously for a Mountain Rescue Team.

Sending for Help

A reliable member of the party should be sent for the Rescue Team, with full information about the nature of the injuries and the position of the incident (including, if possible, the map reference). **He should then find the nearest telephone, dial 999, and ask for the Police**, who will notify the most readily available team. The sender of the message should stay by the telephone until he receives instructions from the Team Leader, who may want further information or may want his help to guide the team to the incident.

General Treatment

Pending the arrival of the rescue team, basic first-aid treatment should be given. The patient should be examined as far as is possible without unduly exposing him. Wounds should be covered and external bleeding controlled by pressure of dressings. Application of tourniquets can be very dangerous and often make haemorrhage worse; they should only be used by experts and then only in extreme cases. Fractures should be immobilised by the most simple method available. The patient, if shocked, or suffering from actual or potential exposure, should then be put in a sheltered place, protected from the rain and wind, wrapped in as many layers of clothing as possible, encased in a 'poly bag' or other impermeable material, and, if conscious and not suffering from abdominal injuries, given warm drinks containing glucose. If available a tent should be erected around him.

The majority of cases will respond to this treatment and their condition should have improved by the time the team arrives. The more serious cases, where such an improvement may not occur, include head injuries, spinal fractures, chest and abdominal injuries with possible internal haemorrhage, and multiple injuries with consequent severe shock. They require urgent expert treatment, and every effort should be made to stress the urgency and the nature of the injuries when the 999 call is made. The use of a helicopter, by courtesy of the R.A.F., can be quickly obtained through the Mountain Rescue Team Leader and the Police.

Treatment of special cases

Fractures of the limbs are usually best treated, in the case of the arm, by padding it and bandaging it to the chest, and in the case of the leg, by padding it and bandaging it to the other leg.

Severe head injuries run the risk of death from asphyxia with deepening unconsciousness. The position of the patient, his head and tongue should be adjusted to facilitate breathing. Apparently less severe head injuries should be continually and carefully observed as the condition of the patient can rapidly deteriorate.

Fracture of the spine, if suspected, means that the patient should not be moved and should be made to keep still. If he is in a dangerous position, a difficult decision will have to be made as to whether or not to move him. If he has to be moved to save his life, then obviously every care should be taken to prevent movement of the spine.

Internal haemorrhage should be suspected if the patient has sustained blows to the chest or abdomen. It is confirmed if, despite the measures adopted for the treatment and prevention of shock, his condition progressively deteriorates. All steps should be taken to facilitate the rapid arrival of doctor, team and, if possible, helicopter. A record should be kept of pulse rate to facilitate subsequent diagnosis.

Lack of help. The most difficult decision has to be made when the patient is severely injured, possibly unconscious, and there is only one climbing companion present. He should try to summon help from nearby climbers or walkers by shouting, giving the distress call on his whistle, flashing a torch, or sending up a red flare. If there is no response then he has to assess the relative dangers of leaving the patient, or of failing to get help, and should act decisively in the interest of the patient.

INDEX

	Page
Hind Cove	104
Hind Cove Buttress	105
Hind Cove Gully	105
Holly Tree Groove	185
Hook, Line and Sinker	38
Horizon Climb	116
Hun, The	91
Icicle	182
Imagine	196
Incantations	154
Injection	190
Innominate Crack	144
Interceptor	127
Iron Crag	184
Iron Crag Buttress	184
Iron Crag Ridge	184
J.C.B. G.T.	200
J.P.	211
Jabberwock, The	130
Jaga	158
Jamie	194
Jewel, The	205
Jim's Wall	194
Joanne	205
Jockey	205
Joint Effort	193
Jordan Bastion	61
Jordan Gap	61
Josephine	206
Junkie	201
Just Good Friends	191
Kafka Syndrome, The	225
Kern Knotts	139
Kern Knotts Buttress	143
Kern Knotts Chain	145
Kern Knotts Chimney	143
Kern Knotts Corner	146
Kern Knotts Crack	144
Kern Knotts West Buttress	141
Kern Knotts West Chimney	141
Kestrel	193
Kipper's Chimney	65
Kirk Fell	110
Kirk Fell Ghyll	111
Klingsor	83
Kraken, The	141
Labyrinth	34
Lakeland Pioneer's Buttress	211
Lakeland Pioneers	212

	Page
Landlubber	116
Larboard Arête	113
Lassitude of Hedonism, The	226
Last of the Summer Wine	202
Late-Flowering Lust	224
Latterbarrow Crag	223
Ledge and Groove Climb	95
Left Central Slab Climb	51
Left Edge Route	213
Left Face Climb	217
Left Face Route	109
Left Gully Arête	182
Left Wall	33
Left-Hand Buttress	183
Left-Hand Route (Black Crag)	54
Left-Hand Route (Moss Slab)	200
Lepton	68
Like It or Lump It	37
Limerick	54
Ling Chimney	165
Lingmell Crack, The	162
Link, The	74
Little John	166
Living in Sin	201
Long Chimney	55
Long Climb	215
Long Crag	188
Long John	166
Lothlorian	192
Low Adam Crag	229
Low Man	76
Lower Crag	186
Lower Kern Knotts	146
Lower Kern Knotts West	147
Lower Slabs Climb Direct	50
Lower Slabs Ordinary Route	49
Lower Slabs Super Direct	50
Lucifer Crack	157
Lucifer Ridge	157
Lycanthrope's Fang, The	226
Magic Rainbow, The	72
Magic Roundabout	210
Main Ridge Climb, The	49
Mainline	201
Mallory's Left-Hand Route	122
Mallory's Right-Hand Route	122
Mark Twain	204
Marriage, The	32
Megaton	86

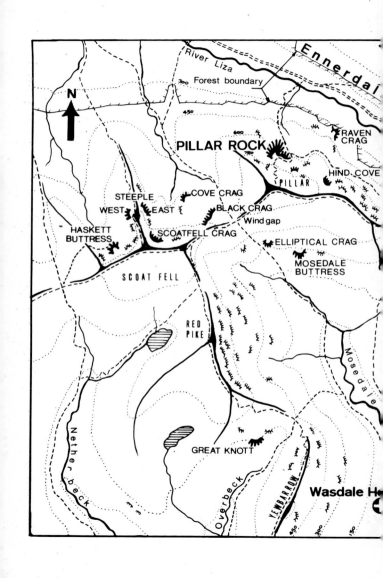